School Drop Out To Multi-Millionaire

A Copy And Paste Guide To Getting Seriously Rich...

The Long-Awaited Autobiography And 'How To' Manual:

Samuel Leeds

Legal Notices:

The information presented in this book herein represents the view of the author as of the date of publication. Because of the rate at which conditions change, the author reserves the right to alter and update his opinion based on conditions. This book is for information purposes only. While every attempt has been made to verify the information presented in this book, neither the author nor his affiliates or partners assume any responsibility for errors, inaccuracies or omissions. Any slights of people or organisations are unintentional. You are responsible for and should be aware of any laws which govern business transactions or other business activities in your country or state.

Every effort has been made to accurately represent any products referred to in this book and their potential. Examples in these materials are not be interpreted as a promise of earnings. Earning potential is entirely dependent upon the person using any product, ideas or techniques. We do not in any way purport any schemes referred to in this book as 'get rich schemes'.

Your level of success in attaining the results claimed in this book or any materials referred to therein depends on the time you devote to the programme, ideas or techniques referred to, your finances, your knowledge and various skills. Since these factors vary according to individuals, we cannot guarantee your success or income success – nor are we responsible for any of your actions.

Any and all forward-looking statements here or within any of the materials referred to in this book are intended to express our opinion of earnings potential. Many factors will be important in determining your level of success or results – and no guarantees are made whatsoever that you will achieve results similar to ours or anybody else's, in fact no guarantees are made that you will achieve any results from the ideas or techniques referred to in this book or the materials referred to therein.

Samuel Leeds

Contents

Introduction

Who Is This Book For - And What Is It All About?

Put simply, this book is for anyone who wants to take control of their finances, replace their regular income, become financially free, and be able to live their life as they wish to – and without being tied to a regular job. If this sounds attractive, then read on; this book is for you!

The pages that follow will give an account of my life so far, in which I will tell you how I went from being a penniless teenager with few prospects (as most people saw things!) - to becoming a multi- multi- millionaire in less than ten years. My purpose is to tell you *how* I did this, so that you can do the same – but without having to learn by trial and error.

This book is intended to be a cross between a biography and a 'how to manual' or 'guide'; you could call this an 'info-how-to-biography'. My hope is that if you follow in my footsteps, you will enjoy the same or even greater success.

Many people reading this will be already be thinking, '*I cannot do this*'; if you are one of these people, *please* trust me; you can do this if you will let me show you how. Actually, <u>anybody</u> can take control of their finances and become financially free, so long as they are open minded, are prepared to learn - and then follow this through with action.

Think about this; many things appear difficult when you do not know how to do them, but once you have mastered something, these no longer seems difficult.

Let me give you an example: The fact that you are reading this book means that at some stage (probably as a child) you learned to read - and this may have seemed difficult at the time. If you have learned to drive or play a musical instrument, you will at the time have probably felt much the same. Of course, the same can be said of many things in life. The sad truth is that fear puts off *so* many people from picking up and following through on opportunities - and fear is the thief of success.

So, why am I writing this book? Well, one of the most satisfying things in life for me, is being able to help others learn how to become financially free; I know how liberating and life-changing this can be! I have over the past few years helped many thousands of people become financially free. My hope is that in writing this book, I will be able to reach out to a far wider group of people than would otherwise be possible. I dearly hope you will be one of them.

If this book helps you, please do get in contact with me personally; I'd love to hear of your success and have included e-mail and contact details at the end of this book.

I have a second motive; you will as you read on, see that I have made a life decision to use my wealth to help provide for necessities such as clean water, food, medical care and education in a number of African and other developing countries – and this led me to establishing the *Samuel Leeds Foundation*.

Many of my students have gone onto become financially free so that they too are able to help fund the causes that are most important to them; this is where wealth creation and financial freedom can help drive each person's *mission* in life. For many people this might involve helping either their family or loved ones - or putting something back into their communities. Again, if this touches a nerve with you, I will try to provide you with some pointers to help you power ahead in these areas.

Being short of money is one of the greatest causes of stress and suffering that exists – and is often caused by people not knowing how to either manage or make money. In most cases this is simply because they have never had the opportunity to learn. In this book I want to change all of that, through the telling of my story.

I will in the next few pages challenge many misconceptions about money that prevent people from creating real wealth and becoming financially free. Please do approach this book with an open mind; you will need to be prepared to 'unlearn' many concepts about money that are widely accepted in society as being financial 'truths'.

Most people have absolutely no idea how to change their financial prospects. Some dream of winning the lottery. Others believe the way to being free of money worries is to 'work your way to the top' and secure a highly paid job. It is this way of thinking that leads to people becoming caught up in the 'rat race' and trapped in jobs they hate.

For many people who do get caught up in the rat race, it is as if they almost have an internal 'financial thermostat' that they are not aware of, in which whatever happens to them in terms of their income, the amount of money they have at the end of each month always ends up being the same. Let me explain by unpacking this...

Imagine a room thermostat set to a temperature of 22°C. If someone opens the windows or doors, the temperature may for a short while fall to let's say 20°C. The thermostat will turn up the heating and within a few minutes the temperature will again rise to 22°C. Conversely if a group of people enter the room, body heat may cause the temperature to rise to 24°C; again, the thermostat will respond by turning the heating down until the temperature falls back down to 22°C.

Most peoples' finances follow very similar patterns. If for some reason they find their finances being stretched, such as when starting a family, they trim their finances by eating out less often, taking only one instead of two holidays each year – or making their car last another year before changing it. Their finances will then settle down, so that they make ends meet with the same amount of money at the end of each month. Conversely, when they receive a pay rise, they will for a short while find themselves being better off each month, but in most cases, will then decide they 'need' a new car, will treat themselves to the holiday they have always wanted or buy a bigger house. They will again, shortly find that they have the same amount of money left at the end of each month. If they were struggling to make ends meet each month before their pay rise, the chances are that within six months' time they will be struggling again.

In this book, I will show you to *override* your financial thermostat by making money work for you until you have all the income you could ever want – and no longer have to work to earn a living. This is how financial freedom can be achieved - and being financially free means that you can spend your time how you wish to. You see, we all have the same number of hours in the day - and so in reality financial freedom means *freedom to spend your time and live your life, how you wish to.*

One more thought about time; all of us need to spend our time wisely. When faced with choices I have to make in life, I try to put them through the so-called 'Rocking Chair' test. It goes something like this: Imagine yourself as an old person. Then sit yourself down in your rocking chair, get comfortable and look back at your life. Then consider all of the options with the choices you are considering now. Which will you be happy with? Consider which opportunities you might wish you had taken, if you let them slip by? How would your decisions affect other people? – and which do you feel you might look back on and feel were the right choices? The rocking chair test, really can help you make better choices in life that you will look back and be content with over the longer term.

In many ways this book could be thought of as an account of the life lessons I would like to go back and tell my teenage self if I could. Obviously, I can't (!), but I can tell you, so you can learn from what I have learned along the way.

Let's get started.

Samuel Leeds

Part One:

From School Drop Out With Few Prospects - To Being A Multi-Millionaire In My Twenties … How It Happened

Chapter One: Let's Start At The Very Beginning...

The title of this book almost says it all; I did indeed go from being a School drop out to now being worth more than £10m within my twenties. Many, many, people have asked me, *'Samuel, how on earth did you do this?'*

I have shared with as many people as I can my path to success and tried to help as many friends and students of mine to become successful. However, this book for the first time describes my life journey to date - and how I as a kid who many had written off is now a multi-millionaire. You see, this is part of my mission in life; to use my success and wealth to serve and help others.

This book tells a very personal story – of how I built my wealth – and my ongoing mission to help others. Everybody has a different story that is unique to them, but I hope to share in the pages that follow some of, 'what makes me tick' – and how anyone with the right information, education and mindset can become financially free.

In the words of John Donne, *'No man is an island unto themselves'* – and nobody can call themselves self-made; this is certainly true for me. Other people did indeed help me. Nobody however gave me money to get started, nobody gave me handouts – but a number of kind hearted and generous people did share their knowledge with me, did give me encouragement, did believe in me when most of the world did not - and did give me opportunities, which in turn I made the most of.

One of the key drivers for sharing my story is to help encourage you along the path of your own unique life journey; you could think of this as almost a form of putting something back. Your idea of what you might think of success and happiness may be very different from mine – and that is fine as we are all individuals.

This book is deeply personal and it is meant to be! Firstly, it is of course an autobiography – a tale of my life to date. Secondly, it is a book written to help you be financially free and be able to follow your mission; that's also personal – but to you!

So, if it isn't too corny - in the words of the song from the *Sound of Music*, *'Let's start at the very beginning…A very good place to start'*.

Chapter Two: My Early Years - Schooling Didn't Really Work For Me

Like so many kids, I just did not get on too well at school. The problem was that I never really felt that I understood or that I was managing to keep up. I was always getting into some type of trouble. Generally speaking, I never felt as if people believed in me or thought that I was going to do well.

Here is an example: There was a desk - a big desk in my form room – that was positioned right under the nose of the teacher; it was almost as if this was 'the special needs desk'.

There had previously been a pupil who had been put to sit at this desk who actually did have special needs - and when he left the school, they put me on 'that' desk. You can imagine how that made me feel. Now even to this day, I do not exactly know why they put me on the desk; I don't know if it was because maybe they thought I had special needs - or maybe because, it was just that I had a really short attention span. It is possible that the teachers just wanted to keep an eye on me as I was the pupil who was always getting put into detention for silly things like flicking glue and generally being low level disruptive. Who knows? (I'm not sure), but in any case, that is where I was placed.

From my perspective it felt like most people just generally did not really understand me. This led me to believing in myself that I was not going do well in school or go on to get a good job, so I just thought *'You know what, I'm going to have to just rely on something different; maybe using my hands? Maybe I could be a builder or something like that?'*.

In most peoples' eyes, I had few if any prospects ahead of me. If you are familiar with Charles Dicken's book, *'Great Expectations'* – the story of a young man in which all who knew him anticipated would have an amazing future ahead of him, then I would have in most peoples' eyes have been the exact opposite; I would have been the child of *'Few Expectations'*.

Looking back at the situation now, this could have really set the course for a life of underachieving, always being poor – and just about surviving or getting by.

Somehow and by the grace of God (literally), life worked out really well for me in ways that nobody who knew me at the time would have ever imagined.

To this day, I am so grateful for the way things have worked out – and this is one of the drivers that has made me want to 'put something back'. I can never forget how easily and differently things could have turned out – and if I can help anybody to find success, freedom and happiness, then that seems like a worthwhile thing to do.

Schoolboy Years...

Now, by being made to sit on 'that' big desk, an expectation was set that I would not do well; guess what? I thought I was not going to do well either. In the classic book, *'How Children Fail'* by John Holt – so many examples are given of how children live out the expectations of others being instilled into them during their most formative years. We often become what others expect us - and we believe what others say about us.

In my case – possibly because I had a short attention span, I ended up being the child who was always flicking glue and constantly getting into some form of low level trouble. This was a natural way for me to behave; I didn't always understand, so I messed about, therefore failed to listen as well as

I could – and so got bored – and then messed about. But… that of course was what was *expected* of the kid who was placed to sit on the 'special needs desk'.

My Secondary School

If you are unconvinced of how the expectations of others shape lives, then consider this; there are areas in the UK where you are three times more likely to go to Higher Education or University than other areas. The children from the more deprived locations are clearly not any less intelligent than those from more affluent areas – but the expectations and aspirations of these groups of young people are very different - and this has a huge impact on life chances and outcomes. This is so very wrong.

Education of all types is so incredibly vital and important – it shapes our very thinking and what we think, we become. Tony Blair the ex-UK prime minister famously made his top three priorities, '*Education, Education and Education*'.

So - why do so many people fail at school? Is it due to what is taught? Does what is taught suit everybody? Does school, equip people well for life? These are complex questions, but let me share some personal thoughts.

Firstly, there are many different forms of intelligence from cognitive intelligence that will be reflected through IQ scores, through to emotional intelligence and creativity.

We are all different – so it would be helpful if society valued the different gifts, we each had. So often we are told by our peers and others about what we are *not* good at. I personally have always had a natural gift as a speaker; at school I was told to concentrate more on the areas of school work that I found difficult – but was rarely encouraged to develop my speaking and debating skills. Today, I regularly give training to large audiences – using those skills I am naturally good at.

History is littered with examples of people who were nearly written off when young. Richard Branson as a prime example, was a child – who in his own words was seen as the 'dumbest person at school'. He clearly wasn't, he was actually dyslexic. Anyone who knows anything about child development and education knows that many people who are dyslexic are often highly gifted - in ways others are not. The problem is that dyslexic children are often not understood since their brains process information differently from most of the population. What acts as a barrier to understanding some information for them helps them process different forms of information that most other people find difficult. Few would disagree that Richard Branson is exceptionally gifted in finance – and yet it was not until after he had become a millionaire that somebody managed to explain to him the difference between *gross* and *net* profit by drawing a diagram (as overleaf). In this sketch all the fish in the sea represent gross profit – while the net profit was what was fish you could net and take away after expenses:

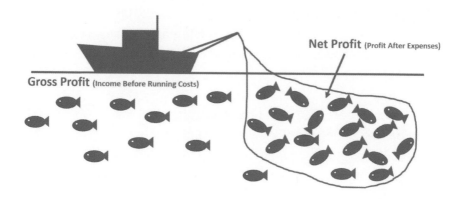

A Diagram Illustrating the Difference Between Gross and Net Profit

While Richard Branson is universally recognised as being exceptionally talented, he was nearly written off as a child simply because his brain operates in a different way from most of the population. Interestingly, forty percent of entrepreneurs are typically dyslexic, in comparison to around ten percent of the general population.

Going back to my schooling, nobody expected me to do well – actually nobody expected very much of me at all. I had loving parents and a great brother and sister – but my parents split when I was seven years old which probably didn't help either.

My parents both knew the meaning of hard work – but it was work that was never going to make them well off financially, with my Mum being a mobile hairdresser and my father a gardener. Again unwittingly, this set expectations in my head – whilst also stirring up a desire to make money and do better for myself. To me this was the way forward – but I had no idea of exactly how could I make 'good' money.

Society told me the way to succeed and be wealthy was to do well at school, get good grades, go to college or University and have a great job. This door was all but closed to me – as it is to so many. Looking back, I realise that many people who do, do well at school and get a good job – actually do not do so well financially. They become trapped in jobs they do not like, then become chained to mortgages – and end up working for forty years, all of this time looking forward to retirement, when they will then end up living on 40% of what they could not afford to live on throughout their working life. This is not a pretty picture!

Now please – please, do not get me wrong; I am not knocking traditional education: we all need doctors, dentists and pharmacists, engineers and other professions of all types. In my own life, doctors and surgeons have put me back together after serious accidents on two separate occasions (more on that later!). Most of us drive cars designed by engineers and rely on architects for designing bridges and buildings that we live and work in. My point rather is that, many of these highly skilled people that society needs, still become financially locked in to a career and lifestyle that becomes a burden - and that does not give them the freedom or lifestyle that they thought they would achieve. One of the things that traditional schooling does not teach is financial literacy - and this can be a key to freedom.

It is so very sad to see highly gifted people who have studied and worked hard all of their lifetime becoming trapped in jobs that they have grown to hate – all to pay a mortgage for a house they are pulled away from for forty or more hours a week. So many people I know, long for the weekends and holidays. This is no way to live. This is why one of my missions in life has become to help people obtain true freedom and quit the rat race - if this is what they would like to do.

My mindset whilst at school could not have been further away from understanding any of this. I just knew that I wanted to make money. Looking back, this was the first inkling of an entrepreneurial mindset, one of the gifts that I did not realise (nor did anybody else for that matter), I had at the time.

At school, I took on paper rounds; as many as I could - and diligently saved as much money as I could. Society had told me saving money was good, so that was what I did.

My father did 'alright' as a gardener and so I thought I could make a living doing the same. Other thoughts included using my hands such as working as a plumber - or on a building site - or something similar.

My Father, 'Dad' Worked as a Gardener and Then Later as a Magician.

At about the age of thirteen, my Dad decided he would switch tracks in life and become a magician. Now to a teenager, this seemed really 'cool' and indeed my Dad wanted and expected me to join him as a magician in the business he was starting. This sounded exciting.

I was by this time always looking for new ways to make money – so I used to buy tricks from my Dad using the paper round money I was earning – and then sell these tricks to other children at school. My teachers just did not understand – and I remember my poor mother being called into the school to explain as they thought I was selling drugs.

My poor mother explained that I really wasn't selling drugs, but actually selling magic tricks, which only added to their view of me as being the child who was a little 'odd'.

My Mother, 'Mum', Who During My Childhood Years Worked as a Mobile Hairdresser

I did actually try to work hard at school and got a half decent set of GCSEs (sixteen year old – UK high school exams) and was a B/C level student; I was not a total write off - but not a high flyer by any standards. By this time, my mindset had disengaged with traditional learning and school – and most of the staff with the exception of one or two teachers, thought I would end up just working in a factory or a building site or similar. While there is nothing wrong in this, there was something in me that wanted so much more.

Schooling in the traditional sense had not really worked out for me so well – and school hadn't taught me anything about finance, business, entrepreneurialism or making money; it was going to be down to me to make something of my life.

Chapter Three: What They Didn't Teach Me At School About Money.

Many people dream of having enough money so that they do not have to think about it. Most people think that the route to this is to have high flying - high earning careers.

There are so many problems with this approach: For a start most of these people do not end up earning what they hoped they might – and then quickly find themselves trapped in jobs that they grow over time to hate. Then they feel that they cannot leave and so become trapped into a rat race paying down a mortgage – and funding a lifestyle that goes along with the job. It is so tragic to see, so many people seeing what was once a dream slowly become a living nightmare.

School and society taught me that the way to get on and succeed was to earn enough money so as to get a mortgage, to get onto the property ladder, then pay the mortgage off as quickly as possible and look forward to retirement.

What I saw was that most people considered to be 'successful' longed for weekends, their holidays and retirement - often they had grown to *hate* their jobs - and were continually worn out to the point of exhaustion and always on the edge to burn out.

I am not blaming my school or anybody I know for one moment for teaching this way of thinking, as this is the way 99% of the population have been taught - and so pass on to the next generation. Most people mean well and all almost all parents want the best for their children; in most cases they simply do not know any other way.

I discovered almost by accident other approaches for making money – other strategies in fact to becoming financially free without having to be chained to a high paying job.

Remember – in my case, the normal route for 'success' was all but closed down for me by the age of sixteen, when it became clear that I did not fit the academic mould. This meant that either I had to find other routes to being successful – or just put up with being poor all of my life. This latter option didn't sound too appealing to me and so I had to ask myself what was I going to do. They say necessity is the mother of invention – and in my case it proved to be the making of me.

Most people get stopped by negative thinking and focusing on what they do not have. Many people will be caught up by and believe the negativity they hear all around them and that is spoken over them. Many young people with their life ahead of them will internally think, *'Well I just wasn't so bright at school, my parents always struggled for money and had low paid jobs, I came from a council estate where nobody went to university etc. – that's just the way things are'*. This way of thinking is so tragic. Things really do not have to be this way for any person; moulds can be broken.

Somewhere deep inside me, I thought that life did not have to map out in this way – and I had an inner belief that I did have in me, what it would take to succeed. The only thing was that at this stage I had absolutely no idea of how to be successful. What I did know was, was that I had a lot of motivation and courage.

I have always been an optimistic and a hard worker with a natural 'can do' approach. From an early age I had a firm belief that life is what you make of it and in the words of the UK special forces SAS (Special Air Service) moto, *'He Who Dares – Wins'.*

At an early age I came to the conclusion that if you took someone who has been extraordinarily successful in business - of the likes of Grant Cardone, Richard Branson, Warren Buffett, or Elon Musk - and if you took all of their money away from them, that they would within a few short years become just as wealthy all over again. The thing that nobody can take from someone else is their personality – and it is what lies within someone that will ultimately determine whether and how successful somebody becomes. To put it another way, you cannot keep a good person down.

So, at this stage, I had found the two most important ingredients to be successful were; first belief in myself – and secondly, drive. I still did not know *how* to be successful.

I had started selling magic tricks at school and started saving money. Selling magic tricks was all well and good, but I was hardly going to become wealthy doing this.

Next, I took on a few paper rounds and this allowed me to save some more.

The two problems were of course that firstly paper rounds don't really pay very well – and secondly what I was doing, but didn't really realise at the time was *exchanging time for money*; this is what most people do. This is hugely significant!

Most people go to work and get paid. When you don't go to work, you don't get paid. Most people think that is just the way things are – i.e., you have to work to get paid. While there is nothing wrong with the concept of being paid as a reward for work, you are never going to get truly wealthy via this approach.

The *model of exchanging time for money is very limiting*. For a start, there are only so many hours in the day that you can work – and if for any reason when you cannot work, you will not get paid. This of course often includes, when you retire – or if you are self-employed when you go on holiday.

At the age of sixteen, I was still of the mindset of working and getting paid for exchanging my time at work for money. It would be sometime before I understood the concept underpinning recurring models where you can get paid – even when you are not working.

My next line of thinking was to look towards learning a trade that could be well paid – and while this was not to be the answer for getting paid when I was not working, through a mixture of good luck, serendipity and a willingness to learn, it did actually take me a step closer to finding a formula for financial freedom: let me explain.

I considered training for a trade where I thought there would always be a demand such as becoming an electrician, plumber or bricklayer – and by chance, I stumbled upon a three-day, 'Crash Course' in plastering.

As part of my final year of school, I had to obtain a work placement– and so I signed up for this plastering course instead of opting for a placement within a bank or solicitor's office as many of my year had done.

I had heard that plasterers were typically paid £100-150 [US$140-210] per day which sounded like all of the money in the world to me at the time. I knew plasterers were always in demand and so I signed up, paying for the crash course with the savings I had accumulated from my paper round.

The course was excellent; I learned a lot and loved it, thinking in my mind that I had my future career path all mapped out ahead of me. I tried to make contacts and network with people who might be able to help me – and started to do some small jobs for free just to gain some experience. Once I had built up a little bit of confidence, I started to advertise – and to my delight was commissioned by a lady to plaster a large room for £500 [c.US$700]. This gave me such a boost in confidence – but it was not to last.

The entire room was to be plastered and this included the ceiling; the only problem was that the crash course had not covered how to plaster ceilings. The lady had paid me £500 [c.US$700] up front and I didn't want to give her the money back and admit that I couldn't complete the job.

I thought and thought and thought about this – and had an entrepreneurial brainstorm... I advertised for other plasterers who could work for me for an agreed rate of £70 [c.US$100] a day.

Someone phoned up - an experienced plasterer called Thomas (Tom) (and although I am not proud of this, looking back), I said the job interview would involve him plastering a ceiling for me. Tom came round to the house and I watched him plastering the ceiling for me for free.

I really do not know what Tom thought of me; here was a teenager of fifteen, who mixed up the plaster for him and managed to mess this up by getting the mixture completely wrong in consistency - firstly too thick and then too thin. The lady who had hired me kept popping in to see how the job was coming along – and somehow (I do not know how), we completed the job and to her satisfaction!

This whole experience started me thinking... If I was to advertise for plastering jobs and then got other plasterers to complete these for me, and I could pay them a daily rate of £70 or so I could still make a profit of £100-200 a job without having to actually do the plastering itself.

In this model somebody else would be doing the majority of the work - and most importantly I could employ two, three, four or more plasterers to undertake a number of different jobs all at the same time.

The real beauty with this approach was that I would no longer be limited by the number of hours I could work in the day. In this way I would be able to take on far more work than I could possible undertake myself. This would mean that I could scale the business. This is essentially what I did – and the first business I started was called 'Pelsall Plastering' after the area of Walsall where my business was based.

This slight mishap of not being able to plaster a celling and having to hire somebody else to do this for me, had actually with a little bit of an entrepreneurial mindset, given rise to my first scalable business venture.

I knew I had had much to learn, but this had really taught me that if you are willing to learn and approach things with the right mindset, even setbacks can be turned to advantage.

My entrepreneurial journey to financial freedom had begun - and I now focused my mind towards how I might work smarter, and build scalable business.

In the words of the entrepreneur and author John Rohn, *'Don't wish it was easier, wish you were better. Don't wish for less problems, wish for more skills. Don't wish for less challenge, wish for more wisdom'*.

John Rohn: The Famous Entrepreneur, Author and Business Mentor

Chapter Four: Breaking Away From The Family Business And Working For Myself

My father was making a success of his new magic business and just assumed that I was going to come to work for him. This was so kind of him and his motives were good. Many parents, if they have found a route to success want to pass this on to their children. I did do some work for my father, but the more I did, the more he assumed I would just come and work for him in the long term. He thought that the plastering business was for me, just a sideline.

The problem I had, was that in my innermost heart I needed to work for myself and make my own choices in life. To compound things, he wanted me to work on Sundays when I wanted to go to church; more on that later...

I thought - and I thought - and thought further about this, tossing and turning all night for several nights – but finally decided I did need to make the break, make my own way in life and pursue my own business interests.

If I am being honest, my Dad whom I love dearly, didn't take this too well - and felt quite snubbed. He told me that he was disappointed in me – but I knew this was his hurt talking. Today we are closer than ever – and as the expression goes, 'time heals'. I knew how much effort he had put into starting his business and how much he wanted the very best for me. The problem was that he simply could not understand why I would want to start another business – let alone one in a completely different field.

My Mum and Dad had split when I was about seven – and I think my decision to do go my own way in life probably felt like another blow to him – and from my point of view, anything that put a strain on my relationship with my Dad felt pretty painful too. Blood is thicker than water though and there is nothing like a reconciliation for making the bond closer than it was before.

My elder brother Russell decided at this stage to work for our Dad, which I think probably helped us all. I am very close to Russell and he has shown himself to have real gifts in business; again, more on that later!

My Mum had in the meantime re-married and my new step-dad, Tim could not have come from a more different background – or indeed be more different in personality than my Dad. Tim was an accountant, good with figures and clearly knew much more about money than anybody else I knew. To be honest, when I first met Tim, I did not take to him too well – probably because he was so different to my father in almost every way possible.

What I did see though, was that he was buying houses, renting these out and making money without having to actively work for money – and this really caught my attention!

Separately, I had found through my plastering business a model in which I could find work and then get somebody else to actually to the work – and still get paid - but this was different. Tim was buying houses and then he was getting paid through tenants paying rent. As far as I could see it, Tim was working *once*, by finding the right house, arranging the finance, employing a solicitor who would do the conveyancing - but then he could essentially sit back and be paid each month, month after month. This was another 'lightbulb' or 'eureka' moment for me. What I did not realise or appreciate at the time was that this was the underlying principle behind creating *passive* income – and this is what almost all truly wealthy people do. Instead of exchanging time for money, *they use money to buy things that make money for them on an ongoing or recurring basis.*

Passive income is an incredibly powerful concept. Property is probably the easiest and most lucrative route for creating passive income – but it is not the only way. There are many – many models for passive income that almost everyone is aware of but few people really think about.

Here are some examples: If you buy recorded music to listen to, this will have taken time and effort to create, but every time someone downloads a track, buys an album or a radio station plays a track, the artist and the record label, get paid a royalty. The same is true for books; this book took many hours to write but every time someone buys a copy, I and the publisher receive a small royalty. Many inventions are protected by patents; the inventor will file a patent and then licenses this to a company who produces a product which is sold in volume; every time someone buys the product, the inventor gets paid a royalty.

Many high street stores operate through a franchise system which again provide a form of passive income for the franchise developers. Household high street chains from *McDonalds*, *Costa Coffee* and the optometrists, *Specsavers* operate through franchises in which local business owners buy a franchise for a business model which they have to follow exactly. The public knows and expects each *McDonalds*, *Costa Coffee* or *Specsavers* branch to look almost identical in branding and offer the same service. This means that the chance of the local business owner who buys a franchise license being successful is far greater than if they tried to establish a brand or reputation by themselves, however the franchise developer gets paid for simply allowing the business owner to use their formula. They have essentially worked once to develop the brand – and get paid over and over and over again.

I was hooked by the concept of creating passive income and having seen the success Tim was having, I decided this could - and should be the way forward. The only problem was that I had absolutely no idea of how to get started - and I certainly did not have the money at this stage to buy a house.

So, what should be the next step? Tim seemed to know what he was doing, so I kept asking him questions. He explained that he was buying houses using mortgages and re-financing, but as far as I was concerned, he might have been talking a completely different language; I didn't even really know what a mortgage was.

I had decided by this stage that Tim was actually a pretty decent guy – and he was clearly going out of his way to show me a lot of kindness and was trying to be helpful. The snag was that while he clearly knew what he was talking about, I just was not understanding what he was trying to tell me. Part of this was probably me not being familiar with some of the financial terminology – but also Tim - whilst very kind, was perhaps not the greatest explainer in the world!

I asked Tim how he had learned about property investing. Firstly, he pointed me towards what I now know is a really seminal book on becoming financially free, 'Rich Dad – Poor Dad' by Robert Kiyosaki. Little did I know that a few years later Robert would be personally giving me business advice. When you have read this book, I recommend you read 'Rich Dad – Poor Dad' as there is no better introduction to the mindset for how rich people *think* - which is so different to the mindset of most people.

Robert Kiyosaki and 'Rich Dad – Poor Dad'

Secondly – and just as if not more importantly, Tim said he had gone to some business network training events run by an experienced property investor who had become financially free through developing passive income streams through property. He was now teaching the techniques he had developed - and so helping others becoming financially free and quitting the rat race.

Tim tool me along to the training events; I could now start to make sense of what Tim had been trying to teach me - and I simply loved it. For the first time I could honestly say I had a real thirst for learning – and now enjoyed studying. Everything Tim was saying started to make sense and I was eager to learn more.

Before long I signed up for more training, using the money I was making from my plastering business. I realised very quickly that to be successful in property (or almost any area of business for that matter), you needed two things: education and energy.

If you do not get educated but do have lots of energy then you will almost certainly make lots of (and costly) mistakes.

If you have all of the education and knowledge in the world but do not implement this knowledge then, nothing will happen. This is why you need both to be educated and have energy.

Well, I had lots of energy – now I needed the education and knowledge, so I signed up for almost every property training programme I could find. Some were excellent – some were perhaps less helpful, but every course I took helped me understand the field a little better.

Now let me start to share with you some of the most important lessons I learned to help you on your way.

Chapter Five: Assets And Liabilities: You Probably Think You Know The Difference And You Probably Don't

Apologies if this is a provocative statement – but I say as someone who didn't know the difference between an asset and a liability until I had read 'Rich Dad – Poor Dad'.

Like many people, I thought an asset was something you owned that had financial value. Indeed, if you asked many an accountant, they would say this definition would be just fine. If you look at a company's balance sheet, this will list assets as things it owns such as buildings, cars, equipment etc.

This is a poor definition and I will explain why: Many things that people buy devalue in value over time. In fact, in accountancy, the value of items takes into account the expected lifetime of objects such as cars, computers etc. You could never sell these items for what you paid for them; indeed, many items such as cars devalue by as much as 20% the moment you drive them out of the forecourt since they instantly become classed as being 'used'.

Many people classify the home they own as being an asset – but in most cases, even if the house appreciates in value, this does the home owner no good whatsoever. Most homes if purchased are bought using a mortgage - and this of course will mean repaying the amount borrowed plus interest.

In both of these cases, the car and the house *take money out* of the person's pocket. So, what the purchaser believes is an asset is actually a liability…! Now you certainly need a roof over your head and you may well need a car – but in these examples these need to be thought of as liabilities and not assets.

So, what exactly is an asset? Put simply, an asset *is something that puts money into your pocket*; there are many, many different things that are assets. Examples of assets can include a shop that makes you money, it could be owning a mobile food van, vending machines for snacks, the copyright to a book that you may have written, royalties for music, intellectual property for an invention or some technology that is protected by a patent – and of course property. Property is one of the most lucrative (if not the most lucrative!) forms of asset that exists on the planet. It is also one of the easiest assets to acquire and make money.

One of the most striking things, if you look at almost any newspaper 'rich list', is that more people have made their money through property than almost any other way – and those that made their money through another way such as business, then have invested this money in property.

There are many ways in which you can make money from property - and I will within this book describe the strategies that I have personally used.

Chapter Six: Why Poor People So Often Stay Poor – And Rich People So Often Continue To Get Richer

First, I want you to ask yourself the question, how would you define what it means to be poor and how would define what it means to be rich?

Now before you turn over the page – write your answers down on a piece of paper.

I suspect that in answering the question of how you define being rich or poor, you wrote down two figures of money or income.

This is the wrong way to answer the question. OK, you will have realised I am toying with you a bit, but please let me explain.

You see, remember that I said, if you took all of the money from someone such as Richard Branson, most people would agree that in a few years he would almost certainly become a multi- multi- millionaire all over again. In the same way, most poor people will expect that they will still be poor in ten years' time and see no way of changing their prospects.

This shows that being rich or poor actually has more to do with your *approach* to money than how much you actually have to your name at any given time. Just think about how many times have you seen stories of when someone who was poor, won the lottery but ended up penniless within five years or so again.

I have a lot to thank Richard Branson for, as it was his book, 'Screw It, Let's Do It' that was so key to helping open my eyes as how the rich create wealth. Little did I know it that in a few years' time, I would meet up with him and be able to thank him in person!

Meeting Richard and Being Able To Say 'Thank You'

You see, money *finds* rich people – and money *slips* through the fingers of poor people. How is this so? The answer to this lies in how people view and use money.

Most people (and most people are poor in this context) buy *things* with their money that they think will improve their quality of life whether these be cars, holidays, clothes, electronics or whatever. When they have spent their money, the money is gone and they are left with goods that depreciate with time.

Rich people by contrast spend their money and their time on buying or creating assets; these assets make them money. There are many forms of asset that once acquired will continue to make income without the need for extra or ongoing work. This is the definition of passive (sometimes called residual) income. This is the next thing I learned – and it is the magic underpinning the concept of 'passive income'. Passive income occurs when an asset genuinely makes you money without having to do any work whatsoever. There are many assets that can create passive income streams that we have already mentioned such as book or music royalties but – property can be set up to pay you passive income as well.

Whatever your faith background, there are good moral strands for using resources including your money prudently and wisely. Think of a farmer, who sows, seed, tends for the crop while it grows – and then reaps a rich harvest sometime later. The Bible gives a parable how some seed gives 'a return of ten, some a hundred and some a thousand fold'.

Having read *'Rich Dad – Poor Dad'*, then having been to a number of property training events – I was able to piece together in my mind and understand what Tim was doing. Slowly but surely, I was starting to see how I might just become financially free. So many people have dreams that have no realistic prospect of ever coming true. I now by contrast had a desire and an outline strategy for becoming financially free – in a way that was actually completely achievable.

I said earlier, that nobody had given me handouts of money to get me started on my road to financial freedom but that had been a number of people who had helped me, had believed in me and encouraged me. Throughout this book I will give a call out to say thank you to those who have helped me, since without them I well may not been enjoying the success I am doing today. You see - one of the other life lessons I learned very early from my Mum and my Dad was to have a positive outlook on life and be grateful to people who show kindness; living in a state of gratitude is a positive way of approaching life.

If you are by nature grateful, you will be in a more positive frame of mind, which means people around you are far more likely to warm to you – which in turn means you are far more likely to have people help you. Just think about this; who would you rather associate with? People who you would describe as being grumpy – or people who are friendly and grateful in their outlook? Positivity – really does make such a difference to our own happiness, the happiness of others around us – and indeed to outcomes. Strive to be a 'can do' person – and you may be surprised by what gets done!

Chapter Seven: So Why Is Property Such A Great Way Of Earning Passive And Recurring Income?

I now had a grouping of people who I could go to for advice for how to get started in property as a route to creating passive or recurring income streams.

First, there was Tim who really understood finance, those who ran the property networks who really understood property investment – and my Mum who had been the person who had gone into school when I had got into trouble and who really understood me! You could think of this as my first property support power team!

Tim together with some of those who he introduced me to helped me understand how so many incredibly wealthy people had made their money through property.

Firstly, you get paid through rent (typically monthly). As a landlord you keep getting paid month after month; this is of course how and why property is a great way of setting up a residual source of income. But this is only half of the story. Property in the UK (and most other countries in the world) has continued to historically increase in value decade after decade – and century after century. There have of course been falls in property prices from time to time, however property prices have on average doubled every decade over the course of the last century. If you think about it, this is astonishing. There is no other asset on the planet you could have invested in that would have given this consistency of increasing value.

Now if you buy a property with a mortgage, you will invest a small percentage as a deposit, (this typically might be 25% of the value of the property for example). When the value of the property doubles over time, then your 25% stake does not double – rather the *whole* value of the property doubles. To illustrate how this works, let's look at an example.

If a property were to cost £100K, then you will put down a 25% stake as a deposit. If after a decade the property doubles, then the value of the property will be £200K. Your stake in the property remains £25K). The increase in value will belong to you. This means that your equity or stake in the property is now (£25K + the £100K or increase in value) which is £125K. While the property value has doubled, your wealth has increased from £25K to £125. This means that your wealth has increased fivefold – or by 500%.

This simple illustration shows the incredible power of *leverage*. If the majority of the population understood how profoundly investment leveraging could be harnessed, their approach to money would so completely different.

I was now seventeen – and it is not an understatement to say that this lightbulb moment truly helped change my life.

So, the next two questions I needed answers to were: How to buy my first house using a mortgage? - and then how to rent it out?

Well, the people to ask were - of course, Tim and the property investment trainers he had introduced me to...

Chapter Eight: But I Can't Get A Mortgage - !! Well - That's Stopped Me – Hasn't It?

Newly equipped with my understanding of how rental properties can be a great way of producing passive income streams – while harnessing the power of leveraged investing, I thought (perhaps rather naively) - that I really had all of the knowledge that I needed to unlock unlimited wealth! In reality, I still had so many lessons to learn – both in terms of knowledge – and understanding for how to approach and overcome the inevitable problems that life will present.

My bubble of newfound confidence was quickly burst, when I approached a number of banks who informed that I had to be twenty one to obtain a mortgage. I was seventeen; I knew that I did not want to wait four years – this seemed like an eternity and was nearly a quarter of my lifespan! I was upset and frustrated and went back to the property investor and asked him for my money back for his tutoring. He was about to teach me my next lesson; he said that *'Of course I could have my money back, but wouldn't it be far better to think of ways and find out how I could obtain a mortgage and purchase my first property?'*

He continued to explain that while the banks would not lend to me if the mortgage was in my name – that that would not stop me buying the house with someone else who was aged twenty one or over.

This way of thinking, suddenly offered many other potential ways for moving forward. Firstly, if someone else, such as a family member would agree to put the house in their name (essentially as a guarantor) then there should be no barrier. This is of course how many parents help their children buy their first houses. Alternative approaches could include buying the house with another property investor, who might contribute a financial stake and would act as the first name on the house ownership deeds.

This way of thinking would not only solve my immediate problem, but – again would change my wider way of thinking and approach how to tackle what could look like problems or obstacles. This is so important: You see, many people when they face unexpected problems, see these as complete road blocks. Successful people look at the blockages ahead of them and think of ways to get around them and move on. This problem solving type of mindset and how you approach problems can completely affect your life chances.

To illustrate this point, think about this analogy. If you are on a long journey and you find that a road ahead of you has been closed off by the police because of a road accident, you are unlikely to say, '*Oh dear – well there is no way forward, we had better go home*'. You are far more likely to find a new route using your sat nav (or if you are old fashioned – a map!) and then continue on your journey.

Since it is inevitable that you meet obstacles along your way, you need to develop a habit of thinking of ways for how to get around problems and so move on.

I had the deposit saved, but still needed the mortgage – and this needed to be in someone else's name, so equipped with my new way of thinking, I went home and asked Tim if he knew of other property investors who might be willing to host the mortgage.

Tim (and again I am so grateful to him), offered to act as a host for the mortgage *himself*. He did not lend me money – but he did *lend his name* - and this was enough to get me going.

Not only was I set to purchase my first property – a beautiful little house that I still own, but I had learned another lesson: when faced with a problem you need to look for a way round it so that you become a winner and not a loser!

When people said to Henry Ford him, *'I think I can'* – or – *'I think I can't'*, he was known for smiling and saying to both, *'I think you're right. I think I agree'*.

This could be a really good point in my story to tell you something I have learned about how to overcome problems in life and being successful from King Solomon, Ants and Winston Churchill.

Samuel Leeds

Chapter Nine: King Solomon, Ants And Winston Churchill...

I have a question for you; so, what do King Solomon, the humble little ant and Winston Churchill have in common? This isn't a Christmas cracker joke I promise...

King Solomon was noted in the Old Testament of the Bible as having been the wisest person who had ever lived – and indeed people travelled from many other nations to seek council from him and listen to his wisdom. His legacy included being the author of the book of *Proverbs* with many snippets of wisdom still being part of daily speech. One of King Solomon's observations was what remarkable little creatures, ants are – and how much we as humans could learn from them. This needs some explanation. Many people know how ants can lift or carry objects many times their own body weight – but it was how they go about tackling problems that Solomon noted and commented upon.

For a start, ants work together collaboratively with no leader to guide or rule over them. If they decide they need to bring a leaf back to their nest, then they all work together without oversight in a co-ordinated and disciplined manner; we have all seen this on nature programmes. Humans have much to learn from this - and yet, it is their sheer determination to keep going and not be deterred by anything, that is arguably their most amazing feature which most of us as humans really could learn most from.

Ants, just like humans will occasionally meet something along their way that blocks their path. Many humans are easily discouraged and defeated at the first sign of resistance. Some people have more resilience than others and we call these people 'driven', but ants are in class of their own!

If an ant meets a brick wall in its path, it will first turn to the left and try to walk around the obstacle. If it finds its route blocked again, it will turn the other way and try to walk round the obstacle the other way around. If this fails to work, it will climb up the wall and try to go over the top. If the little ant finds that way blocked – it will come down and then start digging its way underneath - or even straight through the wall. Now if you think I am labouring the point, anyone who has ever had an ant infestation in their home will know how ants do drill through just about any material - and blocking the holes up with filler or concrete just does not stop them. If they are coming into your house through a wall to access food or for another reason, then they will just endlessly keep drilling holes – and will not give up. Just think of what the average person could achieve if they had this level of determination...!

So - what have ants and Winston Churchill got in common? Well not a lot actually as far as I know, other than their unwillingness to not let obstacles that would defeat most people put them off from doing something they had put their mind to.

It is said that when asked by his old school to address the boys at an assembly, he raised himself with purpose, and very slowly said, 'Young men, never give in. Never give in. Never, never, never, never - in nothing, great or small, large or petty - never give in, except to convictions of honour and good sense'. He then sat down. Nobody ever forgot what he said.

If you are feeling like you could not have Churchill's determination and drive (or indeed think you would not behave like an ant!) take heart; there are practical approaches you can take for developing persistence and determination. For a start, surround yourself by other people who are driven; it is said by psychologists that we all tend to emulate and slowly become like the five people we associate with the most. If you surround yourself by people who easily give up, the chances are you will become a quitter. Conversely, if you surround yourself by optimistic, positive and driven people, some of this will rub off of you too.

Next make yourself accountable to both yourself and other people who wish to see you succeed. Choose carefully who really you wish to make yourself accountable to; this could be your partner, a brother a sister or a trusted friend. Tell them what you want to achieve and by when – and then ask them to *keep* following up with you to check how your plan is going. A critical friend can be a great asset as they can often help you keep going when you are feeling tired, offer practical suggestions - and above all offer moral support when you need it most.

Lastly – if you really do have a problem in believing in yourself, think of someone in your life who you know believes in you (again perhaps like a parent or sibling who really has been a backer of you for a long time) and believe in the fact that they believe in you...

So – just remember, think of King Solomon and his observation of little but mighty ants – and then when you commit and focus towards a goal, never, never, never, ever give up.

Samuel Leeds

Chapter Ten: My Very First Property Purchase As A Seventeen Year Old – A Little House Which I *'Bought Low And Then Rented Out High'*

So, back to my life story.

You may have seen one of my earlier books, *'Buy Low – Rent High'* This is a dictum I still stick to today. I have never bought a house for the full asking price or that is not below the true market value; why? The reason is that there are always houses to be bought where a discount is to be negotiated. These are the houses to seek out and buy. Nobody wants to (or should) pay more than needed for their energy, or car insurance – or anything else, so why pay over the odds for a house? (Especially when it is for an investment). There are always discounts to be found, so this is what any good investor should focus towards buying houses at Below Market Value (BMV).

My First Rental House

This little house in the picture, my first purchase, had a market value of £120K (c. US$168K); I managed to secure an agreed market price of £100K (c. US$140K). This was back in 2008 – and the rules have changed since then, but at the time you could purchase a house and refinance it on the same day. This meant that you could buy a house with a bridging loan, refinance it with a mortgage and then pay the bridging loan back all in the same day; this is exactly what I did.

The next step of course would be to rent the house out to tenants. There are two obvious approaches here: The first and most obvious way of course would be to rent the house out as a family home. There is nothing wrong with this. At the time, this little house would have attracted a monthly rental income of approximately £500 (US$ 700). Another and far more profitable approach, (which is what I did) was to rent the house out room by room. There are many people who want to rent a single room within a shared house such as, students – or professional people who are often transient to an area; these might include nurses, physiotherapists, accountants – or indeed any other people who are working but who do not wish to rent out an entire apartment or home. People like this often would rather live in a house with other people than live alone – and would like the convenience of having all their bills paid for them on an all inclusive basis within a single monthly rental payment.

This little house had three bedrooms upstairs and two reception room downstairs. I converted one of the rooms downstairs into a bedroom by simply putting a bed and a wardrobe in it - and so my little three bedroom house suddenly became a four bedroom house. Rooms in the area were renting for around £350 (US$490) a month – and this meant that my little house could now attract a monthly rental of around £1,400 (US$1,960) – this could bring me more than twice the rate of simply renting it out as a family house. This is one approach for renting out 'high' – in which you can very easily obtain 'super rent' – instead of just 'standard rent'. This is just the tip of the iceberg – but captures the essence behind, *'Buy Low – Rent High'*.

Houses that are rented by the room are known as 'Houses In Multiple Occupancy' – or HMOs.

This was a real breakthrough moment for me; I was seventeen and a landlord; the same person who only a few months earlier been on the 'special needs' desk and for whom nobody expected anything to come of.

Life is surreal at times when you look back at the way things sometimes turn out. Suddenly I was signing up for every educational programme connected with property that I could find, absorbing all the information I could, enjoying education and learning – and suddenly finding myself being taken seriously as a business person, a landlord and a property investor. Life can at times be strange in the way things can develop and turn out –

but I was in the process of learning yet another lesson in that, life is often what you make of it and that you need to create your own life choices.

Chapter Eleven: You Reap What You Sow – So Sow Carefully And Generously….

As a child, my Mum and Dad took me to church every week. To be honest, I found it a bit boring and irrelevant at the time - and I went because they took me.

As a teenager I had a spiritual experience and I committed my life to God as a committed Christian, I decided to live my life with a grateful heart and do whatever I could to help other people. This was a life changing moment to which there could be no turning back.

Now many people who are reading this book will be of no faith – or other faiths, but with your permission I hope you do not mind me sharing with you a little of what makes me 'tick' – as this helped shape the person I became and indeed who I am today.

As I explained earlier, I grew up in a working-class household where money was tight and where being careful with money was an approach I grew up with.

As a teenager an opportunity came through my church to travel to Kenya to help with some humanitarian projects. So, with my new found faith and with an enthusiasm to help others, I volunteered; what I saw when I got to Zambia completely and utterly broke my heart – it truly did.

I found kids walking five kilometres each way to the nearest well to collect water as this was the nearest place where there was a water supply without the risk of it carrying cholera or typhoid. I saw kids looking hopefully to see if there could be second helpings for porridge who were going hungry – with one meagre and insufficient helping being all they would have to eat till the next day.

It still chokes me up now every time I think about all of this. I could not return home and be the same – I just couldn't. I committed in my heart to return when I could and fund the installation of a bore hole and water storage tank for this village.

I looked back at my years in Wolverhampton in a completely different light. As a young child I turned my nose up to crusts of bread; the kids here in Zambia would have given anything for these and would have been so grateful. In the UK there is a schooling system where everybody gets a free education and is taught to read and write. There is a free health service where everybody is offered free inoculations - and if you have an accident, the health service will give you world class emergency care.

In Africa, the single largest cause of death is due to infectious disease, with much of this being due to waterborne and largely preventable disease; this is real inequality and a world away from what most people in the developed world experience.

Now – I know that there is real deprivation and lack of opportunity for many in richer countries as well. What I saw in Africa made me all the more determined to help others - wherever I could in anyway, so that they could to live life to the full.

Back in the UK, peoples' life chances are hugely influenced by the upbringing you have, what your parents do and the socio-economic background you are born into. Many people grow up living in sub-standard accommodation and live with damp and mould etc.

There is no need for any of this; I came back to the UK to help everybody I could in every way I could with a new found passion – and this would be through providing excellent accommodation for people, helping other people to become financially free – and putting something back into society.

There is a saying that the two most important days in your life are the day you were born and the day you find your purpose or mission in life. I discovered my purpose in life through a commitment to use my God given skills to the best of my ability to make the most out of my life; to be the best version of myself that I could be – and to do all I could to help others.

It is said that you get out of life what you put into it – or that *'you reap what you sow'*. Actually, my own experience is that you reap far more (far more, way and above) what you sow in life.

Those familiar with the gospels will know of the parable of two instances of Jesus feeding the five thousand when people offered up two fish and five barley loaves; this was one of the inspirations of my first book, *'Do The Possible, Watch God Do The Impossible'*.

My advice is to sow both carefully and generously... It will pay dividends.

Chapter Twelve: Returning Home From Africa With A New Sense Of Personal Mission

I returned home to the UK and viewed my own circumstances in a completely new light. I had developed a new sense of what was wealth and poverty meant - and indeed what was really important in life.

The question was what to do about it... I shared my feelings with my Mum and Tim who had quite separately developed a very similar desire to help those less fortunate than ourselves. As a family we moved from quite a nice part of Walsall to a more deprived area that suffered from high levels of unemployment, petty crime and drugs.

We helped run food banks, youth clubs and often hired a hall where kids could come and socialise somewhere that was safe and where they were less likely to get themselves into trouble. Helping others does bring out the best in most of us and gives you a sense of satisfaction and a good feeling about yourself. The strange thing is that your own motives can become slightly selfish to some extent – but to quote Jesus, '*It is better to give than receive*'. Another more worldly perspective is to think of this as a form of win-win; either way, it has to be a good thing!

Foodbanks, youth clubs and most voluntary services rely on the good will and generosity of others. You only have to go to any high street on a Saturday afternoon and see people with collecting tins for charity to see the commitment of so many people. All of this nevertheless did get me thinking; there is only so much money one person can collect in a tin on a Saturday afternoon – or indeed time that one person can commit. There had to be another way as the needs of those at home – in Africa – and indeed most parts of the world are vast and obvious for all to see.

There were real parallels in my mind with how the majority of people are limited by exchanging their time for money to earn a living. whereas I had already seen that if you develop scalable passive sources of income then you are not limited by time.

This is where my two lines of thinking started to come together in one of those 'what if' – or even 'eureka' moments. If I could grow a scalable business built on developing passive streams of income and then donate 10% (this is the figure suggested by the Bible and is known as a tithing) and reinvested the rest, then the business could continue to donate more in an essentially ever-growing and sustainable manner.

The business though had to be of value and improve the quality of lives of others or add benefit in some other way. In my mind there were two main ways my business interests could provide real value.

The first approach was to provide high quality housing that people would want to live in and that was of a much higher standard than most of the other housing available - and yet which would still be affordable. If you look at the standard of much of the rental housing stock in the UK, this is sadly not a terribly high bar to meet. The second approach was to help *others* grow businesses themselves to help them fulfil the missions on their hearts that are most important to them.

Over some time, I really formulated and shaped these thoughts in my mind and came up with a three step financial stepping stone journey with three intermediary goals. This is a strategy I teach to all of my students.

First: Aim to Become Financially Free. The threshold for becoming financially free is simply that you grow your passive sources of income to equal or exceed your outgoings. This means that you will not have to go to work, you will not be tied into the rat race and you do not have to exchange your time for money. This gives you freedom in so many areas or aspects of life – and in this way you can use your time to use this in the way you see best.

Second: Aim To Become Ultimately Financially Free. Being ultimately financially free means having sufficient money to live your ideal lifestyle; we will look at this in more detail, but most people are surprised by how low this figure may be. There are after all only so many holidays you can go on, fancy clothes you can wear or meals out you can eat.

Third: Think About What Your Own Mission In Life Would Be. There are no right or wrong answers to this – but it is truly fulfilling to work on a mission that is important to yourself. It might include providing a childhood for your children that you never had, it could be helping disadvantaged communities, supporting the victims of violence, or helping stop people trafficking and modern slavery. What matters is that you have a sense and purpose that you know you are passionate about and committed to. Everybody has one thing (sometimes several), that they truly would wish to see changed for the better. If that is so - make this your mission.

Now here is a strange thing about human nature: most people find it easier to commit to helping others than helping themselves. If this is true for you, then as you start to take action to improve your own life, look two stages ahead and think of your mission and how you will be able to help others when you become ultimately financially free.

Interestingly Rick Warren, author of the New York Times best seller, *'The Purpose Driven Life'*, that that looks at these very issues of knowing your purpose in life, started out donating 10% of his income to charity. His book sales which have now exceeded 30 million copies - are such that he now *'reverse'* tithes, giving 90% of his income back and keeping 10% for himself.

Earlier I referred to the quote that the two most important days in your life are the day you were born and the day you worked out what your mission in life was to be. Well, I had just worked out what my drive and mission was to be (at least for the next chapter in my life).

I want this book to be as much about you as myself, since I have made it a part of my mission to help others become financially free - so next let us look at how you can get started on this journey.

Chapter Thirteen: Becoming Financially Free...First Steps

We have already seen that financial freedom involves creating passive income streams that exceed your outgoings or expenditure.

Most people focus first on growing their income. This is a great start – BUT – you can in many ways cheat a little here, by lowering the income you actually need to live on by simplifying your lifestyle and cutting down on your outgoings.

Becoming financially free is a dream that for many people - and one which seems beyond reach. Have you heard the expression that every journey starts with a single step? The first step is to look at and gain control of your spending. What you do not spend does not need to be earned.

I have seen many people be able to halve their outgoings and this means that the passive income streams you need to establish to achieve financial freedom can be halved as well. This is a legitimate 'cheat' and a great stepping stone to achieving financial freedom.

To cut your expenditure to a bare minimum, you need to approach this with the right mindset. Many people start by thinking that they have no room to cut down on their living expenses, when in fact they could cut down on a number of unnecessary outgoings quite easily.

The first thing to do is to think what you would do if you were to lose your job tomorrow. Is there really nothing you could cut out of your lifestyle? Do you spend a lot on clothes? - do you buy your lunch at a coffee shop? Do you pick up a latte every morning on the way into work? Do you have a gym membership you never or rarely use? (This is an interesting area – since the business model of most gyms work on the basis that 70% or more of people fail to use their membership properly and if most people did, they would be overcrowded all of the time).

I would suggest you go through your bank account and check really carefully for standing orders or direct debit payment orders that you had forgotten that you may have set up. Many people are often shocked to see money going out for things they had completely forgotten about. Sometimes people only realise they had been paying for something when they come to change their bank for some reason. One of my students who had been happily married for some time was shocked when he realised that he had been paying a monthly subscription to a dating service for several years, simply because he had forgotten to cancel the subscription once he had found the love of his life...!

Next look for things that are 'nice to have' but not essential; do you need two cars when you could survive on one? If you normally go on holiday twice a year, could you mange on one holiday? – or even skip going on holiday for one or two years? If you and your partner normally go out for a meal at the weekend, could you commit to having a date night at home to save money? Look to see if you have the best energy deal or if you could save money by switching provider.

Do look at your monthly bank statements and look at where your money goes. Try to do something about minimising monthly outgoings in areas such as these - and cut down unnecessary spending.

It might be worth looking at a book such as Martin Lewis', 'The Money Diet' which gives a whole host of ways to saving money. Remember every bit of expenditure you manage to cut back on is income you do not earn to become financially free and quit the rat race.

If living a simpler life does not sound like too much fun – keep two thoughts in mind. Firstly, think of the sacrifice you will make almost as an investment; secondly just think of not having to have early morning starts on a cold winter's morning or not having to work for the boss who is a nightmare to answer too. Thoughts such as these, help make living a very simple lifestyle for a while well worth it.

When I first became financially free, I drove a tatty old purple *Ford Ka* and lived in a rented two-bedroom terrace house. I remember being asked to speak at a property event and showing pictures of my house and car. I remember the person hosting the event looking at me in way that almost said, *'What on earth is that meant to say when talking about financial freedom?'* But that was the point – I had made it my mission to be financially free and actually this was quite easy in the first instance to achieve. I now live in one of the most expensive areas of the country, drive a Range Rover and am a multi-millionaire because I used my money to invest wisely and have my money work for me – and not to spend it on things that were frivolous or necessary.

The next stepping stone is to calculate how much income you would need to become ultimately financially free. Being ultimately financially free means having the income to live the lifestyle you would really like to lead if money was no object. One caveat to bear in mind; you do need to have a dose of common sense here. If you decide you want two ocean going yachts, a private plane and your own golf course, then the figure you come up with might be astronomically high – but would this really add to your happiness? You may find that you need a surprisingly small annual income to provide for all you would realistically ever want. You could decide that you want a private plane. I do not have a private plane but I still get to travel on them – quite simply I would not want the hassle of having to look after it. Robbie Williams some years ago went on a shopping spree and bought a string of luxury cars on a shopping binge – and very honestly (and actually very humbly) said that the next week and wish he hadn't.

My wife and I have just one car each and that suits us just fine. Similarly, there are only so many cruises or holidays you can take – or fancy meals you can eat – or clothes you can wear. There comes a point when extra things are not going to add to increased happiness.

Make a list of all of the expenditures you might like for your ideal lifestyle. Include things life the running of your car or cars, holidays and other entertainment, clothes, etc. You may well be surprised at how low this would be. Different people will come up with figures of their own but for many people this figure may be in the region of £10k a month (or US$14K) or lower after tax.

Chapter Fourteen: My Quest To Learn – And Learning Through Doing

By the age of seventeen I was a completely different person I had been when I left school with shaky confidence; I was now on a mission.

I had made a commitment to myself that I was going to become financially free through business, that I would build passive streams of income through property and when I was wealthy, that I would use this to improve the lives of others.

I had learned so much already from Tim and those I was now networking with, but realised that there was so much more to learn. I enrolled on a NVQ (National Vocational Qualification) course in business – and signed up for almost any and every property and business related training programme I could find – spending over time, many tens of thousands of pounds.

Some of the courses were good – others less so, but I do not regret spending one penny of this as I think I learned something from every course (even if it was how not to do something). Overall, I found that many different nuggets of information or areas of knowledge I learned did help cross-link, help make sense and re-enforce each other. Above all of this, learning got me thinking about strategies and ways forward.

I remember vividly looking back only a few months earlier at the first ever networking event which I attended, wearing a cheap rather ill fitting suit and trying to hide at the back of the room behind my cup of coffee. Someone walked up to me and asked me what my strategy was, I hadn't got a clue what he was talking about. Now less than a year later, here I was actively planning ways of developing passive income streams.

My First Ill Fitting Suit

I was devouring information from any source I could find and was now really enjoying learning. Earlier you may remember I said, I had heard that different people learn in different ways. I am one of those people who learns most easily when I can see the sense or logic behind something. Maths is a good example: When I was at school some pupils could be enthused by abstract maths; such as the rules of trigonometry or algebra; this was hard work for me. Now I was actively enjoying and devouring how to programme spreadsheets for profit and loss accounts, as I could instantly see the application to real-life and business.

Friends I know in education tell me that there are four main types of learners: those who are visual learners, auditory, reading / writing learners and kinaesthetic in their approach to taking in information. Visual learners tend to learn by watching, auditory learners learn by listening to others, reading and writing learners turn to books or other written material – while kinaesthetic learners learn most easily when doing things. We all have a bit of each in us, but tend to lean to one of these styles. I now understand that

I definitely am more of a kinaesthetic type learner – and now I was reinforcing my learning through 'doing' I was now for the first time in my life truly thriving in education – and loving it.

I wanted to learn from other people through doing – and so I took a job for a few months as an estate agent to learn everything I could about selling houses. I then signed up to be a sales representative with *Utility Warehouse* – a company that provides utilities such as gas, water, electricity and the internet to households and landlords. Again, I am so grateful to *Utility Warehouse* for giving me this opportunity – so much so that I am still a customer of them to this day. This was a great company to work for – and in addition to giving me some great training, they really helped boost my confidence and so build me up as a person.

I continued to learn through doing: Very early on in my property journey – a local builder who seemed to know what he was talking about told me that Houses In Multiple Occupancy (HMOs) only worked in Bournville (where my first house was) and where he was based. He also told me (again with some confidence!), that rooms should all have ensuites – or otherwise it would be nearly impossible to rent rooms out and that if you did the only people you would get would be undesirable and dreadful tenants that nobody else would want. I believed him – why shouldn't I?

I realised that I needed to learn more and so I decided I would offer to help people find tenants for their HMOs – and manage their properties for free. People used to say to me, '*Why would I want to do this – what was the catch?*'. I explained there wasn't a catch, I just wanted to learn through doing; for me there was no better way. So, I would create a little add on *SpareRoom*.co.uk, take pictures of the room, find a tenant. Several people signed up for me – and I helped them while I helped myself learn everything I could about property; this was a perfect win-win for them and me.

Tim had recently bought an HMO property in Walsall and asked if I could find him tenants; I was dubious and said I would try but had been told that

HMOs only worked in Bournville. He did look a little surprised and I was a little nervous, but Tim then had helped me out so was keen to help him if I could. To make matters worse, none of the rooms were ensuite. This looked like a mini 'mission impossible'. I placed a few advertisements – and to my amazement, surprise and delight, all of the rooms let out really easily. Over time I met other property investors who offered HMOs in many different places – and then of course I realised that what the builder was really doing was trying to generate work for himself. There was nothing wrong in the quality of his work; it was that his advice was biased.

I had just learned a bit more through learning on the job – i.e., through the kinaesthetic approach. We actually all need to learn a little through all four approaches; visually, through reading /writing, listening and doing – but understanding how *you* learn most easily is really important, so that you can then focus on this to accelerate your learning process. When I work with students, I now try to ensure that material is provided to help all four different types of learners. We are all different as people and need to understand ourselves and focus on our strengths. It is worth remembering how so many people such as Richard Branson were early on in their lives mis-understood and how thing could have so easily tuned out very differently for him.

I started to get a little bit of a name for myself at property events as the person who could find tenants for rental properties. Now that I knew a bit more about finding tenants, I felt a little more confident (or should I say less cheeky), about offering this service out for a fee. So, I started charging £100 -150 [US$140-210] a time to landlords for finding them tenants - and tenants a small £90 [c.US$130] admin fee. Both the tenants and landlords found what they were looking for – and so this was another win-win. This was another source of income whilst still learning on the job. While this was never going to make me rich, I was making many connections with people in the property world, looking on at what they were doing, learning from how they were making money and all the time thinking.

My plastering business was by this stage starting to wind down, as I realised the way forward to finding true financial freedom was for me to be through property.

Chapter Fifteen: Then A Recession Happened...

I was just about to turn eighteen and everything in the world was about to turn upside down for me – or it so at least it seemed at the time.

The credit crunch started in the United States but quickly swept across the globe and of course reached the UK in 2007 to 2008. Banks across the globe ran out of money; many smaller lenders went out of business while the larger banks required government bails outs. What followed was a bloodbath for many – caused in part by fear in the financial markets, a slump in consumer confidence and the failure of many business across a range of sectors. A deep and lengthy recession followed.

It is said that recessions happen when either banks or individuals across society run out of money. In 2008 – first the banks and then people ran out of money. To make matter worse, governments essentially ran out of money - and had to resort to printing money to stay afloat through a process known as quantitative easing; a term that became a household phrase.

Many property pundits along with columnists in the financial broadsheet papers proclaimed that property investing was finished. Many people tried to exit and of course when this happens, prices fall and properties become harder to sell as the market became swamped.

Before the crash, many mortgage lenders had been offering 100% mortgages – and in some cases even 110% mortgages. This meant of course, that when prices crashed, their houses were worth less than the price they had paid. This is the definition of negative equity – and for many this was horrific. In reality this meant that many people could not sell – and would be left owing money to the bank if they did.

Now – here are two strange and crucial facts I had learned along the way. The first was that more millionaires are made during recessions than during periods of economic growth. The second was that while property prices periodically had crashed, they always rebounded with time to reach new heights later on. Why? Quite simply this is because people need houses to live in, the population keeps growing and housing construction has never caught up with demand over decades. So, my thinking was – why should things be differently this time round? The last recession had happened around 1990 and prices had again risen to all time new highs by 2007. This pattern been repeated time and time again as far back in history as you want to look.

There are lessons to be learned about how human beings behave during cycles when financial markets, property prices or other commodities rise and fall over time. Many people when they see something starts rising in value think, *'Oh – such and such is rising this must be a good time to buy'* - and so they do. Then the market gets overheated, a correction in time happens as prices fall back. The same people then rush to sell and this drives the price down further. Sometime later, the prices will fall too low and the cycle begins all over again.

There are many historical examples including the famous Dutch 'Tulip bulb' bubble back in 1836-1837 when the price of tulip bulbs reached a truly ridiculous level due to many ordinary people seeing tulip bulbs as being a great investment due simply to the price rising and rising. If this sounds utterly ridiculous and irrational that is because it was.

So, what about housing and house prices; house prices certainly rise and fall cyclically, but remember prices and the value associated with them are for properties that people need to live in – and this commodity is limited in volume, while the growth of the population all of whom need somewhere to live, keeps rising in most western countries at a rate that continues to outstrip growth in supply.

We have just looked at the way the majority of the human population thinks about rises and falls in commodity prices – but how do wealthy people – and how do skilled investors handle cycles such as these? True investors tend to look at and respond to rises and falls in markets in an almost completely contrary way.

Warren Buffett, one of the world's most successful investors of all time has been quoted on several occasions as saying, *'When most people are greedy be scared – but when most people are scared, be greedy'*. You see, when prices have just fallen, this is the perfect time for you to buy for the very reasons that the price is low and will most likely rise over time. This is true for many commodities – but is especially true for houses and property as their intrinsic value will never diminish for the simple reason that people need to put a roof over their head. So, while buying housing stock tends to be a good investment over the long term whenever you buy - buying at the bottom of a cycle can be an especially good time.

So – when I saw many property pundits saying the days of property were over, I was thinking of how to make the most of falling market and 'buy low'. I remember discussing all of this over with my Mum and Tim (who were of course also property investors). I think all three of us had similar thinking; I later learned that Tim had said to my Mum that living with me was like living with a 'mini Richard Branson'. Well, I certainly was not a millionaire at that stage – or anywhere near it, but I did have a mindset that was determined to make the very most of the opportunity, which most viewed to be a crisis.

I am not a Chinese speaker, but I am told that in traditional Chinese the symbols that are used to make up the word for, 'Crisis' – are made of two characters, one of which is for 'danger' while the other represents 'change point' with the same character being a component of the word for 'opportunity'. The way you view things really can have a profound impact as to how you approach a crisis – and ultimately to long term outcomes.

The housing crash, certainly did pose challenges for property investing. Borrowing suddenly became a lot harder as banks tightened up dramatically on their lending criteria while buyers found it difficult to sell properties, even to cash buyers, since they often could not sell at the new market values without taking large losses associated with negative equity. These were obstacles sufficient to put off most property investors. My mind was by contrast focussed to looking for ways to make the most of a difficult situation (or at least how most people perceived it to be).

Making the most of the situation was for a while to be my new focus...

Chapter Sixteen: Making The Most Of A Difficult Situation

When teaching at live events, I often point out that newspapers and the press love to report bad news; sadly, bad news sells far better than good news. We all know this to be true, just look at the headlines for the news for the day you read this and you will see what I mean. People lap this stuff up – *'tut tut'* – and say things like, *'Well, what is to be done about it'* and then get depressed.

Entrepreneurs (and almost all rich people) read the same headiness and think – well that's not great, but how could this be turned around for good? What advantage could be gained from this? How could I help address the problem?

Let me illustrate the point: the Covid-19 pandemic turned the world upside down. Very soon after the lockdown that closed many restaurants, I noticed that one restaurant set up stalls at the front on the pavement / sidewalk and were selling all of their freshly cooked meals to take away in containers. Their business was thriving with a really long queue, while everybody else was focussing on how their business was being hit.

In a similar way, a few clothing manufacturers responded by making face-masks and simply could not make them fast enough, while the majority of clothing manufacturers complained that retail fashion sales had fallen badly.

I do a lot of face to face training at live events; this of course had to stop, so I recorded all my material and put it on line. You see... wherever there is a crisis there is also an opportunity if you adapt and respond in an appropriate way – but this requires the correct mindset.

So, being faced with a housing market in 2007/2008 in turmoil, where was I to find the opportunities?

It is in situations like this that character counts. Now it could be easy for anyone to say some people are born with a particular mindset but this really need not be the case. If you do something frequently enough, this becomes a habit; habits shape character - which in turn will help you move forward. Everybody has gaps in their skill sets, so do not worry if you see these; knowing what you need to move forward can be half of the battle.

In my own mind, I firmly believed that there must be a solution associated with every problem. I decided the approach should be to network like crazy and talk to as many other investors, landlords and anyone else I could talk to, to find ways of hunting out properties that might offer opportunity. This is really where an entrepreneurial approach and mindset is invaluable.

Entrepreneurs do not just follow tried and tested routes – rather when the rules of the game change, they find new solutions. This really can be a test that separates the sheep from the goats. Entrepreneurs create chances. If you don't know where to start when the rules for the game change, then do as I did. First talk to everyone and then start thinking of ways in which you could create new solutions. Above all, do remember that *you have to be in the game to win it*, so do not disqualify yourself by sitting on the side-lines and thinking you cannot see a way forward and that entrepreneurialism is for other people.

I set about travelling the length and the breadth of the country to view as many houses as possible. I viewed dozens of houses every week - week after week. I knew many people were desperate to sell, so my first line of thinking was to try and find houses that could be purchased at below market value. I think many estate agents must have thought I was crazy given the number of house viewings I was doing.

I remember one weekend where my Mum and I travelled to Blackpool to see countless houses – just to look for that illusive house that could be secured for a below market value discount. This time was difficult as so many people were asking prices way and above the true market value and would not (or could not) accept lower offers. I didn't manage to find a single deal in a year; I was eighteen and in danger of losing confidence, but I didn't give up. My Mum supported me all the way and came with me on many house hunting trips.

My brother Russell had gone down the path of magic and was working for our Dad. Dad had teamed up with his business partner Craig Petty; the three of them were making a real success of this business – which was impressive. All the while I was feeling an increasing internal pressure to succeed in property – especially given all of the support my Mum had and indeed was continuing to give. Later on, my Dad actually went to Brazil and left the business and my brother and Craig joined up and became business partners.

Eventually, I had an offer of £65K accepted on a perfect little house that had a true market value of £100K. Now the next problem was how to fund the purchase. I knew I would have to put down a 25% deposit which in this case was approximately £13K [c.US$18K]. I did not have this sort of money and now that the crash had happened, I could no longer raise the deposit via bridging finance as I had previously. I had seen other property investors work together as joint venture partners in which one would lend money to the other for a fixed rate of return; so, this seemed to me like a good strategy. I went to all of the property events and networked like crazy with everyone I knew trying to sell a deal in which I would give them 10% interest on the money they would lend. This would be a great deal with a far higher rate of return than the 1% or less interest rate that the banks were offering. I expected someone to jump at this – but nobody did. I tried and tried to sell, but with no luck. There were two problems I hadn't really anticipated: Firstly, most people (and that included most of my investor network) were scared and very wary of deals however good they looked on paper. The second problem was that I was coming across as 'needing' the investment to proceed (which I did), but there is nothing more off-putting than someone who appears desperate. It is human nature to run in the opposite direction.

The estate agent was pressing me to show proof of funds and I managed to satisfy them by persuading my brother to lend me £13K for a few minutes by asking him to send the money across to me, taking a screenshot and then sending the money straight back to him. Now I am not proud of this and would absolutely not advise anyone to do the same – but I was getting desperate and I am just telling you the way it was... and what I did. I would never do such a thing again.

Time was marching on... and I had two weeks to raise the money – or I would lose the house. If I did lose the house through not being able to raise the deposit, I would let the seller down, lose all credibility with the estate agent, be back to square one and feel pretty awful.

The weekend before the due date, when I was supposed to be finalising the purchase, I had in my heart almost given up hope and resigned myself to the deal falling apart. My Grandma and Grandpa had invited me round to Sunday lunch as they often did. My Grandma sensed that I looked a little crestfallen and asked what was wrong.

I explained the whole situation and said to her that I could not believe that I could not get someone to lend me the £13K when I was guaranteeing an annual interest repayment of 10% that would pay them £1,3K [c.US$1.8K] a year, especially when the banks were offering less than 1% interest. I really poured my heart out and explained that I really could not understand what the world had come to, or what was wrong with people? I explained that without the money what would be a wonderful deal would fall apart and that I would end up looking like an idiot.

My Grandma was really sympathetic and kind as I knew she would be - but what followed I was not expecting...

She asked me about the deal with questions such as, *'Why I could be so sure I would be able to guarantee the 10% annual return?'*. I explained that, I would be renting the house out on a room by room basis and that this would mean that the rent would be four times or more than the mortgage payments, that I knew the area and that there was a high level of demand for rooms in the area – and that I had of course considerable experience and track record of HMO management.

I caught a glance between my Grandma and Grandpa – and to my utter amazement I realised that she was asking questions about the deal as *SHE* was interested in supporting it. We had unbeknownst to me been having a roundabout conversation, where she had been probing me questions about the deal and the possibility of be a joint venture investment partner without actually talking about it directly. This was surreal. Here I was thinking I had run out of options and suddenly my Grandma of all people was thinking of investing in this deal and we were not even talking about it directly – even through all three of us realised that was exactly what we were actually doing.

After several more questions, my Grandma looked at my Grandpa, he nodded back and then she said, *'Actually we have some savings – could we invest and provide the deposit; this seems like a good deal to us and we know you know what you are doing'*. I could not believe my day. I had gone round to see my Grandma and was genuinely looking forward to all of the love and warmth she always showed – and a lovely Sunday lunch as consolation at the end of a difficult week. What I left with was all this – plus a recused deal.

Monday morning came – and I was in for another roller coaster of emotions. I had to have the money by Tuesday but come Monday morning and then Monday lunchtime there was no sign of the money. My emotions plummeted again. I could not phone my Grandma up and pressure her for the money – but time was running out. I resigned myself to the deal falling through and internally braced myself to having to explain and make excuses to the solicitors and estate agents the following day. Then sometime later in the afternoon, I received a text from my Grandma saying that she had transferred the money across and wished me well. I checked my bank account and there was indeed the money; the deal was on.

I bought the house and as before I soon had all rooms rented out. The deal with my Grandma and Grandpa was to borrow the money for five years and each year I would pay them £1.3K - and then I would pay the £13K back. The next five years was completely transformative in my life - and my Grandma and Grandpa saw my property portfolio grow and grow to many dozens of properties in multiple towns and cities all across the country.

Five years on from the initial loan, my Grandma phoned me and as she often did, asked me round to Sunday lunch; this was normal but she also said in a slightly quizzical way that she had had been talking with my Grandpa and would like a chat about the loan when I came round for lunch.

I turned up for lunch and my Grandma and Grandpa both sat down to have a 'chat' with me. I was worried and thought that having seen how much money I was now making, that they might be thinking of asking to re-negotiate the deal retrospectively.

For the second time I was not prepared for their response. They explained that they used the £1.3K I paid them each year to go on an annual cruise. They viewed the money as 'free' money – as the lump sum was not diminishing. What they asked for was for me to *keep* the money on loan and for me to keep paying them 10% p.a. interest. They realised that the rate of interest I was paying them was far greater than they could get from any bank and building society and that this was a great deal. I have to say I was relieved and was really pleased that they had not been asking to re-negotiate the deal having seen how well I was doing.

They knew that they could only get around 1% interest in the bank and that this would not even keep up with inflation; she knew that she didn't have investment knowledge - and to her, I was I doing her a favour. In fact, she was so pleased with the deal that she wanted to lend me another £13-15K.

My Grandma and Grandma – Enjoying Their Earnings!

Ten years later on, I have still not managed to pay the money back... I am happy with this and happy for them – as I know how much they love their cruises – and after all they had trusted their savings to me. This was and continues to be a true 'win-win'.

This purchase was my second house; and again, I had learned a lot along the way.

So, what are the take home lessons from all of this?

Firstly – situations do change with time; when they do, if you find that earlier tactics or strategies are no longer appropriate, then you need to 'think outside of the box', find new ways forwards – and above all develop an entrepreneurial mindset to find new solutions and was forward.

The second lesson, I learned was how *not* to sell. If you come across as being desperate, there is no better way to be able to make people run in the opposite direction. People need to enquire of information surrounding an opportunity, so as to make their own decision in their own time without feeling pressured. One approach I discovered by accident in the discussion with my Grandparents was to let a roundabout, *'What if'* type of conversation happen where people can ask questions in an abstract way. I have since used this approach on many occasions and found that people often in this was feel far less pressurised by this type of approach.

There is an analogy I have realised with feeding pigeons in the park. If you run towards the pigeons with the bread, they will run away; conversely if you hold the bread out in your outstretched hand and stay still, they will come to you when they do not feel threatened.

Chapter Seventeen: Buying A House Now But Paying For It Later: Lease Option Agreements And A Strategy For Recessions

As I was experiencing, trying to find good deals was proving hard in the midst of a recession, in which people were suddenly finding themselves trapped in negative equity and unable to sell their houses for the price they had originally paid.

Then I discovered another solution that could allow me to buy a house in negative equity and help the house seller escape the negative equity trap. This was not going to be a tactic that would work for everyone trapped in negative equity – but really could help some people.

The tactic is essentially based around buying the house but paying for it later. This is an approach of course that is used all the time by many people for buying cars, furniture, holidays and almost everything else – including of course, houses.

Lease option agreements mean that you lease the house – but have the option of buying the house later. Let me explain how a lease option operates and how it can help the seller.

Imagine the situation where a home owner buys a house with a mortgage but loses their job - meaning that they are going to struggle to pay the mortgage. The first obvious solution is for them to sell the house; if the value of the house has however fallen in value, then they will not be able to pay the mortgage back by selling the house. This type of scenario happens sadly all too frequently in recessions.

The next option open to the home owner would be to move out of the house and rent the property to tenants. In most cases this would not only allow them to continue to pay the mortgage, but to actually return a profit. Ethically if you find someone in this situation then this should probably be the best advice to give them. You will not benefit from this yourself – but you will have helped someone - and remember what 'goes around tends to come around'. If you had a family member – or a good friend, this is probably the best advice you should give them – and in a similar way, you should try to help a stranger in the same way if you can.

The only snag is that many people really do not want to become landlords – and no matter how much sense this makes, this is not a path they wish to go down. It is in cases such as this, that lease options can work to the benefit of both parties.

If the house owner cannot sell for the price they want (to pay off for example their mortgage) and does not want to become a landlord and rent the house out – one strategy is for you (the potential house buyer) to offer to buy the house for the price they want – BUT – at a later date when the housing market has recovered and prices have risen once again. In the meantime, you can offer to lease the house for the same monthly payment as the mortgage payment while you then you rent the house out to tenants. Essentially you free the house owners from the burden of the mortgage payments, while you do exactly what you advised them to do – by renting the house out to tenants.

You win, as you gain control of the house as if you had bought it with a mortgage but without having to put down a deposit – and all the time you are renting the house out you make a monthly rental income just as if you had bought the house. The house owner meanwhile is freed from the burden of the mortgage payments – and gets to sell the house for the price they need to clear their mortgage. This is another classic win-win scenario.

If the house prices in an area have slumped badly, it is quite probable that this will be in an area where there are many properties in negative equity.

Moreover, the larger the dip in prices, the greater will be the re-bound when it comes. This will often mean that the increase in the house price will allow you to re-mortgage the house for more than the agreed sale price that was set some time earlier. Imagine for example that you agree a lease option agreement for a house for £75K, but the house value in five years' time rises to £100K, then you will be able to take out a 75% mortgage on the house for £100K to give you £75K to the house owner, thereby effectively buying the house for free. This deal will have helped free the home owner from negative equity, will have paid their mortgage off and will have allowed them to move on with their lives. As a property investor, you will have effectively bought a house for free – and in the intervening period made a rental income from a house you have been leasing by paying the mortgage on behalf of the house owner.

There are several lessons to be learnt from this sort of creative approach: First, in periods of recession or economic hardship there really are ways in which you can create wealth while helping those in difficulty. Second, this type of approach underlines the importance of thinking creatively and thinking out of the box; when the rules of the game change so must you in order to thrive – and when you thrive so do others; this is the way societies pull themselves out of recession, by entrepreneurial, creative and innovative thinking.

Next… and this is an interesting point; you do not necessarily need to own assets to make money from them. A lease option agreement is an option to buy a house – and not a commitment to buy the house; I have actually never failed to buy a house at the end of the lease option period – but I could choose not to. If for any reason the house had not increased in value sufficiently to justify the agreed sale price, the option holder could hand the house back. Alternately of course both parties could re-negotiate an extended period of time for the lease, which would continue to help both the house owner and lease holder.

It is worth remembering that many successful businesses make money from assets they do not own but have control over. *Uber* for example do not own any cars; the drivers do. Franchise developers do not own the businesses they sell the franchises to. *Deliveroo* do not own any restaurants. Each of these are examples are where businesses control and make money from assets without owning them. John D. Rockefeller – was often quoted as saying *'control everything but own nothing'*.

As the recession continued and deepened, my next deal was a lease option agreement. I had sent many... many... letters of enquiry to home owners wanting to sell, but who were trapped in negative equity and were trying to sell for completely unrealistic asking prices in comparison to very similar houses in the same neighbourhood which were selling for far less.

One day, I had a phone call from a man we will call Jeremy (not his real name). Jeremy was a lovely guy who had tried to help his son buy a house, but everything had gone wrong for him. The first thing he had done wrong was try to 'kill two birds with one stone' – which when buying property is almost always never a good idea.

Jeremy had a son who had been living in a rented flat in a bad area and was mixing with the wrong company. Jeremy decided a good tactic would be to buy a little house in a nice area and then rent it to his son for the same monthly rent he was paying for the flat. The rent would be more than Jeremy would be paying for the mortgage – and his plan was to save up the excess rent, put this in a savings account and then when this lump sum had grown in value, to give this back to his son to use as a deposit for his son to take over the mortgage. This seemed to him like a really clever strategy.

The next thing that went wrong was that Jeremy's son didn't like living in the nice area away from his friends, so he moved out of the house his father had bought and moved back to the rough area again. This left Jeremy with a house to sell. In the meantime, however, house prices had fallen and Jeremy could not sell the house for what he had bought it for as the property was now in negative equity.

When I met Jeremy, he was paying a monthly mortgage for an empty house that he could not sell – and was pretty low in spirits. I wanted to look at the figures and realised that he could rent the house out for considerably more than he was paying for the mortgage. I explained this to Jeremy and suggested that he rented the house out and wait for the housing market to recover with time as it most surely would. Jeremy could see the logic of this argument, but to him this house had become a complete nightmare. He did not want to become a landlord – and viewed this as being just another headache on top of all of the other troubles he was experiencing.

I really did try to convince Jeremy that renting the property to tenants would be the best way for him to help himself, but he was absolutely adamant this was not something he wanted to do. As far as he was concerned, he just wanted to be rid of the house.

I explained to him that I could not buy his house for the price he wanted (and needed to pay back his mortgage borrowing), but could possibly offer him a deal I which I would lease his house for a seven-year period – during which time, I would rent the property out and make a profit and at the end of this period of time, I would have the option to buy the house for the price he wanted and needed. This would effectively free him from the mortgage.

At the end of the seven-year period I did indeed buy the house – and the increase in its value during this time meant that I could buy the house with a mortgage that allowed me to pay Jeremy back while leave me with a house without ever having had to put down a deposit. It is worth remembering that Jeremy actually received seven years of mortgage payments that he would have otherwise would have had to pay – in addition of course, he received the price he wanted for the house.

My First Lease Option House

Here are how the figures stacked in this real-life example as a case study for how a lease option works.

This really was a win-win situation for both of us.

Case Study:

- **In 2008 Jeremy Buys a House for his son in for £95K – with a mortgage of £81K**

- **The father pays monthly mortgage payment of £145 p.c.m.**

- **The father charges his son rent of £450 p.c.m.**

- **In 2008 after his son has moved out the house is put on the market for £85K – but will not sell**

- **Jeremy receives offers of c.£70K but this would not allow him to clear the mortgage**

- **Samuel advises he puts the house out for rental of £550 p.c.m. reflecting the true rate – but Jeremy does not wish to be a landlord**

- **Samuel offers a lease option to purchase the house in 7 years time for £81K**

- **In 7 years time the property is worth £125K**

A Lease Option Case Study in Figures

Chapter Eighteen: A Huge Car Crash – A Humbling Lesson That Life Is So Fragile

My portfolio of houses grew over time using a range of strategies. I lived a simple life and was still helping out in a range of social projects in Walsall. I had now become really committed to making as much money as I possibly could – and to use this to help as many people as I could.

I was nineteen and I had a real sense of mission and purpose – and then in May of 2011 I had a horrendous car crash. My car was crushed like a fizzy drinks or soda can with the front almost folded back on itself. Somehow, and I do not know quite how, I crawled out of the wreckage and when the emergency services arrived, they found me semi-unconscious on the ground. I am so grateful to the paramedics, doctors and nurses for their amazing care - and indeed God for looking after me.

While I survived, I was not in great shape. I had earlier made a conscious choice to live a life of gratitude; things could have been so very different. It is at times like this that one realises just how very lucky we are in a country such as the UK where we have emergency services that are there for everyone 24/7. In so many places around the world, healthcare is rudimentary if it exists at all, the nearest hospital may be hours away - and care has to be paid for. Put simply there are many people who if they do not have the funds to pay for treatment simply die.

Really serious accidents, near death experiences – or critical illnesses can make you take stock of your life and really make you think about what is most important to you.

This motor accident did just that. By this stage I had eight properties and while not rich was by now financially free. The car accident was one of those 'life' events – I still wanted to be rich, I did want to build my property portfolio far more - but this crash made me realise just how fragile life could be. I knew my faith; my Christianity was important to me and I wanted to explore this further – and to gain a deeper and better understanding of scripture.

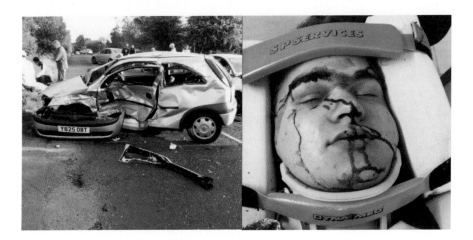

Not A Day I Wish To Remember...

Chapter Nineteen: Going To Bible College

I along with my Mum enrolled upon a three year programme at the Birmingham BBI New Bible College. My school education had ended at the age of sixteen which could have prevented me from entering but one of the tutors, a lovely man - Dr Reverend Robert Pickles accepted me into the college; again, I am so grateful.

Dr Reverend Robert Pickles

Between the ages of twenty to twenty-three, I travelled to Birmingham three days a week – and then as part of the programme undertook a number placements which included, for example, volunteering in care homes along with a number of working trips to Africa.

Working In A Care Home

During that time, I climbed Kilimanjaro to raise some money for *Compassion* charity - and those three years was where I really found myself and had the space and time to mature in my faith and set this into the context of life.

Many people go to University after school – and pay for this through student loans in order to obtain qualifications to build a career. I did things completely in a different order. In my case, I was able to take time out - and to pay for college through passive income from my property portfolio.

The course was, as you might expect was focused towards theology, faith and ethics.

At the end of the course students had to write a dissertation – and I decided I wished for mine to be focused towards biblical economics – and the Bible's view and perspective towards making money and entrepreneurialism. When I left, I expanded this into the form of a book called, '*Do The Possible, Watch God Do The Impossible*'. The writing of this dissertation and then book gave me a real release from a sense of feeling conflicted as I had beforehand about making money and helping the poor and needy - in a rather similar way to how I had felt between feeling torn between working for my Dad and the excitement of wanting to be a businessman and property investor.

My First Book!

Now that I had chosen to be an investor, I had been feeling a real sense of internal tension and of moral dilemma again, around not knowing whether to just be doing full time doing charity work and helping the poor in a Mother Theresa type model - or pursuing success in business. I had felt really torn between these two models because many Christians put across an attitude that if you wanted to help the poor, then you almost had to be poor yourself - and in the process, you would have to shun business and wealth creation.

I knew that there was something inside of me that really wanted to do both – but could I do this and not be hypocritical and true to my faith? It was when I was at Bible college that I realised that I actually could do both – and that the real issues are how you view money – and how you use it. Money is a tool - and like so many powerful things in life can be used for good or evil. It is what is in your heart that dictates how you view and use money.

I came to the conclusion and reconciled in my own mind and conscience, that I could be wildly successful in business while also helping people – and indeed came to the belief that the more successful I became, the more I could help people. Do you remember me saying earlier on in the book that Rick Warren who had always tithed 10% of his money to charity – had through the royalties from his book, '*The Purpose Driven Life*' reached the stage of *reverse* tithing in which he kept 10% of the royalties from this book and gave away the other 90%.

I came to the conclusion that anyone who says money is wrong has not given enough of it away.

I realised that so long as money made is made ethically and held with open hands and a generous heart, that it could truly be used for good.

To my amazement, this book, '*Do The Possible, Watch God Do The Impossible*' became an Amazon best seller – selling tens of thousands of copies.

People started contacting me from countries all around the world, asking if I could teach them both how to make money while helping other people – as well as sharing with them my thoughts about biblical economics and Christian entrepreneurialism.

In response, I set up a Christian business network called *Training Kings*, although everybody was welcome from all different walks of life and of all faiths or none. This grew to be nationwide network across the UK with thirteen different training centres – with people regularly flying in to attend events from all over the globe.

One Of The First Training Kings Events

I organised a series of regular training events and arranged for all of the hospitality for breakfasts, lunches and dinners. I charged a token fee to make this as accessible, but somebody had to pay for this which I was happy to do as I was by now financially free. The organisational side of things for making this happen was demanding – but hugely rewarding. I remember seeing many people overcome their own moral dilemmas in the minds – and I enjoyed being able to share my journey with people along with the business lessons I had learned along the way to help other people set up their own businesses, become financially free and use this in turn help others.

I felt like a man on a mission. It really is funny how things can turn out. The car crash was horrific, but this resulted in me going to Bible college, which helped me organise and prioritise my thoughts, reconcile some internal previously unresolved moral dilemmas in my mind, deepen my faith and helped me write a book. This in turn led me to establishing '*Training Kings*' to help other people become financially free and help others!

Samuel Leeds

Chapter Twenty: On Being A Christian:

This is probably a good point for me to say something more about my Christianity; now this book is absolutely for people of all faiths and none – but my faith has helped shape areas of my life and who I am, including how I do business and my mission for helping those less fortunate than myself. Not mentioning this would be a bit of an obvious omission.

Whenever you find something good in life, whether this be a recipe or some music (or anything else that is fantastic), a natural response is to want to share this with others; now you can of course skip this chapter – but with your permission, I would now love to share something about my Christianity with you as my faith is a key part of who I am.

I grew up in a Christian family and was made to go to Church – something that I found a bit boring. It was not until I left school at the age of seventeen, that I had a spiritual experience. People often ask me what I mean by this; for me this was going from *knowing* about Jesus to having a *personal experience* and relationship with him. This changed my life and my love of people. Before this, I wanted to live life on my terms. When I accepted Jesus into my life as Lord and saviour, I found that I let go of all my internal anger and frustrations that I had been carrying around with me. I know I am far from perfect and not a saint, but I know Jesus loves me unconditionally and continues to forgive me.

All of this meant that I suddenly went from not wanting to go to church with my parents – to having to push back against my Dad who now wanted me to work with him on Sundays as an entertainer - in preference to going to church. Ironically one of the biggest reasons for me wanting to get into property was to be able to leave my father's business and have the freedom to go to church on a Sunday and pursue my faith. You may remember I said something about this earlier.

An additional but connected reason, for going down the route of property investing was so I would not be trapped within a job - and in this way would to have more time to work with my church and go on mission trips and similar. One of these trips as a teenager was to Spain to help with a drug rehab centre, offering practical help and support; I knew that this was something I really wanted to commit and contribute to.

At eighteen, I spent a month in Zambia working in orphanages and spending some time working at a Christian school. I wanted to dedicate my life to the cause of helping people, loving people and loving God. Whenever I went on trip it was from a position of legitimately wanting to help people and make an impact. I always came back, however, feeling as if I had been more impacted than the people I had gone out to help.

I had an overwhelming feeling of a sense of injustice that there are so many people who have so very little, when most of us in western developed economies have so much in comparison.

There was a real spiritual aspect, in which I found that when you constantly look inwardly, it makes you miserable - but when you look outwardly to God with a view to helping others, it makes you happier and brings a far greater feeling of fulfilment.

Now to bring clean water and food to people costs money – since money can make things happen. This is why I really do not believe that money is good or bad, in itself, but rather what really matters most is who's hands it is in - and how it is used.

I saw a lot of people in my church who had a heart to do good things, who were always fundraising for one project or another, with some almost becoming full time fundraisers!

I knew I did not really want to do this, but would rather build a business that could fund the projects I really wanted to see happen. This is where my property business began to work hand in hand to philanthropically fund work in Africa and other developing countries.

My mother, her new husband Tim and my bother, were all really involved with the church. We often used to go to Walsall town centre to be of help to those that were destitute, provide for them food or find a place in a shelter. At night we would help those who got drunk and couldn't get home - or just be there and be a listening ear for those who have been left by their friends and were in a really miserable and lonely state.

As time went on, I became more and more convinced I wanted to grow my property business as a vehicle for funding the work and projects focussed towards helping others. By my early twenties I had a reasonable number of properties – but then some of my church started to say to me that I should not have too many houses and that this did not align with being a Christian.

It was this poverty mindset that ultimately led me to writing my first book, *'Do The Possible, Watch God Do The Impossible'* based on my college dissertation after I had resolved this conflict in my own mind and come to the conclusion that if you created wealth and used this to help others, then money could be used a tool or force for good.

I believe that ultimately you must hold money lightly, be selfless in the way you use this as an enabling tool for bringing about good – If you are blessed with money, you should use this so as to bless others by providing for their needs.

We made a decision as a family to move from Pelsall, a nice part of Walsall to a council estate in a poorer area of Walsall, Leamore, where there was a lot of unemployment and deprivation. We bought a minibus and worked with the kids on the estate - many of whom were quite traumatised either emotionally or psychologically. We took many of these youngsters to trips such as to theme parks or the seaside to ensure they were given days out - as indeed all young people ought to be able to experience and enjoy.

During my time at Bible college, I continued to grow my property portfolio – while also for my own personal development attending business network meetings, training courses and a number of other programmes

At one of these meetings, I was really struck by one of the speakers saying many things that were as if they were almost taken straight out of the Bible with quotes like, '*As a man is, so he thinks*'. Many of the things he was saying aligned with quotes I knew from the bible, but he was not acknowledging them as being either biblical or Christian. Meanwhile, I noticed that several people in the audience who I knew were Christians, thought much of what he said was a little worldly or even sinful. It struck me that many people seemed to think that there was a real separation between business and making money with being a Christian or even just being a 'good person'. I could see no reason why there had to be these two lines of thought that could not be reconciled with each other.

I wondered whether the person who was speaking was actually a Christian? Whilst on stage he never gave a hint or acknowledgement that he might be. Later I managed to make contact with him and found out that he was indeed a passionately committed Christian whose life had been transformed by his faith. This did surprise me – and I really felt God say to me, '*Don't judge him but if you find yourself on stage giving business talks, you could take the opportunity to mention that you are a Christian and not be ashamed of your faith*'.

During my time at Bible college, I increasingly became convinced that I wanted to love God, love people and to do this through using money as a tool for helping others - and that there was no reason why there should be a conflict between these ideals. It is true you cannot serve God and money, but you can serve God *through* using money.

One of the things that so often goes wrong in our society is that people *love things and use people*; by contrast we should *love people and use things*.

As I mentioned in the previous chapter witing '*Do The Possible, Watch God Do The Impossible*' convinced me that you can be a capitalist with compassion. The more money you make then the more people you can help – and even with growing a business you must have a product that brings benefit and value to people, so even this can be an enabling tool for helping others.

It was after publishing this book and having sold thousands of copies I began to be approached by increasing numbers of people asking me to speak on the area of Christian or biblical principles of business. It was this that led me to launching the Christian business network, '*Training Kings*' in 2013.

Training Kings was set up to train people with good hearts – specifically for Christians – as we found many Christians did not understand money, although we were careful to not make this exclusive or a condition of membership; we had Muslims, Sikhs, Jews and indeed atheists as members with the network.

Christianity has touched every part of my life and it was at a Christian church that I met my wife, Amanda. Amanda was originally from Zimbabwe and was brough up in a very traditional family. At first her father was a little unsure, with concerns about differences in culture and background, but when I said to him that we are 'one in Christ' he smiled and totally came round to giving us his blessing. My father in law and I could not be closer – and we are indeed one in Christ...!

When I started to run property training events, it was natural to sometimes mention my faith - and what my core values are.

Property training events are of course focussed towards property – but I did promise God some years back that I would not be ashamed of my faith or indeed him - as I firmly believe it is to him that I have everything to thank for.

Chapter Twenty One: A Red-Diamond Moment That Changed My Life...

The car accident was a life changing moment; another was to follow – although this was to be far more fun...

Red diamond moments are moments that can change your life for ever. I was at age twenty two (two weeks' from my twenty third birthday) - and about to experience one...

I was at a wedding - it was an African wedding taking place in the UK in which my pastor who was from Ghana was marrying a Zimbabwean lady. I was at the front of the church singing loudly, as I always do – and I remember glancing back and spotting this really beautiful lady, right at the back of the church. I remember just thinking how she just lit the whole room up with a huge smile and big beautiful eyes. I decided that I just had to speak to that lady and ideally find out her name. At the end of the service, I shot to the back to find her - but she had gone and was nowhere to be seen.

I knew there was an after party; I was not actually invited to this – but I thought maybe - just maybe, she might be there. Rather cheekily I crept in. I remember getting to this little Community Centre, opening the doors and realising that I was absolutely the only white person in the room. Loosing myself amongst the guests was not really going to be possible and it was pretty clear that everybody there was going to spot me.

The groom spotted me of course, looking at me a little incredulously with an expression that pretty much said, *'Oh, what are you doing here?'* – but bless him, I remember his face going from an understandable state of confusion to one of generosity. He smiled and gave me a nod which essentially said *'What the heck – go and get yourself some food'*.

I was feeling really awkward by this point standing at the buffet, but then I spotted that amazingly beautiful lady I had been hoping might be there.

My next task was to speak to her and find out her name if I could; this was not going to be easy. Unfortunately, she was tucked away at the far side of the room as part of a family group with chairs and tables already crowded around in the form of a circle. I was worried that if I was to go up to her, I'd have to squeeze past loads of people and look even more like an idiot than I was already feeling - and then of course if I did go over, what on earth was I going to say?

I was a bit nervous but sensed maybe this could just be a red diamond moment – meaning that what I did next could *just* potentially shape the rest of my life. I know this sounds extreme, but I decided to just go for it – and so I pushed past everybody one at a time; people had to shuffle and move their chairs and it all made for a little bit of commotion. I got to the table and I said, '*Hey*'. She looked up - with everyone else very understandably giving me an expression of '*Who on earth is this guy?*'.

I don't know what I was thinking - and this is where the magic training I had learned from my Dad possibly saved the situation; I had learned a number of magic tricks with coins etc. and so I said with as a convincing smile as possible, '*I'm the magician*'. I had seen entertainers sometimes be hired for wedding receptions. Everyone at the table swallowed this and seemed to think this was great and I remember thinking '*Oh my goodness, what have I just got myself into?*' I did a couple of little tricks and then I told them that I was not really a magician, but a friend of the groom. Somehow, I got away with all of this. Most importantly though, I was now sitting next to this lady. She introduced herself as Amanda and told me that she had been born and bred in Harare, Zimbabwe, but now lived in Leeds. I laughed and explained that my surname was Leeds.

We ended up chatting for two hours and when I had plucked up enough courage, I asked if maybe I could take her out for dinner. To my delight she said '*sure*', - and the next week I took her out for the evening as arranged.

To cut a long story short, I ended up falling madly in love - and quickly realised that I wanted to ask Amanda to marry me.

She was clearly a great person; I knew I needed to tell her about my finances and that I had a million-pound property portfolio which was by this stage continuing to grow. I did not know how she might react, but I knew I needed to be open and tell her everything.

I felt comfortable to tell her, but I approached the topic in an interesting way. Instead of just saying I was rich, I said to her; *'Amanda I've not been totally upfront about my finances'*. She asked *'How?'* I said, *'Well I'm actually £1,000,000 in debt'*. I did wonder how she might respond to this. I remember so well how she said *'OK - maybe I'll see if I can get some overtime'*. She was working as a quantity surveyor at the time.

Now of course, while this was actually true, since I did have £1,000,000 worth of mortgage debt, I also had substantial equity and by now a really healthy passive income.

I remember my heart just melted - and I told her my situation in rather greater depth. I explained that actually while I did have a million pounds of mortgage debt, actually I was completely financially free and that I didn't have to work ever again and neither would she if she didn't want to. She didn't even seem that excited. She just replied with a throw away remark of, *'Oh, that's good isn't it?'*

I am so very fortunate and lucky and blessed to say that Amanda, this lady, ended up accepting my proposal and we got married the following year!

She Said 'Yes'.....

... And The Rest As They Say Is History...

Chapter Twenty Two: A Charity With A Focus Towards Making A Difference - A Promise To Myself And The People Of Africa:

When I visited Zambia as a teenager, I was utterly shocked by what I saw - and I vowed to myself to bring clean water to the village, if and when I was able to do so. I like to think of myself as a man of my word – and if I say I am going to do something – even to myself – that is what I will do. I could not forget or erase from my mind the image of children walking in excess of ten kilometers or more each day just to get clean water. Bore holes and storage tanks could provide a simple solution and I had vowed to myself to provide these to this village when financially able to do so.

By the age of twenty-one, I was now completely financially free and was now in a position to start fulfilling the dream to not only establish bore holes and storage tanks for clean water, but to start thinking about establishing a charity to tackle this crying need for clean water, sanitation, basic healthcare and education for many parts of Africa.

Anybody who has ever established a charity in the UK will know just how difficult this is set up; anybody who thinks it is easy, clearly has not tried to do this! (Establishing a company is by contrast really easy to do – I'll say more about this later...)

I was now primarily driven by my mission to help those I had seen in Africa – and so many in similar need. I also wanted to help educate and train others back in the UK with a similar heart. At this time, I wasn't really working on the property business, but was primarily focused towards developing *Training Kings*.

I was going back and forth to Africa all the time visiting nine different countries across the continent some of them several times. I mentioned earlier that it is common to feel good about helping others, but that this can actually be something that feeds your own feeling of self-worth. This can in return actually make you quite selfish through sub-consciously feeding your own ego and the need to feel good about yourself.

I was getting really addicted to all the projects I was establishing in Africa and I realised that I needed to make sure this was first and foremost focused towards helping others and not my emotional needs.

I have been out to many different countries in Africa and to some of the most rural and needy areas helping in orphanages and schools, helping to bring infrastructure for water that is safe to drink, along with supplying food and clothing. With all of this, you are of course helping people and you are indeed impacting the villagers and providing necessities for them – but, you have to be honest with yourself that you are also feeding your own emotional needs. Whenever I have set out to make an impact for others, I have always been impacted to a greater extent myself. I have gone out to be a blessing, but I've ended up being more blessed myself. The lesson from this is to keep reminding yourself of what your real driver is. Those of you who know the new testament of the Bible will know that Jesus was the ultimate servant king; actually, he came to serve and not to be served.

I decided I wanted to take out a small team from the UK, on one of my trips in Africa. Amanda (now my wife) would of course be coming. I assembled a small team and one of the people I invited was one of my school teachers, Mrs Hey-Smith; she was very special to me as she was one of the very few teachers who had actually believed in me as a child. During all of my time at school she encouraged me and helped build me up in myself; looking back on it she really did have quite a profound effect on me becoming the person I am now today when most people – (or so it seemed) had essentially written me off.

I remember inviting her to come out to Africa to help with some of the projects we had established. True to form, she jumped at the opportunity and was still eager to support me – and in this instance of course, to help others. She was and is an amazing lady – and one of those teachers who is inspirational and who truly changes peoples' lives – probably with a far greater effect than she realises.

We set out as a small team and based ourselves in Solwezi, a quite rural town in Zambia. During the visit, I returned (this time with the group) to the very small village where I had previously met the small boy who did not have any drinking water in his village and was walking ten or more kilometers everyday just to collect enough water for him and some of his family. By this stage, I and those working with me, had managed to provide a borehole in the village; not only was it was it impacting the people, but it was impacting me just by seeing how significant something as simple as this was having on the village. It is worth noting that in many parts of Africa, water borne diseases, still account for the single greatest cause of preventable deaths.

I remember thinking just how incredible this was and desperately wanted to do more of this type of work. All of this had been made possible as a result of my income from property – and this confirmed to me that I wanted to make more money, buy more houses and scale my business. This was now no longer a route to financial freedom – or even ultimate financial freedom, but actually a financial vehicle for funding large scale charitable work.

This in turn led me to thinking, how might I make money faster through property? I suppose this is the way my brain is oriented – to always look for entrepreneurial ways for wealth creation (or in this case to be more precise – approaches for creating further income streams).

While property investing is a great way for creating passive income streams, (and you will have gathered how much of an enthusiast I am for property), you often have to save money first – to buy a property.

All of this started me thinking about possible approaches for how I might generate cash faster – as a means for funding the charitable work.

Going right back to my days at school when I was selling magic tricks, I had enjoyed thinking about new ways of making income by supplying what other people wanted. Little did I know it but I was just about to come up with first one and then a second business model for helping people become property investors. I would be supplying what people needed to start as property investors and these approaches would allow me to increase my own income to help fund my charitable projects, which by this stage had become the principal driver for my mission in life.

Chapter Twenty Three: Finding Properties For Other Property Investors: A New Business Model To Help Others

I had seen through *Training Kings*, how profoundly even introductory levels of training could help change peoples' futures by teaching them how to build passive income streams and demonstrating how property could be a great way to help build long term wealth and financial freedom.

People still of course needed to find the right houses, stack the financial numbers and put into practice everything I was introducing people to. This is an incredibly powerful model – and one in which ordinary people really can change their futures – but this requires action – and for many people this can be difficult if they have busy lives and are time poor.

This started me thinking...

By now I was well known in the property industry and instead of me trying to find deals, estate agents were coming to me regularly with deals – in many cases before they came to the market (often called off market deals). The estate agents knew what I was looking for in terms of returns and as a result many of these deals that were being brought to me were excellent.

After some thought, I had a 'breakthrough' or Eureka moment: Agents were regularly coming to me with deals that others were desperate to find - and in many cases, did not have the time to search for. Meanwhile, I had seen that many people were unsure about how to really crunch the numbers, to differentiate and spot a really good deal from all the rest. If I could put these two groups of people together this could clearly add real value and serve an un-met need.

My thinking was that if I could arrange a series of viewings for houses that looked promising and which could make really good investments, then I could in turn bring a car full of pre-arranged property investors with me to the viewings. If any of the investors chose to buy one of the properties, then the estate agent would make their normal fee through their normal commission route. I in turn would have an arrangement with the people I brought round to the viewings, in which they would pay me a £1,000 [c. US$1,400] finder's fee should they buy one of the properties.

This would be a win-win for the property investors – and for the estate agents. I would earn my money through putting this strategy together to create a win-win-win situation. In this model I would be providing a service to the estate agents since they knew I was only bringing to them investors who were serious. In turn, I was providing a key service to the investors since they knew I would only arrange to show them properties that offered real potential as an investment. I was undertaking the due diligence to ensure that the financial figures stacked up – along with calculating the return on investment so that the investor would know how much money they could be expected to make per year.

This approach grew and grew and led to the formation of a company I named, *'Buy Low – Rent High Ltd'* (which is where the title of my second book comes from). My reputation for deal sourcing over time became quite well known in property circles. I started selling deals for properties I had seen and had stacked the figures for – without in some cases people even seeing the properties since they had come to trust my judgement, due diligence and stacking of the numbers.

If you buy a house for an investment, it is important that you first assess how good a deal might be based on the figures – *and in particular how much money the property will make as a percentage of how much money you will have to invest in the deal*. It is amazing but most estate agents simply do not know how to do this calculation. I am shortly going to show you how.

At live training events I often show the pictures of two properties side by side and ask the audience to say which they would buy. People invariably say *'this one'* or *'that one'* because of reasons such as *'this one looks nicer'*, or *'this one has a nice garden, while the other doesn't'* etc. All of these answers should be irrelevant to a property investor as you are not going to live in the property; it will not be your home..! The correct answer is you should assess which will be the better *financial investment* – and in particular which will give you the greatest cash flow as a percentage of the money you have to put into the investment.

The lesson here is that you should buy an investment property based on the financial figures – and not emotions. If you buy with emotions, then you are not acting as a property investor should.

So how do you do this? I mentioned earlier that even most estate agents do not know how to stack the figures properly.

Most estate agents provide projected *yields* for a property, which put simply is the income the property can make in percentage terms of the purchase price of the property. While this is easy to calculate, actually the figure is not really so useful for a number of reasons. Firstly, this approach assumes that you purchase a property with cash. In most instances, I would suggest this is normally not the best way to purchase an investment property. If you have sufficient cash to purchase a property – the same quantity of money will allow you to purchase several properties through the use of mortgages. In this way you will receive several times the income - even after the mortgage payments. Remember also, that over the longer term property prices increase with time - and leveraging your buying power through mortgaging allows you to greatly increase your equity as house prices increase.

If you do purchase using mortgages you need a far more accurate way in which to calculate or determine how good an investment might be. If you are going to assess a deal with precision, you will need to take into account the deposit you put towards the property; interest rates and mortgage monthly payments; fees, such as those for solicitors; stamp duty purchase tax; the cost of any refurbishment; the cost of any furniture, management of the property if you do not intend to do this yourself – and a percentage of the rental income put aside for periodic repairs. If this sound complicated, this can actually be calculated quite easily. The figure we need to calculate is the annual Return On Investment – or – ROI in percentage terms.

I am now going to show you how yields and Returns On Investment (ROIs) are calculated.

The yield expressed as a percentage, is the price of the property divided by the annual rent x 100 i.e.:

$$Yield \ (as \ a \ Percentage) = \frac{Annual \ Rent}{Price \ Paid \ for \ Property} \ x \ 100$$

This is the figure most estate agents quote.

Knowing the Return On Investment or ROI, however, is far more informative, since this tell you how much money you will make from the money you have invested.

The Return On Investment or ROI, (expressed as a percentage) - is the annual profit divided by the Investment x 100. i.e.:

$$Return \ On \ Investment \ (as \ a \ Percentage) = \frac{Annual \ Profit}{Investment} \ x \ 100$$

To illustrate all of this, let us consider an average house - worth £200K, with an average rent for the house of £1,000 per calendar month.

The yield for this house will be: $\frac{12,000}{200,000} \ x \ 100 = 6\%$

122

Calculating the Return On Investment is a little more complicated, (but still easy!)

Remember the Return On Investment is calculated by dividing the Annual Profit by the Investment and then multiplying this by 100.

We will start by looking at how you calculate the Investment.

The investment, is simply the sum of all of the money you have to put down as an investment for a house.

If you buy an investment property with a mortgage in the UK, you will first need to put down a deposit of typically 25%.

For the average house costing £200K, the deposit needed will therefore be 0.25 x £200K = £50K.

There are however other costs you will need to account for which are likely to include: mortgage brokers fees, stamp duty, solicitor's fees, furniture and white goods etc. – along with any refurbishment, decorating costs and carpets / curtains and furnishings. The exact figure will clearly vary for each property, but as a guide, we will assume an additional 4% will be needed to cover these costs.

The total money invested will therefore be:

25% deposit + 4% additional costs = 29% of the purchase price.

The total money to be invested can therefore be calculated according to:

0.29 x purchase cost, i.e.:

TOTAL MONEY IN = APPROX 0.29 x PURCHASE COST

(For a £200K house this will equal 0.29 x 200K = £58K).

The next figure you need you be able to calculate is your annual profit. This is simply the rent collected minus expenses.

There are typically three main expenses: we will call these the three 'M's; these are:

(1)   *M*ortgage payments,

(2)   *M*aintenance and voids (typically you should put aside 10% of the rent for maintenance, voids and insurance),

(3)   *M*anagement fees, (this will typically be 10% for single let house or 15% for a house of multiple occupancy).

You can purchase a house through either an interest only or repayment mortgages.

The interest rate for buy to let mortgages is typically 2 to 2.5% at the time of writing; let us choose a conservative interest rate of 3%.

Many people worry about fluctuations in interest rates – but interest rates can be fixed for more than ten years; if you are concerned about future interest rates, then simply fix your mortgages.

Repayment only mortgages typically double monthly mortgage payments - as you slowly pay back the loan over 25 years.

This might seem attractive to the traditional mindset of paying down your mortgage as quickly as possible, but for property investment purposes, it is almost always in your interests and preferable to choose an interest only mortgage.

Remember there is a big difference between good debt and bad debt; bad debt is used to buy things that deprecate in value, while good debt helps make you money – and good debt can work to the advantage of property investors. Let's look at how this can work...

Firstly – debt diminishes in value due to the effects of inflation over time; this means that the loan will become a progressively smaller percentage of the value of the house with time.

The next thing to consider is that your mortgage (for our calculations we are assuming an annual interest rate of 3%), may give you a Return On Investment of 20% or more. The money you could be using to pay down the mortgage could be used to pay another mortgage - which in turn will be paying you another passive income stream through another property which will also over time be increasing with value. So why would you wish to pay down the mortgage? By paying down your mortgage, you will be losing out of the opportunity for investing on another property.

This demonstrates that the whole concept of paying down your mortgage as quickly as possible, rarely serves you very well; using good debt can serve you far better...

Some people caution against becoming too highly geared or leveraged – however you should remember that you will always have a 25% deposit stake as a down payment in the property, which will guard against falls in house prices. This is partly why mortgage lenders ask for a deposit.

Leveraging money with good debt builds high net worth; this is so clearly demonstrated by almost all of the richest people on the planet having high levels of good debt – BUT - *far greater* levels of net worth.

Now, there are two take away lessons you need to note:

The first of these is that calculating or 'stacking' the numbers accurately, gives you a far greater insight into how good a potential lead may be.

The second is that *leveraging* good debt allows you to build your residual income streams far more rapidly than simply buying properties with cash;

in the same way you will gain far greater growth of equity within your portfolio by purchasing with interest only mortgages.

These were some of my earliest and most important lessons for helping me obtain financial freedom at such a young age – and these are still principles I adhere to and implement today.

For those of you who have attended any of my training sessions – or undertaken any of my on-line training, you will know that I heavily recommend purchasing properties with interest only mortgages to maximise income and capital growth based on leveraging good debt.

As a rough guide, I will only purchase a property if it will provide a return on investment of 20 % or greater or greater. If you too stick to these guidelines then if property prices fall (as they can at some stage during a typical ten-year cycle, then this need not cause you concern). Your income will remain robust, so long as you have tenants paying rent – and in the long term, the property price should increase.

The reason I have gone into so much detail here looking at how you should calculate or stack the figures for any potential deal, is because calculating the ROI is an approach that I know provides an accurate, predictive and reliable approach for assessing how good a prospective deal might be. While the process does require an attention to detail, the maths is actually quite straightforward and now that I have done this hundreds of times over, my experience allows me to evaluate deals in this way like clockwork.

It was the very fact that I could quickly look at the details for a property for sale, determine the rental value and select those that would give amazing returns that led to the company, 'Buy Low – Rent High' becoming such a success. Very quickly prospective (and indeed experienced property investors) came flocking to me to find deals. The advantage and attractiveness to them was that they knew I would only bring to them deals that offered a great return on investment, with the figures calculated and presented in an easy to understand, yet thorough way. For inexperienced investors this offered reassurance that they would be investing wisely – and for experienced investors who were often busy and time poor, it meant that they could still find great deals without having to do all the work themselves.

Chapter Twenty Four: Taking Training To A Whole New Level – To Educate And Equip New Property Investors Along Their Path Towards Financial Freedom – And Their Mission In Life

In the previous chapter, I explained how you could calculate the Return On Investment (ROI) for a simple buy to let investment.

People kept approaching me - asking me to teach them how to do this, but also how to stack the figures for other types of property deals such as refurbishment projects – as well as a range of other strategies from lease options through to *Airbnb* (serviced accommodation) type lettings. I tried to help where I would - and I included some of the basic principles within my *Training Kings* network meetings. The problem was that the more I tried to help people, the more people came to me asking for instruction; I think that is what is called being a victim of your own success.

I do genuinely have a desire to try to help people wherever I can, so the next question was how to do this in a scalable and sustainable way.

Training Kings was largely being financially supported by myself as I was charging only a nominal fee, which did not cover all of the running costs. I decided that the way forward was to set up what was to become my first series of *Crash Courses*, each of which would be run in the form of an intensive all day event from early till late evening with a £200 [US$380] fee to cover overheads such as the costs for hiring a room and catering.

An Early Crash Course

Looking back on it, I appreciate that I was perhaps not always the perfect host. I remember once turning up to a hotel and finding the room locked even as guests were starting to arrive - while I was trying to phone round frantically for someone to come and unlock the room! If I had booked a better hotel, this probably would not have happened, but you live and learn... Despite all of this, the *Crash Courses* were very well received; this however failed to satisfy demand. The courses started to be booked out faster and faster as their fame and notoriety grew. One of the most common requests I started to be asked, was for me to run some advanced training to follow up on some of the strategies I was introducing during the crash courses such as lease options or buy-refurbishment-refinance-rent approaches.

At the time, I simply did not want to do this - and just wanted to run a one day event to show people what was possible and help get them started on their own path to success and financial freedom.

One of my mentors asked me why I didn't want to run follow-on more advanced training programmes. I tried to explain, but he persisted and asked me if any of those who had attended the crash course and asked for further training had gone on to enroll for further training with other people. I actually know that quite a few people had done just this, as I had received some emails thanking me for starting them out on their property adventure – and that they were now signing up for some more advanced training.

My mentor asked me if he thought I could offer training to a higher standard than some of the people who were offering training courses. Now having experienced some of these programmes myself, I had to admit that whilst not trying to be arrogant at all, I thought in all honesty I probably could. My mentor replied that if this was the case, then by not offering the training, I was actually doing my students a disservice. This was not the response I was expecting and quite simply I had not thought about the matter in this way. I knew I *did* want to help people – and to help them in the very best way that I could. By now I was twenty-five and a millionaire – and did not need to do this for the money.

I went away and thought about it and discussed this with Amanda my wife – and in the end decided to run some advanced training. The first advanced training programme I launched was a three day intensive programme, I called a *'Deal Finding Extravaganza'*. My thinking was that finding good deals underpinned all other strategies. Deal finding was what I was doing as a service for people who came to me to find and then buy excellent deals that I had found. The first time I ran this I had twenty-two people enroll. The feedback was amazing and I started to see, first some - and then more and more of my students become financially free, help their families and start social enterprises. Seeing and watching other people become successful was amazing – along with a feeling that gave me a real sense of self-worth and purpose. There is really no feeling better in life than helping other people – and knowing that you have been able to make a real difference. Again, I do not want to be selfish – but being able to help others and see the difference does give me a feeling that is addictive.

Most of the people on these programmes went on to do deals, became successful themselves and to this day credit me as part of their journey. I loved that feeling - and I was thinking, '*I really want to scale what I do; I really want to grow*'.

The next stage was to develop and launch a whole series of interlinked advanced training programmes covering areas such as: lease option agreements, buy-refurbishment-refinance-rent approaches, deal sourcing, raising money and joint venturing, rent-to-rent and serviced accommodation - to name but a few. These were all strategies that I had successfully used myself.

Like anyone in business I have made mistakes, and to some extent had learned 'along the way'. The great thing about being able to develop these programmes was to be able to include all of lessons I had learned from trial and error – so that other people did not have to. All of these training programmes gave rise to a new training business in its own right.

Just as this new training business was really starting to take off, Amanda my wife became pregnant and we moved into a little barn conversion out in the country near Featherstone in Wolverhampton.

I started to question in my innermost self whether I really wanted to continue running all of the training programmes as to run these properly is quite demanding – and requires (as it should do) – a lot of follow up with students for mentoring and on-going guidance. I started producing daily *YouTube* videos with tips, how to guides and stories of my students' success etc. Again, the overwhelming feedback was positive, but there were sometimes one or two people who would say that I was too loud, or pushy with sales tactics etc. To be honest this did start to really upset and get to me. Amanda and I were just on the cusp of starting a family and becoming parents for the first time – a more peaceful life was starting to look like it could quite attractive.

Now I know I am indeed an exuberant and a 'type A' character; I know that – that is just part of who I am. If I commit to something, I always put 100% of everything I have into it. I cannot help it; it's just the way I am. I really did not want to be one of those rich people who just hides away.

Ironically – one of the things I teach all of my students is that if you want to be successful in property, you absolutely have to give it everything you have when you start out and begin; if you do not then you are unlikely to succeed. This is of course true of almost everything in life. You tend to get out of anything in life what you put in. There is a well known saying that the only place you find the word 'success' before work is in the dictionary; how very true this is!

Ninety nine out of one hundred people who you try to help are wonderful to work with and grateful, but it is inevitable that very occasionally you will meet someone who isn't so positive. I did start to question whether or not I really wanted to carry on doing this – or not? I was back to one of those life dilemmas again about what I should do.

I was coming to the conclusion in my mind that the hassle of running training programmes was simply not worth it and that retirement sounded quite attractive. I had a nice property portfolio giving me an income through which I simply would never have to work again.

I discussed this over with Amanda of course and said to her, that I did not want to carry on with training business - and that I was thinking of doing some deal sourcing, maybe just packaging and selling one or two deals a month. I also had thought that I might do a few charity shows just for fun for my Dad and help run events for one or two other people such as my brother. I did not want any more money, but just wanted to enjoy life and have a fun, free and easy retirement type of life. I was now twenty-six, feeling comfortable and a millionaire.

Amanda was totally supportive and said that would be fine if that was what I wanted. Life was looking good... In October 2017, our daughter Ruby was born. Becoming parents was for both of us life changing and one of the most amazing and wonderful moments you can imagine.

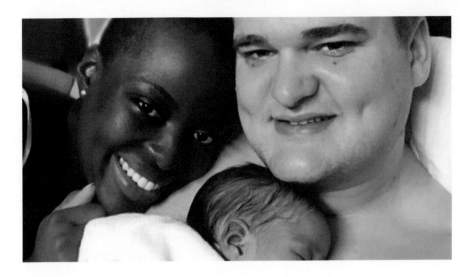

And Little Ruby Leeds Is Born -

Four months or so later, Amanda looked at me in a caring and knowing way, in the way that only those who know and love you really can - and asked me if everything was truly alright with me. It is often the people who are closest to you who can see when things are not quite as they could be; I said I was fine, but I realised that if I was being honest, I was not ready for retirement. I was getting itchy feet and had so much pent-up energy.

Amanda advised that I really needed to go and sell some deals, to start traveling, to start doing crash courses again and to get on stage. I asked her if she really thought that that was what I needed to do; she was adamant that that was exactly what I should be doing!

I spoke to my brother and explained that I was thinking of going back to run crash courses again and getting more involved with property and actually grow my business rather than just lounging around and being lazy.

I asked how he was doing in business; as it happened, Russell was doing really well in his business along with Craig running an entertainment agency that was putting on over two hundred shows a month across the country. I knew in my heart that I wanted to grow, I wanted to scale my business and leave a legacy; I want to help people – and I wanted to register my charity – but also knew I could not really do all of this alone.

I wanted a business partner and so I offered Russell a business partnership. I put a proposal to him that he could come to work with me, to leave the magic business - and together we would grow the property business, scale it and train as many people in property investing as we could. In return I committed to produce a *YouTube* video every single day to help publisise and grow the business. I am delighted to say that after a little bit of persuasion, Russell agreed; this was a real turning point as Russell has turned out to be an amazing CEO.

Russel Joins (Centre Left Shaking Hands) as a Business Partner; Pictured outside Hilton Hall with the Rest of the Team

Russell brought to this partnership his business acumen and his larger scale way of thinking - to work alongside my knowledge of how to make money through any number of strategies in property.

As soon as Russell was working with me, he was pushing for bigger deals. At first, I was not too sure about this approach as I knew the HMO market. However, he kept pushing for bigger deals which before too long resulted in us buying a castle! We bought Ribbesford House, (see chapter thirty) - an absolutely amazing grade II* listed building. with a gross development value of more than £6 million [c. US$8.4m]. I really have to give credit to Russell's vision because he found the castle and without him, we would not have ventured into a project of this scale. Russell kept saying to me, that we needed to get mentors with experience of much larger projects. I kept gently pushing back with thinking along the lines of *'yes - but this mentor that I've had for years is really* good'; Russell was kind and agree we could keep these people who had been so helpful, but was insistent that we also needed new mentors who could push and stretch us. This is exactly what we did. In this way we started reach new heights. Russell kept saying that, *'We are only getting 200 people at the crash course - we need to get bigger venues'.* I asked, *'How big do you think we should get?'* Before I knew it, Russell booked the *Ibis* hotel in London that holds 1,200 people. I was both skeptical and nervous thinking that we were never going to fill this, given that we had never run events for more than 250 people before. To my amazement, the event sold out...

I remember saying to Russell that I believed this was surely just a one-off event and that this was unlikely to happen again. Russell insisted that we should book the hotel again the following week. I remember saying rather incredulously, *'Come on dude - that's ridiculous'*, but ran with it as after all Russell is my brother. Once again, the event sold out. This became the new normal. Russell's much larger scale way of thinking was paying off.

We continued to grow, run larger events - and in this way were able to help many more people become financially free. Meanwhile, of course, we were doing larger property deals ourselves.

I was starting to be invited to go and speak more and more frequently at conferences and I was winning awards that I had not even applied for. I started receiving calls from celebrities I knew from the TV back when I was a child, asking to talk to me about property with requests to see if we could we put deals together. All of this seemed quite surreal.

Russell and one of the other directors of the company next suggested that we move the company's offices. My initial reaction was to say that we couldn't move from Hilton Hall in Wolverhampton as that was where we had always been; why would we want to move? Initially I thought that they were suggesting we move more centrally to the middle of the city. Russell explained that actually he meant that we should move our headquarters to London. Now, I ought to explain at this point that I am a Black Country boy at heart; I was born and bred in Walsall. I could not imagine living in London. After some protestations I said in the end that I would go and have a look at some offices and also houses for rent - and then maybe just maybe we could think about whether we should go ahead with the move.

I knew that I did spend a lot of time traveling to and from meetings in London so I could see that there could be some sense in moving to the capital. In the end we made a really bold move - and even though everything is so much more expensive and really quite different, we moved to London.

Russell and I next approached Amanda's brother, a chartered property surveyor - and suggested to him that he might want to join the business as well. Again, he accepted. Amanda and I, now have a second child, Luke - and as a family we live just outside of London in Buckinghamshire.

A New Addition to the Family: Luke Leeds

The businesses have continued to grow and last year, we made over £2m [c. US$2.8m] clean profit across the businesses from a turnover of just shy of £10m [c. US$14m]. It is important to stress that for me, it is not all about how much money you make, it is about how the money can be made to work for good and practically help people.

I have now had our charity, the *'Samuel Leeds Foundation'* finally registered with a charity commission number, which for me is a real milestone.

We are now in the process of working to build a school in Uganda -and there are just so many exciting projects going on. Has it all been easy? No!! Has it been challenging? - Absolutely!! My net worth is now over £10m [c. US$14m] - and I cannot believe it if I'm honest. As I write this, I am thirty years old; did I intend to become a multi-millionaire? No I didn't. I simply intended to become financially free in property to just give me more time. I intended just to make a decent living since I knew that I would not be able to do that with the school qualifications I achieved.

Now I am on a mission; I want to do a number of things: I want to bring financial education into schools, I want people to realise that if they are not good in school or if they don't like their job and want to escape - that there really is another way.

For me, property has changed my life - and I want to publicly thank those that have stood with me - and thank those that have helped me and have opened doors for me.

No one is self-made; people have given me opportunities. All I have done is take those opportunities and believed in myself that I could be successful. I am so grateful, I am grateful to be alive and am grateful to my family, I am grateful to my customers, I am grateful to my staff and I am also incredibly excited about what the next few years might hold.

Samuel Leeds

Chapter Twenty Five: An Almost Fatal Trip To Africa...

Earlier, I told you the tale of my car crash that really did bring home to me just how fragile life could be. I know how much I owe to the paramedics, nurses and doctors who looked after me. While I made a full recovery, I can honestly say that this was one of those life changing events; one that made me take stock of my life – with one of the consequences being that I went to Bible college for three years – along with my mother Sue. I think it is fair to say that nobody who has ever had a close shave with death will ever quite view life the same way again – at least in the sense that they will never forget the experience!

Little did I know, but I was going to have another close shave with death – the second in just over seven years. Whilst I certainly do not want to make a habit of having serious accidents, I can look back again say that good has again come from this second rather horrible accident.

I mentioned earlier that I had made many trips to Uganda and a number of other African countries to arrange for the installation of bore holes and water tanks. While there are many other needs that need to be addressed and are critically important, clean drinking (*potable*) water represents the most pressing need to help prevent water borne disease. This is the area where money can have the greatest impact for every pound or dollar spent. This is why funding clean water supply projects is one of the highest priorities for my charity, the *Samuel Leeds Foundation*.

Just before going to Africa, we discovered that Amanda was pregnant; this was wonderful news although it meant however that she could not come with us – although I was being accompanied by my brother and his wife Anna and a group of my students.

On 16th July 2018, we all flew out from London Heathrow to Entebbe.

Many of my students have commented that one of the greatest and almost accidental benefits of my training is the number of contacts and the network opportunities that come from being part of a network. Friendships are often formed between students who chose to work together. I have seen many times arrangements where builders contract to work for other students for renovation projects, or in which solicitors undertake conveyancing for other students – or indeed collaborations where students pass deals to each other just to help each other out. Being in a network of like minded people, really can - and does bring many benefits.

It is for these reasons that I always strongly encourage all of my students to network and attend as many property (and indeed other business) events as they can.

As my training programmes really began to expand and grow in numbers, I started to make a habit of inviting a group of students with me on my trips to African countries to firstly see the work I was doing – and to give them the opportunity to get involved by practically seeing what I was doing - and copying, or indeed donating to the charity. It is wonderful to see how many students share the same mission of wanting to help others, when they have learned the secrets of financial independence – and are in this way empowered to help others from a position of abundance.

To help build bonding within the group, I like to arrange if possible some action adventure team activities that will help take people out of their comfort zones as I have found that this almost always helps people to grow. I often say to my students that if they want to develop as people, they need to get comfortable with being uncomfortable – and actively seek out an opportunity each day and every day for something that will take them out of their comfort zone.

I had on this trip, originally planned for all of us as a group, to go bungee jumping before getting started on our work. Having arrived in Entebbe, we found out that due to a fault with the equipment that was awaiting repair, this was not going to be possible. Not daunted, I looked for another activity to take its place and arranged for us as a group to go white water rafting on the Nile in the Jinga region instead; perfect (or so I thought)!

We assembled as a group and our guide gave us some basic safety instructions. We all were supplied with life vests – and were shown how to float on our backs, should we fall into the water. If we did, we were assured all we needed to do was to stay calm, float on our backs as instructed and one of the team would be with us in no time at all.

Our instructor suddenly and deliberately upturned the raft of my friend Charles (much to his surprise), to demonstrate what to do and show that there was nothing to fear.

Charles clambered back onto one of his rafts looking rather shaken but OK - at which point our instructor then upended us all into the water! After this rather salutary lesson, we set off down the river paddling our way along some very calm waters – enjoying looking at and passing a number of villages along the way.

After about half an hour we approached the first set of waterfalls. We had been instructed to go into the rapids leading up to the falls side on and then to back paddle as we passed though. As we approached the falls, the raft I was in with some of the others suddenly and unexpectedly flipped round so that we ended up going into the rapids front nose first; this changed everything and suddenly we were just passengers being taken first this way and then that.

We crashed through the waterfall – with us now being bounced off rocks in every direction as we swept along in the waters below. The raft upended with myself and others now caught under the structure – getting dragged across one set of rocks after another.

I really did think I was going to drown; somehow, I managed to break free, so at least I could breath – but now I was in the water being taken along with the flow of the river. My whole body took a horrible battering against the rocks with my right leg being shattered below the knee taking a compound fracture in which the bone was sticking out through the skin.

We later found out that the raft was overloaded and this was what had led to it becoming unstable, flipping up in the air and heading into the waterfalls sideways on. You live and learn!

I was fortunate enough to eventually be picked up by a rescue boat some distance on from the rapids where the water was calmer. I was relieved to hear that all of the party were safe and sound, with nobody else having sustained any serious injuries – although I think every single person was bruised, battered and pretty shaken up. They were as a group fantastic and looked after me so well. I needed to get to hospital, but this meant waiting for around an hour for a vehicle to pick me up – followed by a two-hour drive. I wasn't feeling too great by this stage and knew I was losing a lot of blood. It was clear I needed surgery and would not be going anywhere for a while.

My brother Russell, his wife Anna (who was also quite bruised and battered but fortunately not hurt too seriously) and the rest of the team had an impromptu meeting around my bedside. Ironically, we had the day before held a group training session to help develop a '*warrior mindset*' in which you choose to carry on despite of any circumstances and how you might feel. We all knew we had come out to Africa for a purpose and unanimously agree that we should - and must carry on with the mission; a lot of people were depending on us – and we knew the need.

I could not lead the trip anymore for pretty obvious reasons and so I passed the leadership batten to my brother Russell. This was a test of a warrior mindset if ever there was, but I have to say that he and the rest of the team not only stepped up to the mark, but utterly excelled.

I had surgery later that day but knew I needed to stay for a few days before being even able to think about how I was going to get home.

This was one of those life situations that really does demonstrate just how lucky we are in the UK with our *National Health Service*. In Uganda, as in so many countries – there is no health service safety net. If you cannot pay for treatment, you simply do not get treated – and if you die, you die.

I was lucky enough to be able to pay – and so I was treated. This level of inequality, with so many poorer people having no access to treatment really affected me. I knew that the hospital wanted to treat all the people they could, but blood products, drugs and other medical supplies cost money and this has to be paid for.

Another area that shocked me was that patients' families were expected to bring food to feed patients. If you did not have family to bring you food, you went hungry. I had sent my party on to complete the engagements of our visit as people were relying on us. This did mean I ended up quite hungry – so much so that I lost quite a lot of weight, which I did actually want to do (just not in this way!); still as the saying goes, every cloud has a silver lining.

My time in the hospital again gave me lots of time to think and take stock of life.

I could not in all conscience, walk away from the hospital and know that others could not receive treatment due to lack of finance. On leaving I told the hospital that should anyone in the future need treatment and were unable to pay, then I would fund this and asked the hospital to put this on account for me. I still fund treatment at this hospital to this day – and again those who know their Bible will know of the parable of the '*Good Samaritan*' [Samaritans at the time of the gospels were looked down upon by the religious people of the day who thought they were better].

Anyone with a heart for those in need can see there is a basic inequality that anybody with compassion would want to help address – and provide treatment where this is possible. Obviously, any hospital will have a finite capacity for care, but most people would agree that the level of treatment should never be limited through a simple lack of finance. I have returned to the hospital on numerous occasions when visiting Africa.

The hospital saved my leg - and in all probability my life as I was bleeding so heavily; I was told that by the time I went for surgery, I had lost about a quarter of the blood in my body. I was anxious to get home and be checked over by surgeons in the UK; the advice from doctors back home was simple – get back to the UK as quickly as possible. I left hospital as soon as I could, hobbling in a cast but trying to get a flight home proved to be quite difficult since most airlines simply refused to take me having had major surgery so recently. At one stage it looked like I might have to charter a plane at a cost of £100K [c. US$140K] or more. Ten days after the accident, I fortunately did manage to persuade the airline *KLM* to bring me home, so long as I could show that I could walk to the aircraft (albeit on crutches). While I had to book two seats in Business class to accommodate for the extra space needed costing me £10K [c. US$17K], this was somewhat less than the £100K [c. US$140K] I thought I was going to need to bring me home on a private charter flight.

Having been assessed by the doctors back in the UK, the prognosis did not initially look so promising – and I was told I would not walk again properly, would need a crutch and would have a permanent limp. Fortunately, I made a complete recovery with the whole experience leaving me with a commitment to look after myself, work out more, get fit and generally look after myself a little better. Those of you who follow my on-line training will know that I often include a workout routine to start the day. I really have learned that we all only have one body and we should look after it with care.

I have done so much soul searching following this whole episode and came away with a few life lessons, that I promised to myself that I would always be mindful of.

Firstly: I mentioned earlier that many people go through life not being able to differentiate between what is important and urgent. Important things can be thought of as those that are likely to matter in ten years' time (such as putting in place systems for financial freedom, your mission in life, relationships and your health etc.) Urgent things by contrast are things like paying a bill, buying your groceries for tonight's dinner or arranging your insurance for your car. The problem is that most people put all of their effort into doing things that are urgent – and then leave many things like their health until they become both urgent and important – by which time it is often too late. An example could include when they have just had a heart attack that could have been prevented had they given up smoking or kept themselves in better shape. We all have done this, but one of the most life changing (and outcome determining) lessons things in life is to be disciplined, so as to prioritise the important over the urgent.

Secondly: When you have a problem... share the burden... When I was told I would never walk again, I shared it on *YouTube*; more than one hundred and fifty supportive emails came back to me with stories in which people had been given very poor prognoses, but had managed to overcome their problems.

Thirdly: Do not bottle things up... Do talk things over with people. A problem shared really can be a problem halved.

Fourthly: Always (and I mean always) stay positive; it may sound like a cliché – but this is actually so important... It changes your outlook and ability to cope when things are difficult.

Lastly: Do seek council; this means finding the best people in the field – and then asking them questions to get the best advice. When I was in Uganda – I emailed surgeons back in the UK; the advice was get home... Always find people who can give you the expert advice and answers to help you. You do not need to know everything; the most important thing is that you know somebody who does.

Chapter Twenty Six: Adapt And Diversify – Or Die...

This is a good point to say something about the importance of adapting to circumstances. You will have noted that when a recession came along, I adapted to the change in market conditions by changing tactics.

Different people approach change in different ways, with some people embracing change - while others hate change, wish things would always stay just as they are - and actively resist having to change in anyway.

Here a salutary fact; change is part of life. Life and circumstances have always changed with time - and always will continue to do so. Those whose mindset is set to resist change always get left behind, while those who embrace change, move with the times, adapt and are far more likely to thrive.

History is littered with examples... when the motor car came along in the end of the 1900's, many people resisted change, citing arguments such as, how it would put blacksmiths out of work. Where there were blacksmiths in every village and town, there are of course now fuel stations, motor repair garages and car show rooms.

All that has happened was that the type of job that was needed changed, from serving the needs of horses to those of cars, vans and trucks. Over time blacksmiths closed while garages opened; those who clung onto the old way of life saw their livelihoods become unviable and in time their businesses closed. The few who understood the inevitability of change opened garages and saw people flock to meet the new demands. With the advent of electric cars, garages may before too long have to adapt.

There is no denying that change can be challenging – but everyone sees change in their lives. The simple fact is that how you treat change will determine whether change becomes your friend through which you thrive – or an enemy which will deny you success.

Moving more up to date, let us consider at something as fundamental as how you pay for things. Internet banking is now universal... Less than two decades ago more – more than 50% of people regularly paid for larger items by cheques; now banks do not issue personal customers with cheque books unless they specifically ask for them – and many businesses will not accept cheques as a form of payment. Similarly, the use of cash is falling away year on year and contactless payment through cards and now mobile phone payment apps is becoming the preferred approach for the purchasing of smaller items in shops.

These examples show how society has changed – but are their lessons to be learned for how some individuals embrace change and thrive?

There are actually many – many examples, but two worth considering are Richard Branson and Elon Musk; both have consistent track records of embracing change and thriving through adaptation.

Richard Branson made his first few millions by starting a chain of record shops selling music and video in the form of vinyl records, music cassette tapes and VHS video tapes. As the technology changed so did his business empire and how he operated. In the area of music and film he sold his chain of shops, just as physical formats for media were just starting to decline in popularity – and now his empire includes *Virgin Media* – offering internet and broadband services with an all digital supply of media. Having started an airline, he is one of the pioneers of space tourism through *Virgin Galactic*. By contrast some high street names committed themselves to carry on selling and hiring physical music formats but have since gone out of business.

Elon Musk is another classic example of an entrepreneur who has always embraced and pioneered change. At the time of writing *Tesla* is the most valuable car manufacturer on the planet being valued at more than the combined value of *Volkswagen* and *General Motors* – this is astonishing given that *Tesla* was only formed in 2003 – while *General Motors* and *Volkswagen* established in 1908 and 1937 respectively represent two of the largest motor manufacturers in the world. How did this happen? Quite simply – Elon Musk embraced the electric car as the way forward – and then strove to develop this as a business model. Was he just lucky? I don't think so. In 2020 Elon Musk's *SpaceX* company beat the aerospace giant *Boeing* by more than one year in the race to send American astronauts to the International Space Station. Again, this is astonishing given that *Space X* was only formed in 2002.

I could go onto give examples of how Bill Gates formed *Microsoft* and then the *Bill and Melinda Gates Foundation* – or how Steve Jobs built *Apple* to become one of the world's highest valued companies but the parallels are clear and obvious to see.

The other lesson that all of these examples also demonstrate is the importance of diversification in business. Elon Musk for example focuses on pioneered a range of new and emerging technologies, while Richard Branson has pioneered multiple media entertainment businesses, finance and travel.

So how about myself? How about you? To date my work has been focused around housing, financial education and addressing humanitarian needs in Africa. In the area of property investing, I have pioneered any different strategies from single lets, though to Houses In Multiple Occupancy (HMOs), refurbishments, lease option agreements and serviced accommodation - to name but a few... In education I have developed a suite of advanced in person training programmes through to on-line courses. In Africa, I have supplied infrastructure for clean and safe drinking / potable water, through to supporting hospitals and teaching financial literacy within schools. I will continue to develop and diversify.

In business, you should avoid solely focusing on one product or narrow an area – if you do, you run the risk of becoming a 'one trick pony'. If circumstances do change and you find that you are a 'one trick pony' you could be left very exposed and at risk.

During the 2020 Covid pandemic, many restaurants and other hospitality outlets were forced to close (or at least prevented from serving food or drink in the way they always had); many businesses suffered loss with others closing – while a few saw an opportunity and started offering deliveries and take-aways when they never had before. The threat to the status quo for many businesses became an opportunity for them.

So, for yourself (and anyone building a business) firstly diversify within your chosen area – and always look out for the opportunities that other people perceive as headaches or threats.

Chapter Twenty Seven: Financial Freedom Challenges

It took me four years to become financially free.

Like so many things in life, doing things for a second or a third time becomes easier since you will have learned how to do things along the way the first time – and so know what you are doing when you come to do it again. This of course holds true for almost anything from putting up flat pack furniture – to becoming financially free through property investing.

If you can learn from other people and 'look over the shoulder' at what other people are doing (who do know what they are doing) - you can dramatically cut your own learning time.

Having mastered all of the techniques I had practiced and taught, I was convinced that I could become finally free in just one week if I had to start all over again from scratch. Whenever I said this to people, they would say that I was being either arrogant – or stupid – or both. I was convinced that I really could show that this was possible and the more people told me that this sounded ridiculous, the more I became determined to prove them wrong and that indeed I could; that is the sort of person I am!

I decided to go ahead and devise a 'financial freedom challenge' in which I would start from scratch with no money in a different city from where I lived and prove that I could become financially free within one week. Specifically, my target would be to earn at least £3K [c. US$4.2] in a week – with at least 50% of this being in the form of on-going passive income. As it turned out, I made £8K [c. US$11K] in the week.

The rules would be that I would move into a hotel far away from home, with no access to money other than pre-paid bills for the hotel, food and petrol fuel costs for transport. In preparation, I formed a company *Lucas*

Ruby Ltd to allow me to trade (which you can do in minutes). Other than that, I would have a mobile phone and my laptop – and that would be that. Since I am quite well known in property circles, I agreed to undertake the challenge undercover and in disguise so that nobody could attribute success on my reputation. For the challenge I would become *'Lucas Ruby'* wearing a black wig and a pair of glasses. The wig was actually one of my wife's cut short; I looked ridiculous, but it helped me to go genuinely undercover. To complete the disguise, I decided to drive an old 'banger' of a car to complete the image – and I was ready to go.

I agreed to take observers with me to ensure that I could not cheat and they in turn would document all that I did in the form of a *YouTube* video of the week. I agreed that this video would be put out on *YouTube* whether I succeeded or failed. So many of my close friends advised me not to go ahead with this challenge as they didn't want to see this go wrong and for me to be embarrassed – or for this to damage my training business. By the end of the week, I was financially free all over again and from scratch – had proved my critics wrong – and indeed proved that anybody could achieve financial freedom from scratch with no money to start with, if they knew what they were doing. I undertook this challenge four months after my accident in Africa – in part to prove to myself that I had just as much drive as ever - and that 'what doesn't kill you can make you stronger'.

I will briefly explain how and what I did... The important point is that you (or indeed anybody else) for that matter could do the same. I wrote this financial freedom challenge up as a book, *'How to get financially free in seven days'*. Inevitably, some people said that I got 'lucky' and that this would not work for whatever reason in other towns or cities. I have subsequently done this challenge all over again several times from scratch, next in the US to prove that the same approaches would work in other countries - and then again in London - where people said this could never work due to sky high house prices.

In each of these cases, I proved that I could from scratch – and starting with no money at, becoming financially free within seven days. It was actually quite important to me to prove to myself that I could do this wherever and whenever I chose, if I was going to tell other people that this could be done. If you have 'walked the walk', then you can instruct others with far greater conviction.

If you, like many people, have decided this sounds ridiculous and that there must be some trick – or that most things that sound too good to be true probably are. I will give a brief outline of how I went about doing just this.

The first step of the challenge involved a city being picked randomly by others out of a hat; the city chosen for my first financial freedom challenge was Sheffield. I did not have any properties in Sheffield, so I would genuinely be starting from scratch in a new city.

Now to secure deals you first need to generate leads – lots of leads; then you have to follow these up with property viewings. You simply cannot have too many leads; it does not matter if you view lots of properties that do not lead to a deal. Along the way you will meet lots of estate agents and others, who will bring you further leads and potential deals.

Having driven to Sheffield and checked into the hotel on the first night, the very first thing I did was to go on-line and to work into the small hours of the morning looking for potential below market deals and motivated sellers. Motivated sellers with houses to sell at below market value can be found by looking for properties that, for example, are being offered with vacant possession, where the asking price has been reduced – or that have been on the market for several months. All of these sellers may be very keen to sell their properties – and may be willing to do a deal.

I have a saying, '*that the person who views the most properties wins*'.

By the time I went to bed, I had booked a series of viewings and had a long list of estate agents to phone in the morning. Day one was spent phoning around to arrange bookings for day two which rapidly became packed solid with viewings and leads to follow up.

One of the most promising leads came through making contact with a letting agent who had a number of landlords on her books who were willing to rent properties as a 'corporate let' arrangement in which the property could be rented on again as 'serviced accommodation' through *Airbnb* and *Booking.com* type nightly lets. This strategy known as 'rent-to-rent', will often provide a route whereby you can rent a property for a standard rate and then rent it out again for a 'super rent' for three to four times the rate at which you rent the property. Serviced accommodation can be thought of as almost running a hotel but without the staff – and as most people are aware, *Airbnb* type booking are becoming one of the fastest growing alternatives to hotels.

By the end of this day, I had a number of HMOs booked into to view along with a development opportunity. The next day was spent viewing all of these… By the time I returned to my hotel in the evening, I had managed to find two potential 'rent-to-rent' deals which offered the opportunities for providing a very healthy passive and recurring income… but I would need to put some money down for rental deposits to secure these… I had however, also seen one HMO and a development opportunity that were clearly below market value; whilst I couldn't afford to purchase these since I had no money to start with, if I could sell these deals for £2,500 [c. US$ 3.5K] each to other investors, then I would have enough money to secure the rent-to-rent deals.

Day three of the challenge was spent attending a property meeting I had managed to book a place for online; you cannot force deals on people and people typically need to get to know you, trust you and like you before they are willing to do business with you. One of the best ways to achieve this, is to try to genuinely help people in the best way you can. During the day, I joined several groups of investors during coffee and meal breaks, listening to their conversations and offering advice and putting helpful suggestions to them where I could. This demonstrated that I was a property expert and that I knew what I was talking about, as well as helping me to come across as a genuinely helpful person.

As mentioned earlier, so that I could sell deals legally and compliantly, I had formed a company called *Lucas Ruby Ltd*. To sell a deal to any prospective investor you need to have shown that the deal is a good one - and that you have stacked the figures rigorously; when you know what you are doing and are experienced, this becomes easy. Never be tempted to make the figures sound more attractive than they actually are - and never try to sell a deal that you would not be happy with to invest in yourself.

The next thing I needed of course was to be able to sell the deals I had found. This requires two things; the first and most important is to be able to present the correct deals that will be a good fit for the person you are talking to. There is, for example, no point in trying to sell an HMO dal to someone who wants to buy a piece of land for development or visa-versa. This is where listening to what people are looking for is so important.

In all of the conversations I was having at the network meeting, I was asking questions and enquiring of people what they might be looking for. The two deals I had were an HMO and a property development project; when I was talking to people who wanted other types of deal, I did not ignore them, but tried to put other people together who could help each other. This just increased my standing as someone who was trying to help people and who was therefore a good person to do business with. When I did find people, who might be interested in either of my deals, I talked about them in very general terms with conversations along the lines of, '*As it happens, I viewed a property just like that earlier*'. If and when they seemed interested, I asked questions such as, '*Did you want to see how the figures stack for a return on investment? - I've been working on these and they do look pretty good*'.

I knew time was tight and not on my side – and I could feel the pressure building inside of me. As Samuel Leeds I knew that I could have sold these two deals in no time at all, but I was starting out as someone completely unknown to this group of investors. My internal stress levels were not helped by the fact that I broke down in my old 'banger' of a car on the way to the meeting the next day; the fuel gauge was showing there was petrol in the car when there actually wasn't, with the result being that I rather embracingly ran out of fuel. I eventually arrived at the meeting and really had to mentally focus and remain unflustered. I exchanged numerous business cards and kept doing what I had been doing all along. To my delight one investor decided he did want to purchase the HMO deal – and this was followed not long after by someone else who wanted to buy the development deal.

I quickly sent the invoices using automated software – and within another 24 hours, I had 2 x £2.500 [2 x US$3,500K] in my bank account. I was delighted... I needed £4,850 [c. US$6,800K] to secure the two 'rent-to-rent' apartments, which I promptly sent over to the letting agents that I had met on day two of the challenge. As these two properties are let out as *Airbnb* or booking type served apartments on a nightly basis the rental income from these would be expected to vary from month to month with anything from £1,000 profit [c. US$1,400] though to £2,600 [US$3,600K], with an average monthly profit of £1,500 [c. US$2,100K] each and every month.

I had now achieved the first goal for the challenge, which was to secure deals that would give me an ongoing passive income month after month. I had however now spent all but £50 [c. US$70] of the money I had just made. I had by this stage found a number of deals other deals that I had packaged for selling and the next day - the penultimate day of the challenge, I received a phone call from one of my new found property investor friends I had been talking to saying she wanted to buy one of these deals for $3,000 ($4,500). Good to her word, within a few hours the money was in my bank account. I had achieved all of my goals – and had without any shadow of a doubt proved that it was possible to achieve financial freedom within one week.

I left for home, feeling very satisfied and content. As I packed up, I remembered the mechanic who had stopped to help me, had taken me to a petrol station and refused to accept any payment. His phone was on its 'last legs' so on the way home I bought a brand-new shiny top of the range replacement and called in to his garage to give him an early Christmas present and reveal who I really was. I did not need the excess cash I had made during the week and donated this to a charity in Manchester I had come across through a Christian network that provide fourteen homeless shelter beds a night in a converted bus; as it turned out, they had been earnestly praying for money to fix the bus which had broken down and was going to cost in excess of £2,000 (US$3,500) to fix. Coincidently another mechanic fixed the bus, meaning that this money could go to running costs for things such as fuel, food and clothes for the guests. One of the most amazing things that I have seen again and again, is that generosity gives rise to generosity in others; if this isn't another case of a 'win-win' then I don't know what is!

The reason I undertook this first challenge was to prove to myself and others that anyone with the right approach and drive can replace their incomes really quite easily; this can be for so many people a complete life changing event. Within days of the financial freedom challenge being put on line on *YouTube* a few people were saying that I had been lucky and this could never be done where they live etc. This was another 'red rag to a bull' – and in the end I decided to do the financial freedom challenge all over again – but in a different country with the location again being pulled out of a hat at random.

As it turned out the county chosen was the USA, so that is where I went. Within a week and again starting with no money I once again become financially free from scratch. When I moved the offices down to London, I undertook the financial challenge for a third time, just to prove that it did not matter where you chose – even in a capital city. Yet again the challenge showed that it was completely possible to become financially free from scratch and quite easily in a very short period of time, so long as you know what you were doing.

So, what does all of this prove? As I pointed out earlier in the book you need knowledge, (which I why I run my training programmes so as to help other people) along with drive and determination. Remember the only place you will find the word success before work is in the dictionary!

Now – I have just shown one way in which you can start as a property investor with little or no money. That does not mean however that money does not help; it does... having enough money to put down a deposit on a house helps you secure a mortgage. Many people see not having a deposit as a barrier to starting out as a purchasing property investor - but again this need not be a road block if you know approaches for how to get around this.

The next question that comes to mind is how might you go about *buying* a house if you have no money to get started? Actually, if you know what you are doing, then this can be quite simple; raise the money from other people. This is what we will look at next...

Chapter Twenty Eight: Raising Money

Do you remember earlier that I said that most people would acknowledge that if someone such as Richard Branson had all of his money taken from him, within five-years' time they would be just as wealthy as before? The previous chapter gives part of the answer to how this is the case as wealthy people know how to set up deals so for making money. Actually, there is more to this; you see rich people *make money work for them* – and they almost always use other peoples' money.

When I was just starting out, one of my mentors said to me, '*Do you know where my money comes from?* With a wry smile he answered his own question, saying '*Other people*'. I protested saying this was dreadful; this sounded like robbery… My mentor patiently went on to explain. It was a lesson I have not forgotten to this day… What he explained, was that money goes around the economy in circles. If you do a day's work and get paid, then your money comes from your employer and this in turn has come from their customers. You see… if you receive a rental income, you receive payment for the service you are offering in the form of a house or apartment – but your money comes from your tenants and their money comes from their income. It does not matter what scenario you choose, yours and everybody else's money comes from other people.

Now most people take their income and spend it on 'things' and when they have spent the money it goes on to someone else. We have already seen how rich people spend their income on buying and building assets that make them money. However rich people, almost always use other peoples' money to work for them. How can this be?

We have already seen one very common example of how you can use a bank's money to buy a house through which will give you a rental income that far exceeds the cost of the mortgage; you are using the bank's money (or actually the banks depositors' money) to make money for you. Actually, the banks themselves use other peoples' money to work for them all the time; they use the money that people deposit with them and invest this to make money. If everybody went to the bank to withdraw their money all at the same time, they would not be able to give it all back, simply because at any one time a good proportion of this will be tied up in investments.

Buying a house with a mortgage normally requires that you put a deposit down, but how could you use other peoples' money to make money, when you have no money to start with?

This is where the art of raising finance comes in. I run a training programme called, '*Raising Finance and Joint Venturing'*, which shows you through a step-by- step approach how you can indeed use other peoples' money to work for you. Almost all of the wealthiest people on the planet from Robert Kiyosaki through to Grant Cardone – all have made their fortunes through raising finance with the help of investors (i.e., leveraging other peoples' money) to work for them. Grant Cardone is another person who has inspired me, written extensively about wealth creation, been a mentor to me and who now I can count as a close friend; he has been so helpful for giving me encouragement, helping take me out of my comfort zone, stretch me and enable me to grow.

I made my fortune through using other peoples' money – and once I had become ultimately financially free, made the mistake of deciding I no longer need to do this. When I told Grant Cardone this, he really berated me and told me in no uncertain terms that I was becoming lazy – and asked me that if I had made my money through raising money from other people, why would want to stop doing this now? He had a point... and I looked at what people like Richard Branson did and realised that he never stopped raising money – and in fact in many of his most successful ventures he had leveraged other peopes' investments – and didn't show any signs of changing his strategy. So that is what I went back to doing – and now intend to do for ever...

I have over the years learned so much about investing from Robert Kiyosaki the author of *'Rich Dad - Poor Dad'* – and he is someone who I always look to for both inspiration – and indeed to learn new tactics and strategies from. Not so long ago, I asked him if he had only $100K to start all over again with what would he do with it. I was completely shocked when he said he *'Would wipe his backside with it!'* When I asked him what on earth he meant by this, he explained that, he had always made his money by raising finance and then using this money to work for him and create wealth.

If you have no money – or do not wish to use your own money to invest, then one of the principal approaches for moving forward is to join venture with someone who has money. In any good business arrangement' this has to be put together in such a way that it is a win-win for both parties.

In the simplest type of arrangement, one person will provide all of the money while the other person brings to the table expertise and might do all of the work. This is of course exactly the arrangement my grand-parents and I had that I described earlier. In this model, they provided the deposit for the house – and I paid them 10% a year interest on the money they had invested. I brought to the deal my expertise from managing HMOs, how to advertise to find tenants for this new property - and then manage it.

There are however many different types of arrangements for joint ventures. In some models you might instead of giving a fixed percentage return on investment, come to an arrangement where the two (or more) parties split the profits either equitably – or according to another pre-defined ratio split.

I have on some occasions lent money to other property investors (including to some of my own students) when I have invested my money to be put to work for me and believed there would be a great return on investment. In all cases the investor will most likely need to be convinced that their money carries little risk of being lost, should things not go according to plan.

Different people have different appetites for risk, but the principle should hold true for all joint venture arrangements of this type.

Remember, before someone will lend you money, they will need to know you, like you and trust you. In some cases, people will primarily invest in a project – and they will want to see how the figures stack. If for example, a four bed HMO stands to make a 20% return on investment when fully tenanted – but will break even if one room is let, then the risk would seem pretty low if the investor knew you had a track record of managing HMOs.

In other scenarios, the investor might primarily be investing in you... If someone lends money to me, then firstly they will be able to look at my track record – but they may well ask me to provide a guarantee that should a project go wrong, then I will be able to pay the money back. Since in my case they will get to see that I am a millionaire, then then a guarantee of this sort can provide the reassurance to the lender to invest with a high degree of confidence.

Chapter Twenty Nine: Why Poor (And Sometimes Stupid) People Pay More Tax...

Alright – this is a bit of a provocative chapter title... I am sure you are not stupid or you wouldn't be reading this book – or indeed to have a determination to change your future.

Let me explain if I may...

Most people if asked, would say that the amount of tax you have to pay is simply what you are liable for – and that would be that. Actually, this could not be further from the truth – and when people think or say that everybody *should* be paying a given rate of tax, all this demonstrates ignorance and a lack of understanding for how tax systems work.

The majority of people when questioned, think that they should be paying less tax - but that people with more money than them should be paying more. All this does is display a poverty mindset.

Taxation rules of course differ from country to country and from time to time, but many of the same principles I am going to talk about are similar and hold true across many economies.

Different tax rates are applied to different sources of income – and these are often to incentivise business growth and the creation of jobs and wealth for the economy. The most punitive tax rates are applied to income earned from paid employment as well as sometimes inheritance and capital gains tax.

It is worth remembering – the vast majority of people (i.e., the poor and middle classes), go to work are paid a wage and their tax is taken at source;

this is why people think that the tax you pay 'is just what you have to pay' - and that there is nothing you can do about it. This is not the case... Rich people (and remember this is far more about a mindset than how much money you have at any given time) – know that the amount of tax you pay is completely in your control. How many times do you hear the same poor people moan about how little money they have and how much tax they pay and then complain with self righteous indignation that organisations such as *Amazon* – or *Google* – or indeed individuals such as Jeff Boaz have paid 'little tax or no tax'.... These people never stop to think about how or why this is possible, can be completely legal and how this helps the economy, by creating investment and employment; they simply say how 'shocking' this is and rant about this is 'wrong'. The point they are missing is that most rich people know how to have money work for them.

Remember I said that Tim, my stepdad was an accountant by training. Accountants do not just add up figures and do book keeping; they know how the tax system work – and how to make it work for them and their clients.

Let me give two examples that will illustrate the point: Firstly, if you buy a house as an investment and its value increases, when you come to sell it, you will have to pay capital gains tax on the money you have made. If, however, you re-mortgage the house for its new higher value and use this money that you have released for the purchase of another property, then you will pay no tax on this whatsoever. Again, if you pass all of your wealth to your children over a period, they will not have to pay any inheritance tax when you die. There are many more examples. You see, if you know the rules of how the tax system works, then you will simply pay less tax. It takes years of training to become an accountant – and accountants are highly skilled professionals with professional chartered status, in the same way that solicitors, doctors or dentists have to be professionally registered in order to practice.

Many poor people think they do not need an accountant; actually, they fail to realise that they are the very people who need one the most! It always seems bizarre to me that almost everybody acknowledges that you need a solicitor to handle the conveyancing for a house purchase – and that you should see a doctor when you are unwell, or a dentist for dental care – *but* - most (and almost all poor) people think they do not need an accountant. I would strongly argue that poor people need an accountant more than anybody else - in the same way that sick people are in most need of a doctor!

It is part of an accountant's job to keep up to date with changes in tax legislation (which change frequently). Just as with doctors, accountants frequently specialise in specific areas such as retail, corporate businesses, property or personal finance. If you are (or thinking of) becoming a property investor, then make sure you choose an accountant who specialises in property.

Accountants will be able to found and establish your company up with a structure whereby you will be able to be paid as a company director through means of dividends at a lower tax than as a paid employee. In addition to this, many items that you may consider as personal items but which are used in support of your business (which might for example include a proportion of the running costs of your car, your computer, electricity, even smart business-ware clothes) can be claimed as tax deductible expenses from any profits. Since it is the accountant's job to know the rules – and by setting up your business and any other income sources in such a way as to be tax efficient, accountants' fees almost certainly pay for themselves many times over. As a rough estimate for every £100 ($140) I spend on accountancy, I benefit by £2,000 ($3,500). I often joke with my accountants that I only wish I could keep running this deal time and time again.

Are you now starting to see why poor (and dare I say sometimes stupid) people pay more tax than wealthy people?

I have tried explaining this to a number of different people and had two reactions. Some poor and stubborn people quickly show that they do not want to listen – often repeating how dreadful they think it is how rich people pay lower rates of tax, then frequently get angry and invariably stay poor; others become intrigued, seek to learn, go to see an accountant and become wealthier.

You should ask yourself which group you would rather be in…

Ignorance is not bliss – it just leads to poverty; willful ignorance is just not sensible – may I say it is just plain stupid.

Chapter Thirty: … And Onto Buying A Castle: Ribbesford House:

In 2018, my bother Russell and I went to an auction to bid for a castle, Ribbesford House - an amazing and beautiful Jacobean grade II* listed mansion in Bewdley, set in eight acres of land with architectural elements ranging from the 16th to the 19th century. The guide price was £500K [c. US$700] – an absurdly small sum when you consider that in some parts of the most expensive parts of the country, this will not even buy you a small terraced house.

The house was in a complete state of dilapidation; we had undertaken some research to allow us to calculate or stack the deal as a renovation project. We went with an upper figure in mind above which we vowed we would not bid above since it is essential to always buy according to formulae and not feelings. As it was, we were outbid on the day and we went home empty handed. I cannot say this wasn't disappointing as both my brother and I love bringing old buildings back to life - but business is business - and if the figures don't stack up then you need to walk away; this was the correct and logical thing to do.

The next day, however, we got a phone call from the auctioneers to say the buyer had pulled out due to complications on his side and would we still like to purchase the castle? Our last bid was £810k and so that is the price we agreed for the purchase. As I always say to my students, property investments must always be determined by formulae and not feelings – and I was so glad we had stuck to the upper limit and not gone beyond; if we had, the price could have risen up and up.

We had done our homework – and we had found out that one of the reasons that this property was being put on the market for such an incredibly low price was that the grounds had been infested with Japanese

Knotweed - a notifiable condition that terrifies many people. We had already assessed that this could be eradicated for as little as £5K [c. US$7K] – and while the property had many problems with extensive restoration being needed, this one factor alone could potentially lead to the castle and estate being sold for well below market value. As a notifiable condition, individuals are not allowed to try to pull up or burn Japanese knotweed – but rather its destruction must be undertaken by a licensed contractor through the periodic injection of a specialist weedkiller over some period of time.

Prior to the auction, we of course had already put in place an outline business plan should we end up being the successful purchasers.

Ribbesford House has an amazing history and had following the second world war had been converted into a number of flats. Our intention was to restore the building to comprise ten spacious and high end self-contained apartments which could be let out as high end serviced accommodation. The scale of the accommodation within the main house is truly vast with, for example, two of the apartments boasting 45m^2 living rooms. In addition to this – the grounds also contain two further self-contained cottages which again we planned to restore – along with a number of outbuildings that could offer a number of possibilities, subject to planning permission.

The grounds are also truly extensive - and this also offers possibilities for a number of development opportunities for further accommodation including the building of some additional houses subject to planning permission, the introduction of some log cabin type holiday chalets and further luxury serviced accommodation for short term stays.

Ribbesford House is located adjacent to the River Severn which runs through the estate - and which is recognised as one of the most sought-after river for anglers who travel from all over the country to fish.

In addition to this, Bewdley and Ribbesford are located approximately three miles from Kidderminster at the gateway of the Wyre forest national nature reserve, offering a truly peaceful and rural setting and a popular holiday and tourist attraction for those who wish to get away from it all.

Ribbesford House is only a 5min drive from the West Midlands Safari Park - and if you visit the grounds early in the morning, you can sometimes even hear the lions roar as they are being fed! All in all, the location is truly amazing!

Nearby annual events include one of the largest in land regattas in the country and the Bewdley festival each October that hosts a variety of artistic performances.

The history of the estate dates back to at least early eleventh century, being mentioned in an Anglo-Saxon charter with separate documents indicating that the estate was presented to Ralph de Mortimer in recognition of his services to William the Conqueror. The house appears to have been rebuilt around 1535 with the inclusion of two octagonal turrets which remain to this day.

Ribbesford House remained in the Mortimer family until the early seventeenth century, when it passed to Baron Herbert of Cherbury, whose coat of arms still are still be found the at the property today. The house underwent some renovation around 1669 - and in 1787 the estate was purchased by Francis Ingram.

The house was visited by both the prime minister Stanley Baldwin whilst he was MP for Bewdley as well as his famous cousin, the renowned poet and novelist Rudyard Kipling. During the second world war, the house and grounds were used as billets and training grounds for British, American and Free French troops with Prime minister Winston Churchill being a frequent visitor during this time. In 1944 Ribbesford House was visited by General (later to be President) Charles de Gaulle to meet with cadets training in the run up to D-day and the invasion of continental Europe. Around one out of every three of the soldiers who trained and were stationed at Ribbesford House were sadly killed and there are legacies from this time that survive to this day including a plaque in memory of those who trained at Ribbesford – along with a circular hole in one of the paths where the free French would place their flag.

As you can imagine, Russell and I are extremely keen to preserve all of these artifacts and memories that are so central to the history of this wonderful and historic building.

Following the war, Ribbesford House was purchased by RAF Wing Commander Alfred John Howell in 1947 – and it was he who converted the house into twelve separate apartments arranged over three floors.

Returning to our purchase, having had our bid accepted the day after the auction, we then of course had to pay the £810K [c. $1200K]. We had just over £400K [c. UD$560] in cash in the bank – and so we needed to raise a further £400K. Now you may remember that I said that one of the habits of wealthy people is to use and thereby leverage other peoples' money.

The next step was therefore to contact our broker to arrange bridging finance. Raising the sum of £400K in bridging finance would normally be a formality for us given that both of us are worth many millions. Our broker confirmed that he would put the wheels in motion for the bridging finance - and so we contacted our solicitor to prepare all of the legal documents and arrange for a completion date.

The days passed and we heard mothing back from the broker – and so we gently chased. Some processes take a little time when buying property so we were not at this stage overly concerned. A little anxiety did start to creep in once we had a completion date confirmed by our solicitor and we still were waiting for formal confirmation of the bridging finance being approved. Then after a series of further phone calls - each becoming ever more urgent, we eventually heard that the bridging company wanted us to provide a number of reports due to the property being listed, each of which would have to be commissioned and would take time. We chased and we chased and we came to the conclusion that we simply could not provide all of the reassurances they were looking for in the time available to us.

I decided honesty was the best approach and we contacted the seller to explain the situation; my suggestion was to pay him the first £400K [c. US$560K] up front as a down payment – and then settle the remaining balance a few weeks later upon receipt of the bridging finance. Despite my very best diplomatic and negotiating sales, he would not agree. Days were passing by and if we could not complete to schedule, not only would we lose the castle, but also £80K [c. US$112K] put forward to cover the deposit and associated legal fees.

Russell and I had called an emergency meeting between ourselves and some of our team to find a way through this. We clearly had to find the money and while we have millions tied up in houses, these would take time to either sell or re-finance - and so this would not be a realistic option with now less than 24hours left.

We knew that each of the flats in Ribbesford House could have retail values of up to £500K [c. US$700K] when completed – and so we decided to see if we could sell two of these flats off plan for £200K [c. 280K] each. This would represent an amazing investment for any property investor – and so we spent the day phoning round our list of property investors with the offer of these two 'off plan' deals. By the afternoon, I had had confirmation for the sale of one – and then Russell receiving a phone call shortly after this, confirming that we had just sold the other.

Within a few hours we had the £400K we needed in the bank. We were back on track – and we had the finance we needed to complete the next day. My next task was to then drive from the Midlands and sign the paperwork in the offices of our solicitor in South Wales the same afternoon before close of business and then drive from there down to London where we would be holding a *Crash Course* the next day. There is a saying that *'all's well that end well'*, but I have to say it is one of the most stressful days I can remember experiencing for some time.

While driving across to Wales, I received a phone call in the car to say that the bridging finance had come through after all - and so all in all we now had £1.2m [c. US$1.68m] sitting in the bank!

The old adage of waiting for a bus to come along and then for three to turn up together did come to mind! My first reaction was one of frustration given the day we had just had – and then the logical part of my brain thought about all of this for a moment. There are situations where cash is king – and we knew that within a few months we would need to have to been raising the finance needed to undertake the restoration. Our plan had been to sell – and or re-finance a few houses. However, what we had just done through a need of necessity and being forced to be entrepreneurial and creative was to raise the money without selling – or even having to re-finance any of our HMOs or other rental income generating properties.

We have actually now re-purchased the two flats we sold off plan, and we can proudly say we own the entire building again. Needless to say the two investors who we bought out are delighted at the return they made - and of course the seller of Ribbesford castle was happy as he received exactly the price he wanted for the site; everybody was a winner!

It's Finally Ours!

Not long after this, one of the surviving French soldiers who trained and stayed at Ribbesford house, having heard about the project decided to contact us, came over from France and took us to dinner in Mayfair. Again, I cannot tell you how amazing an experience and privilege this was to hear of some of the history of this amazing estate, from someone who had lived through so much of its recent history first hand.

Now that Ribbesford House was finally ours, I was desperate to look around with my family - and so at the earliest date we could arrange, I and Amanda, my brother in law (who, as I mentioned earlier is a chartered surveyor), Russell and his wife Anna, our children, my mother and my step-father Tim all visited the property. There are times when you just have to step back and wonder about how some things have come to pass. There we were, proud owners of a beautiful (if rather tired) old castle, one truly amazing deal – and a huge project ahead of us.

While we could gain access and walk around, there were areas where we simply could not access due to safety, the sheer scale of the building, the centuries of history and the sheer majesty of this lovely old house put tingles down my back.

The building had been standing empty for a number of years – and so one of the first practical tasks was commissioning a series of structural and specialist building reports to assess and then prioritise the work that needed to be undertaken.

Ribbesford House: In Desperate Need of Some tender Loving care After Many Years of Neglect

We already knew we had to eradicate the Japanese knotweed – and since this had to be undertaken through a licensed contractor, this was one of the first pieces of work to be undertaken. Several months on – all of the Japanese knotweed had shriveled and died – and the estate has now been officially certified as being free from Japanese Knotweed.

As is so often the case, the first priority was to stabilise the walls, some parts of the roof structure and make the building watertight ahead of the coming winter to prevent further deterioration. Parts of the house were in a very poor state, with one first floor flat having actually fallen in on the one below and so one of the first tasks her was to very carefully sift through the rubble and debris so that bricks and other original materials could be salvaged and re-used during the restoration. Amazingly, amongst all of mess we even found some old paintings that were salvageable and that could have so easily have ended up in a skip.

The entire roof had to be removed before being painstakingly re-built with new timbers but using the original roof tiles wherever possible – and where this was not possible with custom sourced new materials to ensure everything was replaced like for like. Replacing the roof was probably the single biggest issue with the property and making sure this was restored and back in place was to some extent a race against time to have the building water-tight before the on-set of winter. Having the building water tight was going to be pre-requisite for almost all of the internal work - and for many building or restoration projects ensuring the property is water tight a key feature along the critical path for the project to proceed.

When taking on a project such as this, you need to be prepared to be faced with unforeseen challenges; one of these was the discovery of bats nesting in the roof! Like with the Japanese knotweed, there are rules that must be strictly adhered to.

Bats can legally be removed, but you must first obtain a license and then pay for them to be re-housed again by licensed professionals. Another practical point for consideration of course, is that once the bats have been relocated, it is important during the reconstruction of the roof to ensure that they cannot re-gain entry to the high up roof spaces where they love to make their homes.

Again, all of this takes time. It should be noted that here are actually a number of different species including newts that if present must be re-housed when, for example, building new houses on a plot of land.

One of the next things we had to do was to fell a number of trees that were far too close to the walls and that were giving rise to damp and condensation within the building. As well being an eyesore from both within and out outside of the property, some of these wild seeded trees were badly obscuring the view of the house and blocking natural daylight in front of the windows.

We were later to discover that a second and further major cause of damp was due to an underground stream that was forcing water around and under the foundations. This problem had to be fixed through ground works to re-divert the stream to its original path - away from the house and towards the moat!

Despite almost every element of the property requiring complete restoration, one of the most amazing things was that many of the original features such as much of the wood paneling, fireplaces and even staircases remained largely intact – or at least reparable. By way of example, more than eighty sash windows had to be either painstakingly repaired – and where this was not possible new replacement windows had to be made with total authenticity to the originals.

Another priority included treating and where required, replacing structural timbers affected by both wet and dry rot, which was after years of neglect extensive.

As you might have expected, the ancient coal fired central heating system required replacement, along of course with a complete rewire. At the time of writing these infrastructural repairs are continuing - after which we will be able to start the internal refurbishment of the apartments and restore this beautiful building to its former glory; how exciting this will be!

We now have plans to remodel the post-war internal structure of the main building from twelve flats into eighteen self-contained luxury apartments.

The total restoration will cost around £2m [c. US$3.8m]– with the final valuation for Ribbesford House being conservatively estimated to be in excess of £6.35m [c. US$8.9m]; I suspect this figure may rise to £8m [c. US$11m] or more; I will keep you updated in *You-Tube* videos - and of course future print runs and editions of this book. In any of these cases, this should comfortably make Russell and a multi-million pound profit.

While this will unquestionably prove to be a fantastic investment, it is also a labour of love – and it is incredibly satisfying to be able to restore a jewel of a building with such an incredible history to such a high standard.

With the building being grade II* listed, we are taking every step to follow the most stringent of requirements as required – with meetings with Wye

Forest Conservation group and representatives of Historic England taking place each month.

Restoring listed buildings is far more complicated than refurbishing a normal property with almost any change to a listed building in England having to be approved by English Heritage as well as the local conservation and planning officers – even down to the type of paints that are used.

Grade I listed building in general do have to be restored to an almost identical state to the original – and while with grade II listed buildings, changes to the internal structure are often permitted, each and modification must be approved and signed off before work can be carried out.

Conservation and planning officers are normally pretty sympathetic to developers who are trying to save a building which requires restoration and has become dilapidated. There are two golden rules that I would recommend when working with any building inspector, conservation or planning officer: Firstly, since you must gain their approval (and ultimately sign-off) for the work you intend to do, do listen carefully and take on board what they have to say and if you are in any doubt, pass any queries past them; secondly do develop a really good relationship with them and treat them as your new best friend.

I cannot stress the need to take seriously any restoration or conservation orders – along with the need to comply with building regulations when restoring properties. Failure to adhere to the listed building regulations is a criminal offence – and flouting any of these rules, even inadvertently will result in you having to re-do the work – as well as potentially being served with a very significant fine – or even being given with a criminal record and jail sentence if you fail to comply.

Forging good relationships with planning officers has really paid dividends for us; we have through negotiation been allowed to replace the old, cracked flaking burned orange coloured render on the outside of the building - with a far smarter sandy grey colour for the new render, which is far more in keeping with what you would expect for a castle.

Conservation (and indeed all building regulations) are put in place for a reason – so that in all cases work is done in a safe manner - and in the case of listed buildings, is sympathetic to the building, its architecture and surroundings. The best advice is always to seek professional advice from structural engineers, chartered surveyors and the local planning office, all of who will be more than happy to advise. Planning officers like to work with people who are trying to do things properly rather than people who is trying to flout the rules. Our planning and conservation officers have been amazing and totally understand the vision for the project.

We know that people care about Ribbesford House and we care too. In the end we will have restored and saved an historic building back from possible collapse – and we believe we are doing something extremely worthwhile.

After the building, we will turn our attention to the remaining eight acres of the estate which not too surprisingly also need extensive attention.

When we originally bought Ribbesford House we intended to simply restore the house, create ten apartments within the main house and restore the outbuildings that comprise four separate adjacent cottages. The early stage of the restoration started just as the Covid-19 pandemic began to unfold. While this did cause some disruption and indeed caused some materials sourcing and supply issues – as an entrepreneur, I am a firm believer that in every challenging situation there will be opportunities that arise. One of these was that the UK's Prime minister (Boris Johnson) announced a significant loosening of planning restrictions – which has offered us the opportunity to build a number of new houses on the estate, where there were previously a number of old garages full of junk. Obviously, this will be subject to planning approval for houses that will be in keeping with the other buildings on the estate. We do now believe these new guidelines will allow us to proceed with three further developments –

which will both add to the gross development value of the project, whilst of course allowing more people to enjoy this beautiful and vast estate.

The grounds and gardens which again have suffered neglect will be landscaped to the highest of standards, including the refurbishment of features such as the long-neglected tennis courts. The extensive grounds will also allow us to build a number of log cabin style chalets for holiday, short term let - and serviced letting accommodation. Not only will this allow both many other people to enjoy the wonderful grounds and amazing location than would otherwise be possible, but will also very significantly in turn increase the revenue earning potential of the estate and so the financial return on investment. We estimate the estate will give us a passive income of around £10-12K [c. US$14-17K] profit per month after ongoing expenses.

It is anticipated that the restoration will be complete towards the end of 2022, with visitors being able to enjoy the estate for the first time for many years.

When the project is finally complete, Ribbesford House and its grounds will be completely restored - to at least its former glory – and possibly greater than it has ever been.

While this is a business-oriented project, Russell and I are very much aware that this is a beautiful listed building within an historic estate for which many people in the area have a great affection for – as indeed we do. We do feel in one sense that we are custodians of this amazing castle and surrounding grounds. It will be deeply gratifying to not only save the house from collapsing - but actually to hand this building on to future generations.

Chapter Thirty One: Moving Into Property Development:

In 2019, Russell and I branched out into property development with an initial project to build six brand new houses on a plot of land in Lincoln (UK). This should from beginning took approximately – and is now running concurrently with the restoration of Ribbesford House.

The first thing I did when looking for a piece of land was to check that outline planning permission had been granted. The last thing you want to do is to buy a piece of land – and then be stuck with a plot that you are not able to build on. I paid £330K [c. US$460K] for this land. It is important to make sure your solicitor and architect do all of the necessary due diligence and obtain all of the permissions as required before completing on the purchase and parting with any money. One other consideration that you really must be careful with is to ensure that all of the approaches to all of your dwellings – houses or apartments will have full pedestrian and vehicular access across for example pavements. It is amazing how many horror stories I have seen where another land owner will demand a payment for access across a ransom strip of land such as a pavement; again, this is another area very much for your solicitor!

Having looked for a number of sites we chose a plot in the St Anne's area of Lincoln, known as the local millionaires' row – a location that we knew would offer real potential for adding value the houses when complete. The site itself was flat with easy road access which was of real benefit during the construction of the houses – as well of course as being highly attractive to purchasers and residents, whether they be home owners or rental tenants.

The development comprised two rows of three terrace houses. Parking is really quite difficult in this part of Lincoln and the type of residents we knew we would be looking to purchase or rent these houses would almost certainly value allocated parking at a premium, which would be directly reflected in the end valuation of the properties. For this reason we designed the plot so that the two rows of houses have lowered curbs to allow parking in driveways to the front of the houses.

To the rear of the two terrace rows, each house was designed a little garden facing towards the garden of the opposite house in the other block, thereby adding some green and private space for socialising with friends for a barbeque or similar.

It is often the little attentions to details such as parking or gardens – as well of course as school catchment areas that really can make properties more desirable – all of which adds to the final end value. Since with a development project you are by nature starting with a blank sheet of paper, it is so important to speak to estate agents, have a look at other new builds in the area – and do your research to really determine what adds to the desirability – and therefore value and ultimately salability in an area.

It is, as in all areas of business – and especially so in property investing, it is so important to know and understand your potential customers. Speak to at least two – and ideally three or more architects and discuss your plans with them; not only will they help scope your plans, but will be able to bring to the table local knowledge of what will - and will not be likely to be approved by the planning officers in the local council. If the site has outline planning permission already granted, then they will be able to draw up plans that align with this.

Due to all the care we took in selecting the site and in the design and building of the houses, each sold almost instantly on completion of the project. The total development costs for the building of the houses was £500K, [US$650K] and so the total money put into this project was c.£850K [US$1190K]. The end gross development value (the end net worth) was in excess of £1.35m [US$1.9m] leaving us a profit of just over £500K (US$700K).

Now you will remember that I said that this project ran simultaneously with the restoration of this castle. I knew that I was never going to have enough hours in the day oversee this new build in any detail – and so I went into this project as a joint venture with a good friend of mine who I knew could bring to this project huge experience in property investing, including project managing new builds.

My joint venture partner put no money into the deal but who oversaw the builders who he knew well having worked with them on a number of other projects. He made £180K [US$252K] from this arrangement, while I made a profit of c.£320K, [US$450K].

Many people have questioned whether it is possible to really put together no money down deals; in this development I set up and provided a no-money down deal for my joint venture partner! He had to oversee the project, but of course did not have to do any of the actual work himself – while I did not have to even oversee the project, but provided the upfront investment. This is another ideal win-win scenario. At the end of the project, I was left with a very handsome profit.

At the time of writing our latest development comprises a new build of high end apartments in of all places of Leeds! For those interested in property development I have just published another book, 'The Secrets of Property Development: How to Make Six Figure Profits Every Time You Do a Property Deal'.

Chapter Thirty Two: Putting Something Back; How I Taught A Teacher Who Believed In Me How To Be A Property Investor

You may remember at the start of this book I told you something about my secondary school.

One of my teachers who had a great influence while I was there was a wonderful lady by the name of Mrs (Debbie) Hey-Smith who taught me Maths, IT and how to type. Her husband taught History at the same school and was similarly a great person.

My Mum was for a while a teaching assistant to help in Mrs Hey-Smith's class. These three people had some belief in me – above almost anyone else within the school - which was fortunate given that I always seemed to be living on the verge of getting expelled! I was suspended on more occasions than I can remember and collected more detentions, I suspect than anyone else in the history of the school.

Mrs Hey-Smith – a wonderful teacher who had faith in me

For some reason, for which I am eternally grateful, Mrs Hey-Smith saw something in me and used to say to the other kids that one day they would look at the me and say I '*knew that guy at school*'. One of the special things about her was that she always had the philosophy for only looking for the talents each individual had been given and always resisted giving out negative comments within school reports or similar, but rather concentrating on building people up in themselves and focussing on what they were good at.

This in itself is a quality and outlook in approach I learned from her and is one I try to emulate in my own life. Whilst not being the most naturally academic child, Mrs Hey-Smith saw that I was a natural communicator and really helped encourage me in developing this gift, which as things have turned out has had a profound impact on my life as a business and property investment trainer and coach.

After leaving school at sixteen, I lost contact with Mrs Hey-Smith for few years and only properly reconnected when I started the Christian business network, *Training Kings* through inviting her to our first ever meeting. As it turned out she went on to help run the Birmingham branch as the network became established and grew.

Later she and her husband travelled out with me to one of my earlier trips to Zambia to help establish a bore hole well, where she was fantastic and invaluable in helping manage the builders.

When I started running property *Crash Courses*, she was again at the very first event – yet again showing incredible faithfulness in her long-standing support. One of her gifts she believes she has (and that I can also vouch for) is for the encouragement of others; what an incredible quality this is!

When I met up with Mrs Hey-Smith again through *Training Kings*, she had recently lost her mother and inherited a large rather dilapidated house in Yorkshire, the land on which she built three, five bedroom houses which she then sold to give her a pot of money for further investing.

The next property she found was a slightly tired house in Bangor on the market for £110K [US$154K] that she spotted as having potential as an HMO within walking distance of the University and the station. She had learned from the *Crash Course* the importance of buying houses below market value and so put an offer in of £80K [c. US$112K]. The vendors not surprisingly turned this down but said they would accept an offer of £95K [c. US$133K], which is the price she paid for it. She found the estate agents who had handled the sale, a builder who put in new windows and gas along with a redecoration all of which only cost £5K [c. US$7K]. Again, following the formulae she had learned, she had the house revalued for £130K [c.US$182] thereby allowing her to pull out more than £90K [c. US$126K] for the next project. At the time of writing, she now has four rental properties and a full-time income from property - which as it turns out has proved to be incredibly valuable as she was made redundant at an age where it would be difficult to find another position but too young to claim a pension.

Chapter Thirty Three: My Charity - The Samuel Leeds Foundation:

As I mentioned earlier in the book, it was in 2009 that I first went out to Africa and I went to a rural village where there was no drinking water. I met a little boy who was five years old and would walk ten Kms to collect clean water. I just could not quite believe what he was telling me but after some investigation I found that this was absolutely the case and that every word he said was true. I remember as a teenager vowing to myself and God that if ever I became wealthy, that I would return to that village and commission the drilling of bore hole and building of water tanks to provide safe clean drinking water – not only for that boy but for the whole village of 350 people.

A few years later when I had become financially free through property, I recalled this boy and the village, returned and built a bore hole 110m deep. One bore hole together with the holding tank and pump etc. costs around £5K [c. US$7K] which just about covers the cost of putting in double glazing windows in an average house in western Europe or the US – and yet think of the impact to the whole of a village of three to four hundred people or more. I remember the spring water bursting up from this, the first borehole I installed and seeing all of the villagers and the children coming to drink the water and singing and dancing with such excitement. A tank to collect rainwater water from roofs costs even less with a price of around £1,500 [c. US$2.100] or so.

Watching this scene gave me a real sense of fulfillment and feeling of significance. Whilst I had been successful in my property business and knew that success felt good, significance felt greater. Since then, I have been going back and forth to a number of different African countries once or twice a year, finding the most-needy people who have noting and trying to combat poverty in those areas.

I believe when you are successful in business and when you have money and when you find yourself blessed, you should be a blessing to others.

I am extremely excited to say that we now have the *Samuel Leeds Foundation* registered as a UK registered charity. I put off registering this charity for so long as I initially was not intending to ask people to donate to this work; I just wanted to pay for this work from my own business profits. People had however been chasing me for a few years saying they had seen the work we were doing, and how lives were being changed and wanted to help and want to contribute. This is ultimately why I set up and launched as a charity – the *Samuel Leeds Foundation*.

The Samuel Leeds Foundation is focusing on four areas:

The first of these is for immediate aid; for essentials such as clean water and food where this is needed. There are many orphanages in Africa which are constantly in need of aid as they struggle to meet the needs of children who have nobody else to look after or care for them.

The second area is Health: as I explained earlier and as you know by now I had the unfortunate experience of needing emergency surgery in Uganda where like in most African countries, there is no state health care – and treatment has to be paid for. There are so many people who were in serious need and if they had not got the money for treatment, they would just be sent home. So, I have partnered again with the surgeon in Uganda who undertook the surgery on my leg. The foundation is giving money to people in desperate need of surgery and other medical care, but who cannot afford to pay. I can think of nothing worse than being in agony and in hospital and then not being able to afford the treatment.

The third area is Education; I believe that when you grow in your knowledge about business and finance, this is the key to prosperity and can be used to help break poverty. We are teaching kids and budding entrepreneurs to create wealth for themselves and other people - and we are even working with governments across Africa to partner with them to introduce business training into mainstream Ugandan government funded schools. Many adults are in need of business education and entrepreneurial training as well. By way of example in one particular group, we are focusing help towards widows to help them build businesses so that they have the resources to care for, feed and clothe their families and dependents.

Fourthly, we have a mission to provide School Buildings. We have recently started with our first school building programme in Uganda. There are many children who are unable to go to school because either the nearest schools are too far away – or because they have to walk for hours each day so as to bring back water for their family and livestock. Children in these situations often need a bore hole and clean water close to where they live – and a school nearby. I really do have a dream to extend schemes of this type to as many locations as is possible right across the continent of Africa.

Amanda my wife and I now travel to Africa once or twice a year for a few weeks at a time to oversee this work with the foundation's work primarily focused towards Uganda and Zambia. These visits and the work we do in Africa sustain and motivate me for the rest of the year and my work back in the UK.

During 2019, we visited Uganda to look for a site to establish a school staying in a hotel in Bable as a base for visiting a number of villages in the surrounding area.

Many people were incredibly generous and offered plots of land for free if we used this for the building of a school, however the location of the school is critical and must be chosen with care.

Our host and guide, as on a number of previous trips to Uganda was the same person who was our local host and guide when we had our white-water rafting accident. As a child he had been orphaned as a child and grew up in one of the villages we visited. He moved away some time ago to a nearby town where he now has a good job but he has never forgotten his roots has comes back to the village every week. As well as being a warm hearted and lovely person he is one of the most selfless people I know with a mission in life to put something back for others. He is a good cook and every week brings all the food for - and cooks a meal for the entire village; there is a lot of poverty and hunger in the area, but because of him everyone gets a really good meal at least once a week.

We visited a number of different locations to assess where we could have greatest impact for the building – or re-building of a school. There was certainly no shortage of need... One school was operating in buildings constructed by the villages – but the classrooms did not have walls; extremely heavy rain is in this part of Uganda frequent – and when this happens teaching, learning, studying becomes completely impossible. In another location, while there were buildings for a secondary school – there was only a tiny and totally inadequate building for the primary school.

In the end we found one school that was operating without any buildings whatsoever. Students and teachers regularly came together and meet at a site under a tree – and while it is true that a school is primarily a learning community - buildings are needed that are for fit for purpose. We also managed to meet with the head of schooling in the local area – who granted us permission to teach business and finance.

This visit was a great success with us also managing to locate further sites for establishing another bore hole and water holding tank in another nearby village.

I do like to lead a life of gratitude as this is a good way to live and helps your own wellbeing through being in a positive frame of mind. One of my priorities was to visit the hospital where I had been cared for and to meet up again with the surgeon Dr Jamirah who had operated on me after the water rafting accident. It was a wonderful visit and felt so good to be able to return under such better circumstances.

She told me that quite often she had to beg the orthopedic implant companies to donate reparative implants such as metal plates for bone repair since the list price for these (and indeed so many other medical devices) was completely beyond what her patients or the hospital could afford. She told me that sometimes she simply was not able to obtain the implants needed to help repair broken bones in the way she knew these could be. I pledged to Dr Jamirah and her hospital that that I would donate 10m Ugandan shillings (c.£2K or US$2.8K) for her work for the purchase of the medical implants and materials. This is an example where I was able to help because I had the resource to be able to do. It is easier to give from a position of abundance.

Lastly as we often do during visits of this type, we held a business networking and training event to help people establish their own businesses and in this way create wealth for themselves and the local community. In business you become wealthy ultimately by being valuable - and so teaching people to be valuable will help them to create wealth and lead them out of poverty; this is the ultimate 'giving a man a fishing rod instead of a fish' model. The thinking here is to start something that will continue to grow in a sustainable manner with time.

These events are always both fun and fulfilling – and end with a *Dragons' Den* type competition in which people pitch their business plans (which we have helped them prepare) for a number of small business grants we offer to help them get their plans established.

Fortunately this time we could head home without coming to any harm..!

The Samuel Leeds Foundation has been set up as a vehicle so that others can get involved. If you do want to help, you can give and you can do this on-line by Googling the Samuel Leeds Foundation or go directly to www.samuelleedsfoundation.com - and then donating on line. An even more powerful way to help, however, could be to come out to help out with the work as your time can be more valuable than your money. If you have a burning desire to come out to help but do not have much to give, then I would strongly suggest you get yourself educated, become financially free and then you will have the time and the money to help. It is harder to help the poor when you are poor yourself. As I have seen, it is easier to give from a position of abundance – when your time is your own and you are able to travel and help with the work in Africa.

My mission in the UK is to help people to become financially free – and when they do, I encourage people to be generous with their time and their money; remember when we are blessed, we have a moral responsibility to bless others.

Part Two

It's All About You; Freedom Formulae

Chapter Thirty Four: You Can Do It Too...You Really Can

I have told you much of my life story... so far. I have enjoyed extraordinary success – and been blessed in so many ways; I know this. As I mentioned in the last chapter, I truly believe that if you are blessed, you are blessed to be a blessing machine – and that is what I strive to be. In developing parts of Africa, I have a mission to bring water, education (especially in areas of finance and entrepreneurialism), healthcare and the building of hospitals and schools. In rich developed countries, my primary mission is to help people become financially free so that they too can become blessing machines to others.

If you are reading this – and want to become finically free and to become a blessing machine yourself, then parts two and three of this book really are all about you...

I have literally hundreds of students who have become financially free and are now enjoying levels of success that they never thought possible.

I have shown you how I built – and continue to build my wealth through property; now I want to help show you how you can do the same – and more.

I have long held the view that the best investment you can ever make is in yourself through becoming educated. The second-best investment you can make is in property.

Part two of this book is focused towards some of the fundamentals of business that you must grasp; you could view this of this almost as being like a mini-MBA programme. Part three delves into the specifics of a number of property strategies. Do not be tempted to skip part two; this is so important and what I am going to teach and share with you is here for a reason... your success!

So – let me help you become financially free. The first step is to ensure you develop the mindset to allow you to succeed.

Chapter Thirty Five: First - You Have To Be In The Game To Win It

If you are thinking of becoming a property investor and approach this with a mindset of *'Let's see if this works?',* then I can tell you right now and upfront – it won't… it simply won't. Like all things in life, you will get out of property investing what you put in to it in terms of effort and commitment. You cannot expect to experience success by being half-hearted.

You have to approach your learning with a mindset of: *'This is going to happen, I know this is going to happen; I just need the knowledge to make this happen'.*

The strategies you are going to be taught work: I'll say this again… they work!

I am financially free - and every week I have students who are becoming financially free though these approaches and putting what they have been taught into action.

The question you need to ask is – *'Are you going to make this work?'*

No matter how many excuses you may have, whether they be, *'I am too young, I don't have any money, I don't live in a country where this is easy, we might be entering a recession'* or others, you can make this work and it is down to how you approach things. As I often point out to my students, I started investing in property in 2008, as a paper boy - just as the world was heading into a credit crunch and right at the beginning of one of the most significant recessions we have ever seen. I made it work…

If you read something in the next few chapters that you do not think applies to you – do not dismiss this; stop, think about it and make this apply to you…!

The take away message from this *has to be,* to *'Get your head into the game'* - and then you can and *will* succeed; do not make excuses.

Chapter Thirty Six: Why Do People Fail?

Steve Jobs famously said that the people who are crazy enough to think they can change the world are normally the ones who do. How true this is!

Sometimes you have to forget what you have been told by others and think about what would empower you. To take the attitude that things are *'just the way they are'* or that you were just *'born that way'* takes any power away from you – power to change. How much better would it be to realise that you can be whatever you wish to be? You just need to learn how to - and then put this in to practice.

You *do* have a choice. I would not want to judge anyone, but please do not be one of those people who moan and say that *'you are just the way you are'*.

I know a story about two people who grew up together: One was really successful, happy, kind and a great husband. The other was a loser, beat his wife and never had any money. Both were interviewed and asked why they were the way they were. The one who was making a mess of his life, said it was because his father was that way; the other guy by contrast replied that he had seen his father be a loser, beat his wife and did not want to be like that. Both had similar backgrounds and upbringing, but made completely different life choices.

This story illustrates how we all have free will to make life choices – *but* - since we know from psychologists that we tend to become like the five people closest to us, our choices can be influenced with who we mix - so pick your company carefully. If there are people who are likely to drag you down, think carefully about potentially mixing with a different circle of people.

I believe how your life play out is 90% down to what you make of it and 10% down to what happens to us. Let me first explain this: Good and bad things happen to us all; this is the 10% part. Do you get angry towards situations? - or do you see opportunities in situations that do not quite go to plan? Are you always thinking about what you do not have? - or conversely are you thankful for what you do have?

An important part of my daily routine is to put time aside and consciously think about all the things that I need to be grateful about. You see, gratitude as a state of mind makes you happy. If you do this on a daily basis you actually will over time become happier. By contrast, if you are ungrateful, even if you become successful you will never be happy as feelings of entitlement, pride and arrogance will rob you of feelings of contentment.

There is a fine line between confidence and arrogance. I am naturally a confident person. We all, however, need to learn humility; humility is not thinking less of yourself but *rather thinking of yourself less*; the two are completely different.

Think about this: Anybody who says something cannot be done is speaking from a poverty mindset. Why talk about what cannot be done; why not think and talk about what is possible.

If someone says '*something can't be done*', I just tend to switch off. I would far rather someone say something such as, '*The way you are going about that might not be the best way - have you thought about doing it this way?*'

Some people are allergic to success without realising it. I am addicted to success - and am allergic to negativity!

Chapter Thirty Seven: Be Disciplined In All Things And You Will Succeed...

Have you ever noticed that the way in which someone does anything is almost always the way they do everything? Just take a moment and think about how this applies to some of the people you know. People, for example, who are competitive in areas such as sport, are often driven in their careers. In the same way others who are known for being 'laid back' will almost certainly be less competitive in all that they do. There can be few things more important for pre-positioning us for success, fulfilment and happiness than making sure that we approach *life* with the right mindset.

Many unsuccessful people simply do not see that the way they approach life is never going to lead a change in their fortunes. There are a number of reasons why this is the case, with one of the most significant being a lack of discipline to follow through on opportunities or projects.

If you start a project or venture but fail to complete it, then it is pretty clear that this will not lead to a successful outcome – and yet this is something so many people do over and over again. If you think this sounds obvious, just think about how many people who on January 1st each year make New Year's resolutions such as to lose weight, give up smoking, learn a new language etc. Everybody knows that come February the overwhelming majority of these people will have given up on their resolutions - and by March will have in many cases even forgotten what they were!

You see my point is, that outcomes do not happen by accident. If you want an outcome you need to follow through on good intentions with positive actions; actually, you need to be committed to doing whatever it takes. This is a crucial point – since obstacles will inevitably present themselves which can easily deter or put off the faint hearted. If you meet an obstacle, you need to think and have the mindset of how you are going to get around the problem – and not let a problem stop you – or even become a subconscious excuse for giving up.

One note of caution: There is little point in having lots of motivation, but having no idea what you are doing; if you do, you will become 'a motivated idiot'. This may sound harsh but this is an important point. While you may learn through mistakes, success will follow so much more easily if you first become educated and then continue to learn by immersing yourself within networks of people who you can come to learn from through osmosis.

If what you do continues to fail again, and again, you do need to critically look at why this might be – and to be honest with yourself however painful this might be.

If there are gaps in your knowledge or if there are flaws in your approach, then you need to learn so that you do not keep making the same mistakes. In the same way, if you recognise that are not a finisher, then you need to become more disciplined. If necessary, make yourself accountable to your partner, a sibling or a friend, diarise your time and set goals.

It might be helpful to seek out and hire a business mentor; just do whatever it takes and ensure that you are not one of those people who fails to succeed because they do not follow through, are too easily put off, lack sufficient motivation, or end up becoming quitters when things get difficult. Commit to yourself to just do whatever it takes!

When people come up to me to talk with me at training events and are seeking advice, I can normally tell within five minutes, whether they are likely to be successful or not. Unquestionably the two biggest qualities for success are the desire to learn and the commitment to follow through with action.

So... if you know in your heart of hearts that you lack knowledge or know how, motivation or drive to follow through, you need to resolve to not keep making these mistakes in the future – and in this way change your approach so that you succeed.

A final thought... Albert Einstein defined stupidity as *'Doing the same thing over and over again and expecting a different result'*; please do not be one of these people... If you want to succeed, then learn from previous mistakes, put better systems in place to be more organised – be the person who always follows through - and who always finishes. In summary do whatever it takes – and remember the way you do anything will almost always be the way you will be doing everything!

Exercise:

Write down on a piece of paper all of the reasons **you are** going to succeed:

o   What have you going for you?

o   Have you got courage?

o   Have you got experience of business?

o   Have you got faith in yourself?

o   Have you got people who believe in you more than you do yourself?

o   Do you have great drive and determination?

o   Do you know you can get a mortgage?

o   Do you have a wish to change your financial future for the benefit for others?

List as many things as you can...

Chapter Thirty Eight: What They Didn't Teach You At School

In part one of this book, I told you how I failed to get on too well with school – and in fairness I know I was far from being an ideal pupil (and that is putting it mildly).

When I did leave school – and started to learn about business, finance and property investing, I suddenly became hungry for learning and could not study enough. The difference was of course that these areas captured my imagination - and then suddenly everything I was being taught started to make sense to me.

You may have had a great schooling and if you did then this is something to be really valued. Even if you did, the chances are however that you were not taught about business and finance – and what you did learn about money probably came from other sources such as your parents – or indeed generally held views within society.

You may have been told that it is good to save up money, to buy a house and then pay off your mortgage as quickly as possible - and that the model for a 'good life' is to do well, get a job or even have a career with a good income, save and then look forward to retirement.

In reality, most people work hard for forty years struggling to make ends meet - and then have to survive on 40% of what they were struggling to live on during all of their working life.

You need to understand that it is in the banks' interest for you to save money with them. Banks use this money to invest – in, for example, property. If everybody went to the banks and asked for their money, it is clear they would not be able to hand it all back, because it has been lent out as investments to other people.

There is no reason why you cannot become an investor yourself. You may however have to first 'un-learn' some deep seated pre-conditioned misconceptions - and to do this you will need to question everything you think you have learnt about money. As you work through the following chapters, do ask questions of yourself including – *'How could this help me become financially free?'*

To do this, you do need to be educated: Formal education teaches you many essential skills including, how to read and write, to tackle maths etc. Now is the time to become educated about money, finance and wealth creation.

So, let's start by self questioning some misconceptions or preconditioned beliefs that could hold you back.

Exercise:

Write down on a piece of paper all of the reasons why you are going to succeed:

Now make a list of areas where you might have - or have had pre-conditioned assumptions or mis-conceptions in your mind?

Think carefully and be really honest with yourself.

Think about ideas or concepts such as:

o   What have you always thought about property investing? Do you think this sounds exciting – or risky?

o   If you were to say, *'Rich people are...* What comes into your mind? Do you think greedy, do you think selfish – Do you think he or she has done well... Do you think he or she has created wealth for the economy?

o   When you think of money, what do you think? A force for good or bad? Do you think money is neither good nor bad - but how people use it?

o   When you think about becoming wealthy what are your immediate thoughts?

Chapter Thirty Nine: The Importance Of Taking Action...

Nothing will happen to change your life circumstances without taking action; while this is pretty obvious, many people grumble that life has not worked out as they might have hoped - and resign themselves to a status quo they are not happy with, when all along they are not prepared to take any action to affect change.

Just think of how many people who you know who have joined a gym to get fit – and yet never go?

Do not procrastinate – take action; do not wait for everything to be perfect. Waiting for everything to be perfect can easily become an excuse for not taking action. If you say – '*I will wait till next year when I have some more life space, for interest rates to fall, for more certainty in the worlds markets*'... the likelihood is that next year you will find your life is just as busy, other things will be still less than perfect - and then you will most probably decide to wait till the following year.

One of the most important things to remember in the area of property investing is that you have to be 'fully in the game' to win. This is true for any of the techniques I teach from Rent-to-Rent, to Buy-Refurbish-Refinance strategies or Deal Sourcing; success needs action. Remember that the only place that you will find the word 'success' before work is in the dictionary!

To illustrate the point of needing to be in the game – it is worth noting that on average property prices double every ten years. If you procrastinate for a decade, you will miss out on this gain. If it turns out that your timing was not perfectly at the bottom of a house price dip – does it really matter? The most important thing in ten years' time will have been to have taken action, bought a good property, seen substantial equity growth - while of course receiving rental income in the meantime.

There are two approaches for learning how to do something new: One is to just get going and figure everything out as you go along; the problem with that is that you are likely to make some serious mistakes along the way.

The second approach is to gain understanding through training and then take action from an informed position. However, you do need to strike a balance between these two positions; some people want to figure out every detail before taking action – and do not move forward through getting tripped up by a form of 'paralysis by analysis'.

There has to be a balance; if you see a property deal but have yet to figure out how to finance this, do not let this hurdle stop you. Sometimes, you have to walk the A,B,C - and then figure out (you could call this) the X,Y,Z. Follow Richard Branson's advice and say *'yes'* and then figure out the details later.

This second part of the book has been structured and put together in a very systematic step-by-step order. Do not let concerns such as, *'Now I know how to find a deal, but I do not know how to do this, this and this'*, rob you of opportunities as you learn and work your way through the following chapters.

Walk the A,B,C and figure out some of the X,Y, Z as you go along.

Stick to the formulae you have (and will be) taught, and then in the words of *Nike* the sports brand, *'Just Do It'*.

Chapter Forty: Time Management - And Prioritising The Important Over The Urgent:

Time management is critical to the successful running of a business.

As I mentioned earlier in the book, most people do not understand the difference between what is *important* and the *urgent*. *Important* things are those which will matter in the long term – like leading a healthy lifestyle. Many peoples' lives are by contrast completely focussed towards things in the short term – such as wondering, where you will next be going on holiday, paying a bill or even what you are going to eat tonight. A few people prioritise important things with longer term consequences, such as, for example, giving up smoking, eating more healthily or becoming financially free.

Many people only address the important when it has become both urgent and important, when it almost always too late; a good example of this would be when people realise their health is suffering due to lifestyle factors.

Success in business requires prioritising the important over the urgent – and this is achieved by careful time management and setting long, medium and short-term goals focussed towards achieving your desired outcomes.

Practical Steps to Time Management:

First concentrate on what you are good at and pay for others to do tasks that can be outsourced inexpensively; learn to outsource and delegate where necessary. This is a skill you will need to master if you are to grow and scale a business.

One of the key practical steps is to list all of the jobs that can be outsourced inexpensively and then find people to do these tasks. Examples of this could include bookkeeping, hiring virtual PAs to take messages, bookings for serviced accommodation, cleaning, etc...

Chapter Forty One: The Art Of Making Decisions

While it is absolutely crucial to take action - decisions should always be informed by careful consideration of realistically the best, worst and the most likely outcomes.

Extremes might range from becoming a millionaire through to becoming bankrupt.

Risking becoming bankrupt would clearly be unacceptable for most people, but if the worst case scenario would be to possibly loose a modest investment - while the most likely outcome could be to set up a passive income stream for life, then the risk / reward balance would look very different!

Different people have different appetites for risk - and this is an area to consider carefully for yourself.

Next, you need to consider is how and what you might advise my best friend to do? Would you advise them to go through with a deal or not? This often helps clarify the mind, as you mentally step out of the choice for yourself.

If you decide you should take a particular course of action, but still feel nervous, then take what I call the 5-4-3-2-1 plunge – in which you take a deep breath, count 5-4-3-2-1 and then in the words of *Nike 'Just Do It'*. This is really useful when tempted to procrastinate about, for example, picking up the phone and talking to an agent to book a viewing – or indeed even putting in an offer for a property.

Exercise:

If you know you procrastinate – make a list of the things you know you should do – and then start working through this list.

Chapter Forty Two: Develop Goal Oriented Business Plans For Yourself:

There are two types of goals you need to consider:

First: Personal Goals: – these should be fun to plan for:

Personal goals should be focussed towards what your dream life might look like...

Some people would like to live a luxurious life, some would like their life to be simplified - while others might have a passion to help others.

What matters is what *you* might think would be ideal for *yourself*.

Second Your Business Goals: now need to serve your Personal Goals.

Exercise: Planning your Business and Personal Goals:

Spend half an hour (or more if needed), dreaming about what your ideal life might look like and what would bring you true contentment and a feeling of satisfaction.

Make a list of what your ideal life might look like and comprise.

Steps For Achieving Your Financial Goals So As To Serve Your Personal Goals:

1) Calculate how much money you would need to live the lifestyle you wish to have – itemise all costs so that you arrive at an accurate cumulative figure.

2) Work out what the product of your business is going to be: you need to specific and not just say something like property. Examples might include selling deals for investors, or buy to let HMOs.

   What do you sell – what will your customers buy? You need to know your business.

   You need to be able to describe your business strategy in a few words (or one sentence at a maximum).

3) Determine the profit and then the turnover of business you will need to provide this income.

4) Next, think about how much money you could make in a month as if your life depended upon it? This is a challenging question: Think hard, think creatively and think outside of the box about this. Put yourself under pressure.

   To do this – you might have to change your strategy and game plan.

   Borrowing or selling something you already have does not count, since you already have this and so this cannot be counted as making money. Ask yourself how could you create new income streams? Think creatively – this could involve deal sourcing – or co-deal sourcing, it could involve negotiating lease options which you sell on, it could be through serviced accommodation etc... You could, for example, view houses and take people with you with an agreement that if they buy a house that you introduce them to, then they would pay you a fee.

Do not get complacent along your journey – or else you will settle for a little success instead of far greater reward. Aim to be the most successful or best version of yourself that you possibly can be.

5) Market your business; you need to know how to market. Do not chase people. You need people to come to you based on your offering.

Marketing is about telling people about what you do – then you can sell. Selling is closing the deal. There are many ways of marketing and we will take a look at these shortly.

6) You must learn how to sell through first gaining an understanding a person's need. First ask questions and then more questions. Determine what the person needs; remember it is pointless trying to sell something is inappropriate for them. Making sales is achieved first and foremost through asking questions about them and their customers... so that you can offer them what they need and/or adapt the offering to suit.

7) Delivery: First set the expectations for your customer... this will minimise complaints. Make sure you always use a contract that defines expectations and so defines the deal. Always seek feedback through, for example, feedback forms for all of your customers (e.g., tenants). In this way you can address any problems and improve your service.

8)   Re-invent, adapt and develop your product based on feedback.

9)   Finance – You need to be aware of issues such as cash-flow and tax (see point below). You need to you work with you accountants in partnership. You cannot devolve responsibility to them.

You need first to be fully au fait of your monthly, quarterly, half yearly and annual turnover. Next, you need to determine your monthly, quarterly, half yearly and annual overheads and direct costs.

Overheads include staff costs, rental for offices etc. Direct costs include costs such as repairs to properties. Your net profit is the money you have made after overheads and direct costs.

Net profit = Turnover – (overheads and direct costs).

You need to determine your percentage net profit.

Percentage net profit = Turnover / (overheads + direct costs) x 100

10)   You need to be fully aware of tax liabilities that you will have to pay: You only pay tax on profit. Many expenses are tax deductible. This is where you will need advice from a specialist property accountant.

You need to determine in conjunction with your accountant costs that may be tax deductible.

11)   Finally, to grow your business you need to plan for growth through investing in your brand, education, refinancing your properties.

Exercise: Writing the Outline Business Goals for Yourself: Where Would You Like To Be?

a)   Take time and write down exactly where you like to be in 6 months, 1 year, 3 years and 5 years from now.

b)   Now sit down and *honestly* evaluate where you are (what do you have – skills, finance, a power network?):

c)   Next list all of the things your business is missing? This could include items such as a website that attracts customers, a marketing plan or strategy, a customer base or key contacts, cash or investment, an accountant, a broker, builders, key relationships with estate agents? Analyse everything you need to take you to each of your intermediary timeline goals.

d)   Now write the first outline skeleton for your business plan based on a-c above.

e)   Come back to refine this the next day and then again in two days' time, a week's time and in a month; the key thing is to keep refining this again and again and then start to assemble the resources you need such as power team or investors.

f)   Plan a time line that is only just achievable – and do not be lenient on yourself; be driven and do whatever it takes to keep to your timelines. If you meet an intermediary goal early, reschedule your goals and again be driven. Plan to achieve as much as you possibly can in as short as time as you can. Be highly ambitious and do whatever it takes to achieve all of your goals to schedule or ahead of schedule.

g)   Plan 'to do' lists to achieve the goals - and be accountable to yourself for these; even better share these goals with your business partner or spouse or someone else close so that you stick to the goals and do not procrastinate.

h)   The more times you return to your to do lists and goals, the more you will chase yourself to do what you set out to achieve.

Chapter Forty Three: Make It Simpler – Cut Down Your Expenses

Earlier I mentioned that one important approach towards helping you become financially free is to cut out unnecessary expense from your life. Now is the time to be ruthless and work through the exercise below:

Exercise:

You now need to examine your expenses and see where you can make savings; think of where you could make savings if you really had to such as if you lost your job.

Be ruthless with yourself.

Many people find that they can cut their monthly expenditure by 50% if they really had to. By doing this you may be able to very considerably lower your financial freedom goal.

Questions you need to ask yourself could include:

- Can you get rid of a second car?
- Do you use your gym membership?
- Can you do without a foreign holiday?
- Can you cut out of your lifestyle so many meals out?

How much do you spend on clothes each month?

Do be ruthless with yourself and go through bank statements to see where you spend your money. Cutting down on monthly expenditure on unnecessary luxuries is a form of deferred gratification and be thought of as accepting short-term pain for long term gain.

Many people who have gone through this exercise, have found standing orders for things that they had forgotten about. I remember a student of mine - a happily married man who had been paying for a dating agency for years after he had been married, but had forgotten to cancel a standing order!

Samuel Leeds

Chapter Forty Four: Passive Income: Making Money While You Sleep

In part one of this book, we discussed how active income is earned when you work once and you get paid once. This is what most people do when they go to work; they get paid in return for exchanging their time for money.

Passive or residual income occurs when you work once and you keep getting paid over and over again. This is the way in which you can make money while you sleep. There are many ways in which you can make passive income from, for example, royalties on books or music – but property is probably the best vehicle on the planet for making passive income. If you buy a house for renting to tenants, you work once to fund the purchase, but your tenants pay you rent month after month.

You need to train your mind-set into developing passive income streams. There is nothing wrong in earning money through active income, but you need to invest your resources, (time and your money) to make passive income; this is the route to financial freedom.

There are dozens of ways for creating passive income streams.

Exercise:

Sit down and make a list of all of the ways you can think of for creating passive income streams.

Chapter Forty Five: An Introductory 'How To' Guide For Wealth Creation Through Property And Leveraging Finance

Imagine two people: They both have the same job and get paid the same amount. The both save up £50K [c. US$70]. Person A puts his money in the bank where it is 'safe'. Person B uses his £50K [(c. US$70] as a deposit to buy a £200K [c. US$ 280K] property – (the average house price in the UK at the time of writing), with a £150K [c. US$210K] buy to let mortgage.

Now let us look at what happens to these two people over time: Person A receives interest from the bank. At the time of writing interest rates for savings will be 0.1% or thereabouts; this is practically zero. To make matters worse (actually far worse), this person's money is actually devaluing in real terms over time, since inflation decreases the value of money. At current rates of inflation, person A's £50K [c. US$70K] will after ten years be worth approximately £36K [c. US$50.5K] in today's terms.

Person B will be making a net income over and above their mortgage payments and other expenses; person B will already be winning - each and every month.

Houses tend over time to increase in value: Over the last two hundred years in the UK and many other countries, house prices have doubled in value on average every ten years. While future increases cannot be guaranteed, history does tend to repeat itself.

Now when the value of the house increases, the *whole* value of the house increases and not just the deposit with which person B used as an investment down payment. So, when after ten years, the house increases in value from £200k to £400K [c. US$280K to US$560], the initial £50K

(US$70K) deposit has now made person B £200K [c. US$280K]. Person B is now in a position to refinance the property to release this capital appreciation as cash to be used as deposits for the purchase of further properties. By doing this again and again you can you can become a millionaire – almost by accident.

This demonstrates the incredible power of leveraging. This is exactly the way in which I became wealthy... actually very wealthy. While rental income can bring income in the short term, real wealth creation comes through capital appreciation over the long term.

Chapter Forty Six: On Managing Your Money For Personal Growth, For The Benefit Of Others And Empowering Mission...

I have told you much about many of my own personal experiences and how these led me along my own path to becoming financially free. I encourage everyone I meet to strive to become financially free as this helps unlock so many doors, including of course ultimately empowering your mission in life.

At the start, I inevitably got some things right and others wrong, with some of what I learned being picked up along the way being through trial and error. As I invested in myself, success followed and so did growth in my residual income. With greater success, so did the opportunity to help others; you will have seen that two of my missions in life are to help others become financially free – and to help provide basic needs such as clean water, sanitation and education to parts of the world with the greatest need.

One of the greatest lessons I learned was how to *apportion* and manage money not only for financial freedom but also for the benefit of others.

What I now want to do is share with you a formula for sustainable money management for your continued success, your happiness, personal fulfilment personal growth – and your mission.

Some years ago, I heard an amazing talk on money management by T. Harv Eker author of the book, '*Secrets Of The Millionaire Mind*'; at the time I realised the approach could be life changing and vowed to myself I would implement the strategies he taught. Did I do this? No... I went back the following year and listened again - and this time started to put the what he was suggesting to work. I have since further adapted these principles for personal money management – and say more on this in my book, *'Do The Possible, Watch God Do The Impossible'*. I will however give a summary here to help you get started.

This is how it works... The first thing you need to do is open a number of different bank accounts, each for a different purpose; I recommend at least seven: a master bank account and then six more into which you will regularly apportion money for different purposes.

When you are paid, whether you are starting out in business or still in paid employment, put your income into a master bank account and then distribute this money into the six different accounts with a suggested percentage split as below:

- (Main Bank account into which your income is paid)

- Essential Living Costs: 50%

- Entertainment / Recreation: 10%

- Giving: 10%

- Savings: 10%

- Investment: 10%

- Education: 10%

For this approach to work, you do need to distribute your money between the different accounts each and every time you are paid. Human nature being what it is, if you do not put a system in place to make this happen, then the chances are it won't. If you have a regular income the best way to make this happen is to put standing orders in place from the master bank account into each of the other subsidiary accounts so that these money transfers occur automatically.

The percentage split does not of course need to be exact. If you have a relatively modest lifestyle and you have good income, you may wish to put more money towards your education, investment or giving.

At the heart of this approach, is the principle of careful budgeting and valuing putting money aside, over the urge for instant gratification. In this approach, you still allow yourself a budget for entertainment and fun and this can grow as your income grows. Do however resist the temptation to allow your day-to-day living expenses to swallow up any increases in income. It is so easy to convince yourself that you 'need' a new car or 'need' a new holiday when you find yourself earning a little more. Be disciplined and do not allow yourself to fall into this trap.

Let me explain a little more concerning how and why money should be allocated to each category:

Essential Living Costs: (suggested 50% of income)

This is the largest allocation for covering essential day to day living costs and will include housing costs such as rent, mortgage, electricity, gas food and similar.

Entertainment / Recreation: (suggested 10% of income)

This allocation is to cover all areas of entertainment from *Netflix* and *Spotify* to nights out and holidays. It is important to spend some money on fun and entertainment for a number of reasons. First: as the expression goes, 'All work and no fun, makes Jack a dull boy'. If you do not allow yourself some fun in life, then you are less likely to have an optimistic and upbeat outlook. Second: when people live too frugally and deny themselves all fun, they often end up splashing out extravagantly in a pressure value type backlash. Third: if you are in a relationship, it is good to spend an agreed budget - no more and no less - on entertainment; this helps prevent arguments through one person naturally being a 'spender' and one a 'saver'!

Giving: (suggested 10% of income)

Giving is effectively making an investment in others. I have learned that giving blesses and benefits the giver in equal - if not greater amounts than the recipient. I know this to be true from personal experience. Giving again needs discipline if this to happen: if you think to yourself that '*I will commit to giving 10% when I have more to give*', it will never happen. This again is just human nature. Start now, be disciplined about this and it will become a habit – and one you will find will bring happiness contentment and blessing.

Savings: (suggested 10% of income)

This is the 'pot' for saving up for things like home improvements, a new car – and of course reserves to act as a rainy day fund.

Investments: (suggested 10% of income):

Investments should never be spent and are there to provide you with passive income in areas such as housing, stocks and share holdings or systemised businesses. Regular and wise investing will provide you with increasing passive income that will snowball with time and inevitably lead to financial freedom - and in time, ultimate financial freedom.

Education: (suggested 10% of income):

The best investment you can ever make is in yourself and the most valuable asset you will ever have is your brain. Put simply, the more you learn, the more you will earn. Do not skimp on your own personal education and learning, whether this be on spending money on training – or indeed commitment of time and effort. Book up for and attend seminars, read books, network and learn from others – and above all immerse yourself and commit to ongoing personal development.

Remember right at the beginning of the book we saw that most people operate as if they had a personal 'financial thermostat' and tend to always have the same amount of savings or debt however their circumstances change.

Apportioning your money in this way does require personal discipline, but will help you invest for sustainable income growth, personal development and fulfilment of mission.

Psychologists will tell you that the ability to appreciate the value of deferred gratification is a key indicator for future success in life!

Today, I am completely fastidious and disciplined in the way I apportion my money into different 'pots', so that I know my money works for me and my mission in life.

Samuel Leeds

Chapter Forty Seven: Your Next Steps – Understanding The Basics Of Business:

1) *The Art of Selling:*

All businesses sell. They may sell physical goods, software, services or some other product offering – but they all sell products.

All successful businesses employ sales funnels – so let us look at how sales funnels work. A good example could be to look at how this would operate for a car dealership as you may recognise the approaches used.

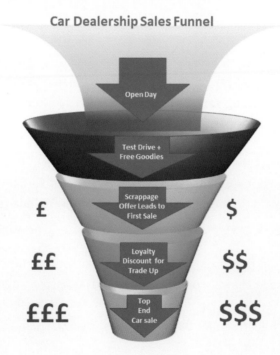

Sales funnels operate by attracting leads (potential clients), then serving them and adding value in some way, before trying to sell; this helps build trust.

People almost always need to get to know you, like you and trust you before they are likely to buy from you. This is how you direct leads into the top of your sales funnel.

The sales funnel then - and only then, should be ready to sell. Repeat business is always easier than your first sale, so long as the customer has a good experience. A good experience can be provided by, for example, under promising and over delivering with incredible service. One of the reasons for Amazon's success is that their mission statement is to be *'The planet's number one company for customer service and satisfaction'*.

Your first job is to attract as many leads (and people) as you can into the top of the funnel.

There are many ways in which you can attract leads into the funnel and these include: offering something for free, such as a book, or daily blog. There are many examples.

The next stage of the funnel is to make the first sale; if this is for cars it might be an entry level car such as a Vauxhall Corsa or Ford Fiesta, the next level might be a VW Golf, after that an Audi TT and after that a Lamborghini.

Repeat sales can be encouraged by offering discounts and incentives: in the motor trade these could include free servicing, trade in deals, scrappage schemes or similar. In other areas of business, common incentives include 'three for two' type deals, loyalty schemes, time limited discounts and other offers.

2) *The Importance of Developing Key Behaviours in Business:*

Earning Trust, Helping People Get to Know You – and Then Like You:

You Must Serve Before You Sell: Remember always set out to serve first before trying to sell; this helps build trust and shows how you can add value.

Make Eye Contact: It is said that the eyes are the window to the soul. Everybody intuitively distrusts people who avoid contact for fear that they are trying to hide something. Conversely people who make eye contact come across as being genuinely interested in other people. Eye contact is important for building trust, so make a conscious effort to always look other people in the eye and smile. If at first you find this difficult, look at one of their eyes when talking to them.

Be Genuine: It is so important to always be genuine and trustworthy in all you do. It takes time to build trust – and it is so easily lost. As Mark Twain famously said, *'Always tell the truth and then you will not remember what you have to say'*, So many people do not behave like this in business. Why do otherwise? It is far easier to always be scrupulously honest and open, as well as being one of the surest ways for building relationships founded on trust.

Ask Questions: Always ask questions when speaking to people and try to answer questions from the other person with a question. The person who asks the most questions always controls the conversation; just think of how an interview is conducted and then ask yourself who is in control of the conversation?

With practice, people will actively come to you like iron filings being attracted to a magnet - and this is the first step to becoming an influencer.

Chapter Forty Eight: Get Comfortable Being Uncomfortable:

We have one life; this is not a practice run and during our time here on earth we are either learning and moving forward – or losing skills and slipping backwards.

If you develop a skill, whether this be learning to play a musical instrument – or learning to speak a new language, you need to keep practicing this skill or you will start to lose it. If you work hard and practice a skill you are developing, you will continue to learn and get better at this. This is why orchestral musicians often practice for hours each day and linguists always try to find opportunities to keep conversing with others in each of the languages they speak. The same of course is also true within sport. When we exercise, we become fitter and our muscles grow and when we don't, our muscles become weaker. This is true for all of us at any age.

Two of the most effective ways to keep our brain sharp into old age is to keep out minds active and our bodies fit. Our bodies and our minds are designed to be used - and we are in all things either growing and moving forward, or diminishing and slipping backwards.

One of the problems we almost all encounter is that we are as human beings, creatures of habit; it is so easy to do the same things again and again. This is why so many people do not believe (or have the confidence to believe) that they can change their life circumstances. Learning of any type takes effort and can make you feel uncomfortable – just as going to the gym can leave you with aching muscles. If you want to get fitter you have to put up with a few aches, but as your body responds you will in time start craving for more exercise.

The process of learning new skills is no different; learning to play a new instrument requires hard work and dedication – and playing this in front of others will almost always at first make you feel uncomfortable. Learning to mix in business circles or speak in public will probably make you feel uncomfortable – but if you keep practicing, you will become more skilled and then comfortable with mixing and conversing with groups in ways that at one time might have felt quite intimidating.

One of the biggest reasons that people fail to reach their full potential is through inaction caused by the fear of failing. If you just stop and think about this for a moment, this is almost always nonsensical. If you fail, you will in most cases have lost little, but may well have gained experience along the way. Most successful people, such as Richard Branson and others, have had a string of setbacks behind them; some even almost wear these as a badge of honour. The difference between those who become successful those who do not is that unsuccessful people call setbacks 'failure', while successful people treat setbacks as experience gained, learn from these and move forward. The Richard Bransons of this world, treat all of life's experiences whether these be good or bad as opportunities for development. People of this mindset certainly do not relish failure, but neither are they afraid of it – and have almost certainly learned to be comfortable with being uncomfortable.

So – how can you train yourself to become comfortable with being uncomfortable? Here are a few suggestions... First list a number of things that you like doing, that you are comfortable with and that you feel you are genuinely skilled at. The list could include absolutely anything from being a natural optimist, to having an appetite for work, to being a good listener, to being skilled as a negotiator through to being great at DIY, being gifted at maths or being super organised. Make the list as long as you can. This list should give you confidence as when you look at these areas you will recognise that you will have become better and more skilled in these areas over time.

Next make a list of things that you do not feel so skilled at – or situations that the very thought of makes you feel uncomfortable. The list might include networking, public speaking, organising your accounts, negotiating deals; again, this list needs to be specific to yourself. Look at the areas on the list that you feel might be holding you back the most – and now make a sub-list and prioritise these. Now start at the top of the list and commit to putting yourself in positions where you have to work at developing these skills so as to grow.

If you have done this properly, you are now probably feeling very uncomfortable! If you are to grow, you need to tackle these things head on. Let me give you two words of encouragement: First, things that seem difficult to you are things that invariably you cannot easily do at the moment; when you have learned how to do something properly, you will no longer find this difficult. When you start to learn to drive, it seems difficult; once you have learned to drive it becomes second nature. When you were at school, learning to read and write will have seemed difficult; once you have learned to read and write, this becomes second nature. In the same way, have the confidence that once you have tackled these areas that you now view as being difficult, you will in due course look back and wonder why you carried such a mental block around with you in your head that stopped you moving forward. This is a mental attitude you can learn to adopt, that will help you learn to become comfortable with being uncomfortable.

So, let's look at some practical examples: The areas below might be very different for yourself, but the principle of deliberately putting yourself in situations where you might feel uncomfortable and in which you have recognised it would be good to grow - really can be life changing.

Let's as an example, say you have identified public speaking as a situation where you feel uncomfortable. Find someone close to you and make yourself accountable to them. This may be your partner, a brother, sister or a close friend. Tell them you want to grow in this area and that you want to be accountable to them and that you want them to periodically follow up with you on your progress in this area.

If public speaking is your area for growth, pledge to your accountable person, that that you are going to find a situation where you will give a pitch at a property or other business networking event. Next, prepare a 2-3 minute pitch about what you – or what your business has to offer. Now refer to your list of skills, and put together a pitch. You may for example, say *'I am a property investor, I am a natural organiser and have experience in managing HMOs – and if these are things that could help you, then please come and find me in the break* and *let's have a cup of coffee'*. Next practice this on your own and when you are ready, practice this in front of your friend, partner, sibling or whoever – if necessary, again and again until you feel really confident: Practice makes perfect – and also builds confidence. Repeat doing this to the point where you can deliver your pitch almost in your sleep. Lastly book yourself into a suitable event and give your pitch. If it goes badly – so what! Do this again and again... As you get more experienced, your confidence will grow and grow. Eventually you will wonder why you ever felt nervous about giving a talk.

The same process of course can be applied to almost any situation; you might always put off and procrastinate with your bookkeeping. If necessary, enrol on a short bookkeeping course, pledge to your accountable person that you will do this - and then ask them to follow this up with you. By being accountable to someone else in this way, you will find it far easier to follow through on your good intentions for personal development.

All of us grow in situations where we are stretched – and you will I am sure, know of the old expression of, *'What doesn't kill you, makes you stronger'*. This whole idea is played out brilliantly in the 2007 comedy film, *'Evan Almighty'* in which the main character, Evan Baxter (AKA Steve Carrel) runs for Congress under the banner of wanting to *'Change the World'* – and prays that he could do just that. Without spoiling the film too much GOD turns up in the guise of Morgan Freeman, takes him at his word and provides opportunities for him to 'change the world' – (although this is not quite what Evan Baxter [Steve Carrel] quite has in mind). There is a great scene when God [played by Morgan Freeman] is talking to Evan's wife and suggests to her that if someone wants to develop patience, would God will just make them more patient, or would he give them opportunities to be patient?' Although this is very light hearted film, there is a serious take home message to be learned from this, in that if you want to grow in an area, then you need to practice at this – and this invariably means stepping out of your comfort zone.

Remember... developing news skills and operating in ways that we are not familiar with often feels uncomfortable – and the reason it feels uncomfortable is that it stretches us. It is when we are stretched and feeling uncomfortable that we grow the most. This whole concept fits with and aligns with the concept and importance of investing in yourself.

Chapter Forty Nine: Learning How To Be A Speaker - A Guide:

Public speaking is one of the best ways to develop your brand and market what you have to offer. Public speaking can lead to people coming to you like iron filings being attracted to a magnet.

Instead of just talking to people on a one-to-one basis, your brand, who you are and what you may have to offer to people, can be presented to rooms full of people at a time.

Everybody has a story to tell - and stories with a personal message add to the authenticity of your message. Learning how to be a speaker is a highly transferable skill that will help you get your message across to anyone you need to work with.

Think about what you do that is interesting and that others will want to hear about. Specifically, what do people most often ask you about?

Again, think about what message you would like to leave the world if you were to die tomorrow.

A story can often be told often in two ways - one of which is positive and one of which is negative, both of which can be true. Here is an example that illustrates the point:

A business that turns over a million pounds but only makes a profit of £50K [c. US$70K] p.a., could be described as making a marginal profit; alternatively, the same business may be described as expanding at a rate of 20% turnover a year, employing twenty people and hugely impacting on hundreds of peoples' lives. Both descriptions may be true, but one gives a far more positive message than the other. You need to learn how to tell the most positive story you can about yourself, your life, your skills, what you have to offer, your successes - and then market yourself and your brand in this way.

Exercise: List all of the positive features about yourself to include in your message

Make a list of the things that you would like people to say about you at your funeral – and include these in the message you communicate about yourself.

Chapter Fifty: Tell The World: A Step-By-Step Approach For Putting Together A Talk – To Bring People Into Your Sales Funnel:

There are two ways to monetise a talk. Speakers either charge a fee – or they speak for free and have a business that they pitch to at the back end. Having a back-end business pays far more than one-off fees and so this is the preferable approach to take.

Three things you should include in a talk are:

1) Answers to the things that people always ask you when they speak to you. Note down these questions that you keep being asked and keep a record of these. Address these in the talk and introduce each in the form of a question that you then answer.

2) Talk about things that you never get bored about – this will bring passion and display energy.

3) Include material that is going to help your business. Think about what the message of the talk is going to be? Personalise the talk by combining your story into the message, since this brings authenticity to your message.

One key to planning a talk is to interview yourself point by point. Think about the questions somebody might ask – and then answer these one by one. Examples might, include, 'What was your greatest challenge... You may then say, 'My greatest challenge was... Another might be, 'How did you secure your first lease option?' You could then say: 'The exact steps I took to secure my first lease option were to...

The most difficult parts of any talk to plan for are the opening and the closing.

One trick for engaging with the room as you begin, is to wait silently for five seconds and engaging eye contact with the audience across the room before starting to speak; this brings the room to silence with everyone looking at you with keen anticipation.

Begin with one, two, three (or more), top level questions asking the audience if they would like to hear about X, Y or Z (knowing these are topics people always ask you about). Examples might be, *'Who want to make a lot of money?'* or *'Who would like more time?'* This helps people engage with you – whilst encouraging them to think.

Thank the audience for engaging with you and sharing their thoughts with you – and say how helpful this is.

Next outline to them what they will have learnt by the end of the talk and how they will benefit. Ensure this is personalised to address any feedback the audience offered when you opened the talk.

This all forms the introduction to the talk and should not form more than 10% of the total.

During the talk, you should obviously only talk about what you know about so as to remain authentic. In this way you will 'have earned the right' to speak about this topic as you will have demonstrated that you are an authority in the area you are talking about.

To earn this 'right to speak' on an area, describe your own journey. People will then believe in you, because you have demonstrated your authenticity and that you are the 'real deal'.

You need to include some suspense in the talk. There are many ways of doing this. You may, for example, refer to something that is of importance

– and say something such as *'We will reveal a really clever trick of how to find the address for any property on Rightmove. We will show you the exact step-by-steps for doing this this afternoon; who would like to know how to do this?'*

Use techniques such as asking everyone to make a list of things they know about a subject – e.g., marketing, or sales, or building websites etc... then ask them to find a partner and then take two minutes for them to share with their neighbour their list.

Make sure you explain to the audience the outcomes for your talk; this is typically what they will have learned from you. An example could be that by the end of the talk everyone will know how to find a house with a Return On Investment (ROI) of more than 20%.

There are at least three key ways that people tend to take in information; some process information primarily through *visual* approaches, some through *auditory input*, while a third group of people are primarily *kinaesthetic or tactile learners* who take in information through tactile or practice based approaches. You should include techniques for all three groups.

For visual learners, examples can include the use of different colours for headings and lists of bullet points on flip charts or PowerPoint slides.

For auditory learners you can speak directly to the audience and explain in detail a particular point or concept.

Here is a tip: If you hit the letter 'B' during a PowerPoint presentation, the screen turns off: hitting 'B' again brings the screen back. This helps you to talk to the audience directly.

For kinaesthetic or tactile learners, approaches can include either passing a demonstration prop around - or including tasks such as sharing their thoughts with a neighbour.

Including different ways for imparting information to others is important and helps engage the entire audience.

Towards the end of the talk and when answering questions, try to position yourself on the opposite side of the stage to a person asking a question, so that you are looking across the maximum number of people to help remain engaged with the entire audience.

Finally, when you finish, include the 'thank you-s' with appreciation of the time that they have spent listening and engaging with you. Finally, thank them for being a great audience.

Chapter Fifty One: So How Do You Get Going?

The first thing to reiterate is that nothing happens without action, so make a vow to yourself to prioritise the 'important' over the 'urgent' – and take real action.

The next thing to remember is that any journey starts with the first step, so again today promise yourself to take the first step – today; not tomorrow but today!

People often procrastinate as they do not know what the first step for them should be. I have therefore put together a seven step plan to start you out on your property journey. These seven steps are just as applicable to a teenager starting out as a property investor as to someone middle aged who wants to escape the rat race and become financially free.

Step One: Get Yourself Into A Good Circle Of People:

It is well known within psychology - and has been shown in numerous studies, that we become like the five people we associate with the most. This is the primary reason why peoples' life chances are so affected by the family or area we are born into. However, it does not have to be this way and we all have life choices.

If you want to be financially free and successful in property, you need to be associating with and networking in a circle of people who are already successful. If you are mixing with people who do not have any life ambitions – or do not know how to be successful, you really do need to find a new group of friends and acquaintances. My recommendation is to join as many property and business networking groups as you can – and start mixing with these people; you will learn much and make crucial friends and connections – all of which will help you.

My experience is that the vast majority of successful people are generous hearted, only too happy to help and want other people to succeed. People who are not successful sometimes become jealous – and while they may not even realise it themselves, often want you to fail as they cannot bear watching someone else succeed when they are not successful themselves. You need to walk away from people like this – otherwise they will drag you down.

Step Two: Do Not Be Intimidated:

Starting out on any new venture can be daunting - but do not be intimidated by the jargon people use, by conversations they may have that go over your head – and especially by people who come across as arrogant or 'know it all's'.

Remember, things are only difficult when you do not how to do them; when you have learned how to do something, it no longer seems difficult.

So... learn to ask questions all the time; if you do not know something, the only stupid question will be the one you fail to ask. If anyone sneers or laughs at you for a question you might ask, then this reflects on them, not you.

Step Three: The Coffee Trick:

If you see someone who knows how to do something – and they have clearly been successful, such as, for example, refurbishing properties, or raising finance etc – ask them if you could buy them a cup of coffee and pick their brains.

This comes back to my point in step one, that many people who are successful are only too pleased to try to help other people be successful. Successful people tend to like to help other people - while unsuccessful people often have problems seeing others succeed; this is just human nature.

Clearly you can only ask people for so much help and advice - and you do not want to push this too far, however many successful people will be flattered by being asked for advice.

Step Four: Do Not Quit Your Job – Until You Are Financially Free:

If you are reading this book, the chances are you would love to be financially free – and would like to not be tied down to a regular job. If you are in employment and want to quit the rat race – choose your timing carefully and do not quit your job *before* being financially free.

You can start investing in property part time – working as the expression goes '5 till 9', by sacrificing some of your free time to become financially free. Having a regular income while you start building your property portfolio is really beneficial. Firstly of course, this relieves financial pressure – and you will have an ongoing and regular income to pay for essential bills and general living costs. Secondly – having a regular income will help you raise borrowing for, for example, a buy to let mortgage.

Step Five: Write Down Your Goals:

It is very hard (if not almost impossible) to plan your way forward without setting clear and well-defined goals. When you know what you want to achieve and by when, it far easier to plan your next steps and plan a way and a route forward. You will in this way be far more likely to achieve success. If you plan a road journey using a sat nav, you will first need to enter your end destination so that the sat nav can plan a route.

If you haven't already done so, go back to chapter forty two and ensure you define and write down your life goals – and then plan a way forward for achieving these. We will look at how to write a detailed business plan in chapter fifty four. So many people want to 'succeed' without actually working out in their own minds what 'success' for them might actually look like.

Step Six: Investing In Yourself Is The Best Investment You Can And Ever Will Make In Your Lifetime:

You have one life; this is not a practice run – and if you want to be successful you need to invest in yourself in terms of time and money. You should never stop growing; you are either growing or shrinking – so make sure you are always growing and invest in yourself. When you have finished reading this book; read other books such as, Robert Kiyosaki's, *'Rich Dad – Poor Dad'* – or T. Harv Eker's, *'Secrets of the Millionaire Mind'*. Listen to podcasts when you are driving – or going for a run. Attend as many business seminars – and property events as you can. Some will be better than others, but always be on the lookout for ways of learning since this is one of the ways you will grow as a person – and success will in this way follow. The more you learn, the more successful you will become.

Step Seven: Do Whatever It Takes:

Many people are good at starting projects – but not so good at following through on these and finishing; please do not be one of these people…! Do whatever it takes. If something needs a bit of extra effort to get it to the next stage – just do it. Sometimes, the very best opportunities (such as extensive refurbishment projects) will take a lot of effort. You may encounter difficulties along the way – but be the person like Winston Churchill, who never quits.

Being easily deterred is one of the greatest reasons why people fail in life; they fail to see life opportunities – they only see what to them looks life hard work.

Chapter Fifty Two: You Don't Need To Be An Expert For Everything Or Do Everything Yourself - But <u>You Do</u> Need To Build A Power Team:

You will need to seek expertise and skills from a range of professionals who are qualified or licensed to operate in their fields. The range of people you will need to work with may include: estate and letting agents, accountants, mortgage brokers, solicitors, builders - and other skilled trades people.

Your power team is the second most important asset you have, the first being your mindset. Surround yourself with positive people, who have a 'can-do' mindset. If you want to grow and if you want to have a hassle-free investment career, you NEED to invest in your power team. I credit my power team for a lot of my early success, because when I did not know what to do, I could lean on their understanding, abilities and experience to get things done for me.

As a property investor it is likely that nearly all of your power team will be on commission. That means if you earn more, they will too and so they have an interest in seeing you become successful. Use your power team to answer your questions, solve your problems and get tasks done: The pneumonic of Samuel can act as a good aide-memoire:

S-A-M-U-E-L

- **S**olicitor
- **A**ccountant / tax advisor
- **M**ortgage Broker
- b**U**ilder / Contractors
- **E**state Agent
- **L**etting Agent / HMO Manager

Chapter Fifty Three: Learn To Network

Networking is essential for making contacts – and this is a skill you need to learn to develop and become comfortable with. There are many different types of networking group from those that are quite formal through to those that are rather more relaxed; if in doubt – ask and determine the dress code. If the dress code is lounge suits, then this will clearly be quite formal whereas if it is smart casual, then you can expect the meeting to be more informal.

When you do attend networking events, *do not* be always trying to sell yourself; instead engage in conversation, ask lots of questions and determine other peoples' needs; in this way you will be able to pitch your replies so as to offer help and add value – and in this way people will flock to you. By way of example, if you find yourself talking to a builder or architect, then offer to introduce them to your network of property investors; they will love you for it and almost certainly will want to engage with you!

You need to look on-line and find a number of different networking events to attend; the more events you attend the more skilled you will become at this essential tool.

Exercise:

Search on-line and sign up for at least one networking event each week for the next ten weeks; do not restrict yourself to property events but attend others covering areas such as investment, social engagement, consultation meetings for the development of a town or local project etc.

Chapter Fifty Four: Writing <u>Your</u> First Business Plan – A Step-By-Step Guide:

Now that you have come this far, you will I am sure understand the importance of the psychology needed and correct mindset for starting and operating a successful property business. You will have set your own goals - and you will have determined who you need to bring into your power team. You are now ready to pull all of this together and prepare *your own personalised* business plan.

This will be crucial for helping you take action yourself - and making your dreams turn into a reality. A carefully prepared business plan will moreover also be crucial for helping with raising finance and joint-venturing.

Before investing your time or money, you need to plan carefully your next steps - and be able to articulate and sell your vision to others. If you do not have a clearly prepared and thorough business plan – you will lose your way and your lack of a vision or plan will be evident to others.

To help you, I have prepared a step-by-step guide: work though this and you will have an invaluable tool to help you. You should refer to your business plan regularly and this should be updated as and when necessary - but certainly no less frequently than annually. During the first three years of any new business this should be no less than every six months.

Now start to fill in the template:

Writing Your Business Plan - Getting Started:

Business and Owner Details:

Business Name:

Owner(s) Name:

Business Address and Postcode / ZIP Code:

Business Telephone Number:

Business Email Address:

Home Address and Postcode / ZIP Code (if different from above):

Home Telephone Number (if different from above):

Home Email Address (if different from above):

Section One - Executive Summary

1.1 Business Summary:

1.2 Business Aims:

1.3 Financial Summary:

Elevator Pitch

1.4 Your Business Name:

1.5 Strapline:

1.6 Elevator Pitch:

Section Two - Owner's Background

2.1 Why Do you Want To Run Your Own Business?

2.2 Previous Work Experience:

2.3 Qualifications And Education:

2.4 Training:

Details of Future Training Courses You Want To Complete:

2.5 Hobbies and Interests That May Be Relevant:

2.6 Additional Information:

Section Three - Products and Services

3.1 What Are You Going To Sell?

☐ A Product

☐ A Service

☐ Both

3.2 Describe the Basic Product/Service You Are Going To Sell:

3.3 Describe The Different Types Of Product/Service You Are Going To Be Selling:

3.4 If You Are Not Going to Sell All Your Products/Services At The Start Of Your Business, Explain Why Not And When You Will Start Selling Them:

3.5 Additional Information:

Section Four - The Market

4.1 Are – Or Will Your Customers Be:

☐ **Individuals**

☐ **Businesses**

☐ **Both**

4.2 Describe Your Typical Customer:

4.3 Where Are Your Customers Based?

4.4 What Prompts Your Customers To Buy Your Product / Service?

4.5 What Factors Will Help Your Customers Choose Which Business to Buy From?

4.6 Have You Sold Products/Services To Customers Already?

☐ Yes

☐ No

If You Answered "Yes", Fill In Details Below:

4.7 Have You Got Customers Waiting To Buy Your Product/Service?

☐ Yes

☐ No

If You Answered "Yes", Fill In Details Below:

4.8 Additional Information:

Section Five - Market Research

5.1 Key Findings From Desk Research:

5.2 Key Findings From Field Research – Customer Questionnaires:

5.3 Key Findings From Field Research – Test Trading:

5.4 Additional Information:

Section Six - Marketing Strategy

What are you going to do?	Why have you chosen this marketing method?	How much will it cost?
TOTAL COST		

Section Seven - Competitor Analysis

7.1 Table Of Competitors

Name, Location and Business Size	Product/ Service	Price	Strengths	Weaknesses

7.2 SWOT Analysis:

Strengths	Weaknesses
Opportunities	**Threats**

7.3 Unique Selling Point (USP):

Unique Selling Point (USP) – Describe In Detail:

Section Eight - Operations and Logistics

8.1 Production:

8.2 Delivery To Customers:

8.3 Payment Methods And Terms:

8.4 Suppliers:

Name And Location Of Supplier	Items Required And Pricing	Payment Arrangements	Reasons For Choosing Supplier

8.5 Premises:

8.6 Equipment:

Item Required	Already Owned?	If Being Bought:		Price
		New Or Second Hand?	Purchased From	

8.7 Transport:

8.8 Legal Requirements:

8.9 Insurance Requirements:

8.10 Management and Staff:

8.11 Additional Information:

Section Nine - Financial Forecasts

9.1 Sales And Costs Forecast

	Monthly Sales Forecast												
Month	1	2	3	4	5	6	7	8	9	10	11	12	Total
Product or Service (A)													
Product or Service (B)													
Product or Service (C)													

Monthly Cost Forecast												
Month	1	2	3	4	5	6	7	8	9	10	11	12	Total
Monthly Cost Forecast													
Product or Service (A)													
Product or Service (B)													
Product or Service (C)													

Assumptions (e.g.: Seasonal Trends)	

9.2 Personal Survival Budget

Outgoings:	Monthly Cost
Mortgage/Rent	
Council Tax	
Gas, Electricity	
Water Rates	
All Personal And Property Insurances	
Clothing	
Food and Housekeeping	
Mobile Phone	
Hire Charges (TV, DVD etc.)	
Subscriptions (Clubs, Netflix, Spotify etc.)	
Entertainment (Meals and Drinks)	
Car Tax, Insurance, Service And Maintenance	
Children's Expenditure And Presents	
Credit Card, Loan And Other Personal Debt Repayments	
National Insurance	
Other	
Total Costs:	

Income Source:	Monthly Income
Income From Family/Partner	
Part Time Job	
Working Tax Credit	
Child Benefits	
Other Benefits	
Other	
Total Income:	

Total Survival Income Required:	

9.3 Cashflow Forecast

Month	1	2	3	4	5	6	7	8	9	10	11	12	Totals
Monthly Trading Income:													
Funding: Other Sources													
Own Funds													
Other													
Total Money In													

Outgoings:												
Trading Expenses												
Salary / Wages												
Loan Repayments												
Personal Drawings												
Total Money Out												

Balance												
Opening Balance												
Closing Balance												

Section Ten – Back Up Plans

10.1 Short-Term Plan:

10.2 Long-Term Back Up Plan:

Chapter Fifty Five: Starting And Running Your Own Business – Key Considerations And A Step By Step How To Guide:

Your Options:

There are a number of ways you can trade: Firstly, as a sole trader, secondly through the establishment of a Limited Company – or thirdly through the establishment of a Limited Liability Partnership (which can be thought of as a half-way house between operating as a sole trader and as a company).

While you should always speak to an accountant prior to setting out in business so that they can advise you as to what type of trading arrangements or company structure you should use – establishing a Limited Company will for the vast majority of people be the route you should choose when setting up a property business.

There are a number of reasons for this:

1)   **Limited Liability:** As a 'sole trader' you are personally responsible for any financial loses or claims against your business, however if you set up a limited company you have limited liability.

Having limited liability means that if the business cannot pay its bills and has to cease trading, your personal assets and finances will be treated as being legally separate and so cannot be taken from you by debtors. This means if your business folds you will not be personally responsible for the debts – and you cannot personally be declared bankrupt. This is the reason that so many business people establish a number of separate limited companies so that if one company fails, this cannot not bring down all of the others.

2)   **Tax efficiency:** There are a number of areas where it far more tax efficient to trade through a limited company than as a sole trader.

One of the most important is through the purchasing of property since the introduction in the UK of 'Section 24' in April 2017. The section 24 tax ruling means that if you purchase a property as a sole trader, you will no longer be able to claim tax relief on any mortgage interest, or any other property finance. Instead, rental profit will be taxed with a maximum deduction for finance costs of 20%. By contrast if you purchase the property through a limited company, mortgage interest payments will continue to be counted as being tax deductible. This can literally be the difference between making a profit or a loss on your rental properties.

The full details of this tax ruling are found in Section 24 of the Finance (no. 2) Act 2015, which has euphemistically become known as the 'Tenant Tax' because of the legal case launched to challenge the ruling.

(Note, also refer to: Chapter Fifty Six: Tax Efficiency - Key Points For Consideration).

3)   **Professionalism:** Trading as a limited company can simply help you come across far more professionally than operating as a sole trader; this can be important when for example, establishing joint ventures or raising finance.

How To Set Up A Limited Company:

Setting up a limited (Ltd) company is not complicated. Any chartered accountant will help you establish a limited company for a fee of a few hundred pounds.

You can also easily set one up online using a number of online company establishing websites such as www.companiesmadesimple.com or similar for as little as £16 [c. US$22] to set up.

In the UK when you register a company at Companies House, you must provide at least one 'Standard Industrial Classification of Industrial Activity' – or SIC code to describe the nature of what your business does.

Some Of The Most Appropriate SIC Codes For Property Include:

68310: Real estate agencies

68320: Management of real estate on a fee or contract basis

64209: Activities of other holding companies not elsewhere classified

68100: Buying and selling of own real estate

68209: Other letting and operating of own or leased real estate

98000: Residents property management

85590: Other education not elsewhere classified

Your Responsibilities As A Business Owner Or Company Director:

I highly recommend working with a specialist property accountant to look after all your tax affairs and company filings, however it is important for you to understand what your responsibilities are:

1. **Filing of Annual Statements and Accounts:** In the UK, Companies House require limited (Ltd) companies to file annual statements with details of who owns and runs the company (i.e., the directors), along with financial accounts. To do this you will need to keep track of your income and expenditure using some form of accountancy software and for you to supply these to your accountant for the filing of the annual accounts, which will then dictate how much tax you will have to pay to Her Majesty's Revenue and Customs (HMRC).

2. **Corporation Tax (COTAX):** HMRC requires to be paid on company profits. At the time of writing COTAX is charged at 19% and it is normally paid on an annually basis for start-up and smaller companies.

3. **VAT registration:** You will need to register for Value Added Tax (VAT), if your turnover exceeds £85k (correct at time of writing) in any twelve - month period. You can check if your product/service is subject to VAT on the .GOV website, alternatively, ask your accountant to monitor your company and to let you know if and when you need to register for VAT.

4. If you trade through a Ltd company, you must trade legally. If your company becomes unable to pay its bills, then you must, through your accountants, appoint administrators; failure to do so may render you liable to your creditors, your company being compulsorily wound up and you being barred from holding any further company directorships.

Understanding the Rules for Success:

Rule Number One: *You Must Treat Property Investing As A Business And Not As A Hobby.*

If you treat property as a hobby, then you will receive hobby like returns. You have to decide whether you wish to commit to being 'all in' or not. Committing wholeheartedly demands energy and discipline. If you adopt a business-like approach and follow the formulae in this book, then you will enjoy far greater returns.

You will learn everything you need to know to be able to treat property as a business within this section of the book – and everything you will learn will come back to this first golden rule; treat property as a business.

Rule Number Two: *To Be Successful In Business You Need To Be Direct.*

You cannot succeed in business if you operate as a 'snowflake'. Always treat people ethically and how you would like to be treated yourself, BUT when you need to be direct - be direct.

There is a saying: *'Say what you mean and mean what you say.'* Many people do not like complaining – but if something needs to be said to address or fix a problem then say it plainly and succinctly.

Chapter Fifty Six: Tax Efficiency – Key Points For Consideration:

The first thing you should do is to engage an accountant specialising in property; taxation rules change regularly and an accountant specialising in property will be able to help you and your business be tax efficient and legally compliant with current tax legislation. Your accountants will also help you prepare and file your tax returns on time. A good accountant will earn the value of their professional services many times over and should be a key member of your power team.

There are a number of key areas where you should be familiar with - and we list some of these below:

'Section 24' – or 'Tenant Tax'

A new rule introduced in the UK in April 2017, known as 'section 24' – or the 'tenants tax' (see above) means that as a sole trader you will no longer be able to claim tax relief on mortgage interest payments. So, if you pay £200 a month in interest on a mortgage and collect rent of £500 a month, you would previously have pay tax on the £300 profit, but from 2021 you will have pay tax on the whole £500!

This is completely different from almost any other line of business where it is standard practice to deduct interest on business loans, since this is an operating expense for the business. It is designed to make amateur landlords pay more tax and deter them from the market.

Section 24 does not however apply to any property purchased through a company. Even if you already own properties in your personal name, you can transfer those assets to a company and avoid the extra tax. In some cases, it may be possible to transfer property already owned by individuals to a company without incurring capital gains or stamp duty land taxes - and so if you own rental properties in your name, I would strongly advise you to speak to a specialist tax accountant who can advise accordingly.

Stamp Duty Land Tax:

Many investors forget to consider Stamp Duty Land Tax (SDLT) when calculating Return on Investments (ROIs) for a property.

Stamp duty is calculated based on the value of the property and falls into several bands.

As of April 1st 2016, stamp duty rates for landlords (and anyone buying a second home including those purchased through a limited company) is 3% on the portion of the property up to £125,000, and then 5% for any residual value of the property above £125-250k, 8% for £250-£925K,13% for £925K-£1.5m and 15% for any value over £1.5m.

Let's look at an example:

An investor purchases a: £500,000 (Buy-to-let) property, either as a sole trader or through a limited company.

a) Stamp Duty for property up to £125k value @ at 3% = £3,750
b) Stamp Duty for property between £125k to £250k @ 5% of 125K = £6,250
c) Stamp Duty for property between £250k to £925k @ 8% of £250,000 = £20,000
d) £925k to £1.5m 13% = £0
e) Rest over £1.5m 15% = £0

So, the total stamp duty = £3,750 + £6,250 + £20,000 = £30,000

Despite the fact that SDLT can add a significant cost to any investment purchase, there are many reliefs and exemptions that you may be entitled to.

The HM Revenue and Customs (HMRC) offers SDLT relief for:

- First-time buyers
- Building companies buying an individual's home
- Employers buying an employee's house
- Local authorities making compulsory purchases
- Property developers providing amenities to communities
- Companies transferring property to another company
- Charities
- Right to buy properties
- Registered social landlords
- Multiple Dwellings

Multiple Dwelling Tax Relief:

In the UK one important tax relief measure for property investors is through the purchase of Multiple Residential Properties that may be connected – e.g., by purchasing a series of flats - or a house with a granny annex, in which the different units operate as separate dwellings. Another example might be when you purchase a number of properties from another property company. Again, a specialist tax accountant and/or solicitor can help you guide you through this process.

To calculate the tax relief that you may be entitled to:

a) Divide the total purchase price by the number of dwellings,

b) Work out the tax rate for each dwelling on this average purchase price,

c) Calculate the total tax by multiplying this average tax sum and multiplying by the total number of dwellings – and,

d) If the total stamp duty using this approach is less than 1% of the total purchase price then – you only have to pay 1% as a flat rate.

Let's look at an example:

We purchase five flats or houses for a total of £1 million

£1 million divided by 5 = £200,000

When purchasing multiple residences within one property (such as flats within one building), no SDLT is liable for the first £125,000 purchase price.

The amount of SDLT you will pay on a £200,000 purchase will be £1,500 (0% of £125,000 + 2% of £75,000)

£1,500 multiplied by 5 = £7,500

As this is less than 1% of £1 million, the amount of tax payable is £10,000

When purchasing any property that you are looking to get a Stamp Duty Land Tax (SDLT) relief, it is always advisable to first discuss it with your solicitor to check what relief you can claim.

The HMRC provides a stamp duty calculator to help you determine the stamp duty you should have to pay.

www.tax.service.gov.uk/calculate-stamp-duty-land-tax

Tax Deductible Expenses:

There are many expenses that your business will be able to claim against tax. Many (and possibly the majority of people) fail to offset all the expenses that they can, simply due to ignorance – and so I would advise that you speak to your accountant to ensure you do claim all you are entitled to. Claiming legitimate expenses can bring very significant tax benefits – and so it is worth taking the time to ensure all of your genuine business expenses are carefully logged and claimed for. You will need to supply the information to your accountant – but they can point you in the right direction and help determine what can and cannot be claimed for as a legitimate expense.

Here is a list of common business expenses that you may be able to offset against tax:

- **Optometry and Eyecare Costs:** If you require glasses or contact lenses to work at a computer, read paperwork or drive as part of your work, you should be able to claim optometry and eyecare costs as a legitimate business expenses.

- **Business Insurance:** this includes insurance for professional indemnity and liability, landlord insurance and critical person or business interruption cover.

- **Advertising, Marketing and PR Expenses:** This can include on-line advertising programmes such as *Google AdWords*, through to the production of leaflets or business cards.

- **Travel and Subsistence Expenses:** If you have to travel on business, you can claim rail travel or use of your car based on mileage – along with overnight accommodation and food and drink as travel and subsistence costs.

- **Use of Your Home as An Office** - If your home is the heart of your business, then you will be able to claim a percentage of your household costs and utility bills as business expenses. This cost could be claimed either at a flat rate of £4 per week - or by working out which rooms you use for your business needs and the amount of time these are being used for, for work purposes. You can additionally claim the costs of lighting, heating, postage, printing, broadband internet, along with mobile or landline phone costs as ongoing office expenses.

- **Equipment Expenses:** The purchase or hire of any equipment along with maintenance costs needed for your business can be claimed;

this can include the purchase of for example damp meters or laser measures used for house viewings – through to the hire of furniture within rental properties.

- **Banking Charges:** These could include admin or interest.

- **Professional Expenses:** Such as legal or accountancy costs.

- **Child Care Expenses:** While childcare costs cannot be claimed directly as a business expense, a limited company *can* claim tax relief on childcare costs up to a total value of £243 each month.

- **Professional Subscriptions**: To, for example industry relevant magazines, journals or books can be claimed as a business expenses.

- **Training Programmes and Manuals:** This can include the purchase of any business-oriented education, or fees for enrolment for seminars or business events.

Value Added Tax: VAT

Value Added Tax, at the time of writing VAT is at a rate of 20% in the UK and this is charged on top of your fee and is usually paid to HMRC on a quarterly basis. Not everyone has to be VAT registered and not every service or product is subject to VAT.

If you do have to charge VAT (if you provide a product or service that is subject to VAT and you are VAT registered) then it can actually work out as a blessing. The VAT you charge on top of your fee is paid by your customers and you can off-set your spending against it. You CANNOT however charge VAT on any sale unless you are VAT registered and have been issued with a VAT number from HMRC.

Chapter Fifty Seven: The Art Of Creating And Cultivating A Brand, Marketing And Selling:

It does not matter what area of business you are in, you need people to first get to know you, trust you and then want to buy from you.

It follows that as an entrepreneur in almost any sector, c. 80% of your time should be focused on sales and marketing.

Sales is not just important when you are trying to persuade someone to purchase directly from you and part with their hard-earned cash, but knowing how to sell and negotiate are both essential skills for you to master when you wish for someone to:

- Work for you,
- Partner with you,
- Buy into your vision,
- Agree a Rent-to-Rent deal,
- Agree a purchase property for a property.

Many people think they are just not very good at sales, or that they are not a naturally born sales person. This normally comes from either previously bad experiences – and / or fears of rejection and negativity from others.

I will in the sections that follow help show you how to overcome these very natural feelings and become both skilled and comfortable at selling.

Marketing lets people know what you have to offer them – to illustrate this, advertising is one form of marketing.

One of the best ways to develop trust in other people is to make sure that you serve before trying to sell to them; this is one of the most effective approaches for marketing what you have to offer as others will see this for themselves if you offer and add value to them before being sold to.

Branding describes who you are, what you do and what your business is known for... People should know you and your company for what you do. If you think of either of the brands *Dyson* or *Hoover,* you will think of vacuum cleaners; if you think of *Mercedes* or *BMW* you will think of luxury cars.

Key Steps for Creating and Cultivating Your Brand:

- Establish a website describing what you do.

- Write an on-line book – describing your life story and detailing who you are and what you do. Everybody has a story to tell.

- Offer content to establish you as a leader and authoritative figure in your field, (e.g., property sourcing).

- Cultivate a reputation of honesty, authority, authenticity and trustworthiness.

- Invite testimonials for inclusion on your website or book.

- Associate with other trustworthy and successful people; this will enhance your reputation for your brand.

- Remember cultivating trust takes time – and reputations can be easily lost.

Key Steps For Marketing:

- Learn to serve before trying to sell via, for example, offering a free book, free spreadsheet or other software, introducing people such as trustworthy brokers, or solicitors or builders. Above all help other people - and in this way add value to help them.

- Use a Customer Relationship Management (CRM) system to build a list of contacts for your sales funnel. This can be coupled to a sign up – 'opt in' page on your web-site.

- Network at property and other business events and ask lots of questions from people, so that you know what they want; you will then be in a better position to serve them.

- In all of these activities, positivity is crucial. Do not allow yourself to give out any negativity - ever; positivity and negativity both say far more about yourself than the person or thing you are talking about.

Two Leading Customer Relationship Management (CRM) Systems:

- AllClients: https://allclients.com/ and

- InfusionSoft: https://help.infusionsoft.com/

Exercise: Branding:

a) Think about and then list what you are going to do differently to brand yourself.

b) First make a video using your phone, describing where you are (e.g., at a business event and that you are working with leading experts putting together business deals). Talk to the camera with high energy... Nobody wants to watch a dull or boring video, so be enthusiastic. Some of the best videos are made at live events, in railway stations, inside shopping malls, at airports or indeed at property events.

Social media and video marketing – are so important for marketing to millennials or generation Z, so whatever your age, work to become comfortable with social media and if necessary, ask for help. Practice, practice, practice – it gets easier with time to make videos and if you don't like the videos - it does not matter what people think, you will get better. You need to stop worrying about what other people think, so that this does not hold you back. This is another example of where 'you need to be in the game to win it'.

Here is a tip – when you make a video, hold your phone out in your outstretched arm and hold this slightly elevated so that you look slightly upwards. Commit to doing at least one video a day for the next three weeks to practice. There are simple apps for editing on phones.

Release your videos at a regular time each week so that your followers check for these at a regular time – this is one approach where you can 'train your investors' and potential leads for joint ventures.

Try to record videos at events with an audience or crowd behind you in the background; examples could include saying in the video what your strategy is, how you are working with others and demonstrating you know your business inside out – and including, *'If you want to join my network use the link below'* – and then point to a link you will include in the video.

c) Write down achievable goals in the next month, four months, six months and twelve months for marketing.

Goals should include how many videos will you will make per month, how many contacts you will have added to your list, how many networking events will you have been to etc.

d) Create a vision board and make it visible either on your phone, your computer or a whiteboard; the important thing is that you place this where you will constantly see it so as to positively influence your thoughts — and thereby affect your behaviour.

Focus On What You Have To Offer - And - Be Focussed:

Examples of what you have to offer, could include:

- Offering a healthy return to investors in return for investing in your business.

- You could be selling your expertise for finding deals through a deal sourcing business; your product here would be finding fantastic deals for property investors.

- You could be selling the best HMO accommodation in a given area.

<u>Selling Always Requires Energy:</u>

You must also have confidence in yourself:

- *Do Not Be Reticent*; remember, after reading and studying this book you will be more knowledgeable than most people in the property business - and therefore you can help others along with their journey. This is something you have to offer and that you can sell for the benefit of others. Many people underestimate the value of what they have to offer.

- *Think of The Sales Funnel*: Think of what you could offer that could add value to others and that will help secure a sale, which in turn could lead to a follow-on sale and another and another.

- *Think Creatively Around Additional Ways for Monetisation:* If you have a regular product to sell (such as deals for investors) – you could also offer preferential VIP access for a monthly fee.

Chapter Fifty Eight: Tips For Being A WINNER:

I have produced an acronym to help ensure *you* will be a WINNER. Do study and work through this check list diligently to help ensure you succeed:

Won Over:

Before you can sell anything to anyone, you (personally), need to be won over by and love the product first. Be the best - and know in your heart of hearts that your business is the best in your sector. This will give you confidence.

If you already have a business and already have customers, start by asking all your existing customers why they decided to buy from you. Write down and record all of this. They might, for example, say price, customer experience, location, friendly staff, convenience. Whatever they say, start making a list. Then write down all the advantages that you can possibly think of, as to why someone might be better off using your business in preference to a competitor. Do be honest because you need to and if necessary, take action to stay ahead of the competition.

What do you do, however, if you have a product or service that you do not believe in?

The easy answer is: find something else to sell.

Investigate:

Make sure you know what your customer needs or wants. Just think about this; there is little point in trying to sell a car to someone who does not have a driving licence. Once you understand this point you will see why it is so crucial to investigate someone's circumstances and needs.

The first thing you should do when you get in contact with a prospect is to ask questions and investigate. If you do this simple thing, you will be better positioned than 99% of 'professional' sales people since unfortunately 99% of sales people fail to do this critical first step.

No-one likes to be pressured into buying something that they do not need or want - or indeed where the benefits to them are not made obvious.

So, if you do not like being sold to, it is probably as a result of bad sales people who have not investigated your particular needs and made their pitch relevant to you.

Think about this; nearly everyone likes to buy 'things'. Why? Because we want new items that will benefit us. We like being sold to when it is something we actually want; we just do not want to be sold to when it is something, we fail to see any value in.

The great thing about the WINNER approach is that you do not need to pressure anyone. You do not need to sell anything that they do not want. It makes sales and selling far more profitable for you and enjoyable for your customers.

Selling is about finding someone else's needs and providing the right product for them.

This is far easier if you have leads coming to you.

The concept is simple and clear, you just need to keep asking relevant questions until you feel you have a good understanding of what the other person wants and whether or not you can fulfil their needs.

The type of questions you should be asking are open-ended questions.

One dictionary definition of an open-ended question is:

"A question that cannot be answered with a 'yes' or 'no' response, or with a static response. Open-ended questions are phrased as statements which require a response. The response can be compared to information that is already known to the questioner."

The key is just to keep asking questions: It is said that that the only way to be interesting is to be interested. It is important to show an interest in other people, let them speak and find out what they want. It is worth noting that sometimes people often do not even know why or what they want or why until you ask - and in this way force them to think about it. So, if they seem a little vague keep asking "Why?" until you get to the truth - and until you believe that you know exactly what they want and how you may be of help.

In essence, you are looking for at least one of two things. Either the customer's 'pain', i.e., what pain are they in that you can solve? Or their 'gain', in which case you need to be thinking about what can you give them that they would like.

At this point if you cannot help them, or if you are unable to solve their problem or provide them with a gain, just halt the process there and then. Do not waste any more time – either yours or theirs.

There is no need to feel rejection.

Negotiation:

You need to be a good negotiator: learn to be the person who always pushes the envelope for negotiation of the price on anything and everything – and this includes property…! There are many approaches you can use to negotiate, such as being a cash buyer, being able to move quickly, factoring in the price for replacing a bathroom or kitchen etc.; be creative.

This is the part that people tend to omit. Most people finish the sales pitch and then just stop, hoping that the prospect will say:

'Yes, I'm in. Sign me up'

I am sorry to break it to you (although I'm sure you already know), but that rarely happens.

It is now time to negotiate and this starts with *'the close'*. Many people are scared of closing as this is where they fear rejection, but this is the time to ask for the sale.

There is a popular sales strategy – *'Always Be Closing'* – this is the ABC of sales. This is however simply nonsense. You should not be attempting to close until your prospect is ready for closing. Never attempt to close unless you are confident that they want what you are selling. If you close too early you risk just annoying them.

There are many different ways of closing.

One of my favourites is the *assumptive* close. This is where you've just finished your sale and then you ask a question. This question is assuming that they are ready to buy, so you would say something like, *'How would you like to pay?'*

I will never forget when someone replied, *'I don't want to pay'*.

Ouch, did I feel rejected and a little embarrassed? Indeed... Why did she say this? Because I tried to close too early. I tried to close before she was ready.

So, before you attempt to close, you need to establish two things:

1.   Do they want and/or need your product?

2.   Do they trust you to provide what you say you are able to provide?

You should have a good feeling for this during the investigation. When you become convinced that they are ready to purchase, then that is the time to close.

Another version of the assumptive close that I really like is the *'Three - Yes - Assumptive Close'*.

You ask three questions that you know they will say *'yes'* to - and *then* you ask for the sale. This will get them in the habit of saying *'yes'* and saying out loud that this is something they do want. An example might be along the lines of:

'So, let me get this straight, you want to get into property investing?' (Yes)

"You are wanting to start earning a passive income?" (*Yes*)

'And you think the training we provide would be of benefit to you?' (*Yes*)

'Well, what are we waiting for? Shall we get you signed up?' (*Yes!*)

Another favourite of mine is the *'Alternative Close'*; this is where you offer two alternatives both of which involve them buying your product. So, you might say:

'Would you like to attend the course this Wednesday or next Wednesday?'

Effectively, you're offering them this Wednesday which will give you a sale or next Wednesday which also gives you a sale.

Be sure to pick a few closure strategies that you feel comfortable with - and then check that they will work for your product.

No Brainer: Make offers that are *'no-brainers'* and are *'win-wins'* for both you and your customer - and explain to your customer why this really will be a no brainer for them.

For example, explain that if they join your VIP list, then you will offer a discount if they make a purchase that will pay for the VIP subscription; this makes the subscription a no brainer.

Another fundamental strategy for selling is that it is important to rely on a script. If your plan is to grow your business, you will eventually have a sales team. Do you really just want them saying whatever they want? Of course not. You want them to be saying exactly what you want them to say. That way, they cannot oversell and promise the earth, or just spout rubbish because they do not really know what to say.

The main reason people dislike scripts is because they are afraid that they will sound robotic. While this may be true with many scripts, if you write a good one and learn it off by heart, this should not be the case.

An inspiring speech delivered by a politician, or a gripping movie, will have been scripted and then delivered in such a way that it is not robotic. Your job is to do the same with your sales script.

It is one of the most important tasks for your business because without making sales you will have no business – and certainly not a business that is likely to make any money.

So, let me take you through some tips on crafting a good script. First of all, the greeting. You do not want to sound like a typical salesman, especially if you are the one making the call.

Each script should be made up of two parts:

1.The Introduction

How many times have you answered the phone and immediately identified that it is a sales call and then immediately switched off mentally? A phone call may start something like this:

Salesman: *'Hello my name is David calling from Premier Insurance Limited. Could I speak to (Your Name), please?'*

You know it is a sales call straight away and normally you can hear other people in the background. It may sound like a call centre.

You want to avoid this type of call.

Start the conversation with something friendly and simple such as:

'Hi, is that Zoe?'

It sounds like you may know her slightly and just using her first name is far more personable.

Then introduce yourself just by giving your name and the company name:

'My name's (Your Name) calling from (Company Name)'.

We do not recommend cold calling. It almost always annoys people; it is time-consuming and rarely get results.

Only call people when they have taken an action first, such as having ordered a book or filled in an enquiry form on your website. This makes calling people far easier as you are only ringing individuals who you already know are genuinely interested in your product or service.

The next step is to give the reason I'm calling Zoe, as follows:

'The reason I'm calling today is I noticed you've recently ordered a copy of Samuel's book "Buy Low - Rent High" and I'm just checking that you've received it'.

Notice that at this point there is no selling: this is now the time for the investigation.

I recommend having a few set questions to start your investigation; you should write these down as part of your script.

2. Selling

This is where you will put together your 'no brainer' offer.

It is now time to highlight the benefits of what you have to offer. Remember you will be helping this person and that you are an expert at what you do, so do not be modest and hold back. If your product is amazing and is going to fulfil their needs, tell them! That is why you should have a script. It gives you time to relay all the benefits and reasons for why they should use you. And that is when you give them the price.

Remember the list that you made at the beginning of this chapter for when you were winning yourself over? You are now going to write some sales copy for each of those points - and you are going to put them in your script.

When you are writing your sales copy, the most important thing you can do is to focus on the benefits and not the features.

Let me give you an example:

I wanted to buy a new laptop recently so I headed down to my local computer store to have a browse. I wanted to see the laptop physically before buying it. The store assistant approached me and asked:

'Can I help you?'

'I'm looking for a new laptop', I replied.

'We've got this one on sale', he eagerly told me. *'It's a Windows 10 machine, it has an AMD a Ryzen 3 3200U processor, it's got 4 GB of RAM and 256 GB of storage'*.

Now for computer dummies, like me, he might as well have been speaking a foreign language. He was just giving me the features. He was not explaining to me the benefits of the machine.

What we need to remind ourselves is that we know far more about our product and the industry than our clients do. We might understand all the features and exactly what they mean, but there is a very good chance that most of our clients do not.

The computer store assistant knew exactly what it meant, but I did not. So, you need to know the features, but then tell the client how that feature will benefit them.

So instead, he should have asked this:

'So, what are you planning to use the computer for?'.

I might have replied *'Well mainly for watching movies on Netflix while I'm travelling, for browsing the internet and editing photos'*.

From those answers, he could have told me the features and related the benefits to me. He could have said:

'Ah we have this one on sale which has an AMD Ryzen 3 3200U processor which means that your Netflix movies will stream almost instantly while 256GB of storage will mean that you will be able to store and edit over 10,000 photos'.

Let me give you another example. Here is a sales copy that I wrote for a three-day programme that we run, teaching people who have no money to start with make an income from property using a strategy called 'Rent-to-Rent'.

Rent-To-Rent Revolution

'How to make £1,000s or even £10,000s a month without even owning any property!';

Nelson Rockefeller famously said, *'The secret to success is to own nothing, but control everything'*.

Multi-million-pound companies understand this very well. For example, Uber does not own the cars that transport you, Airbnb don't own the accommodation you book through them and Amazon do not own the majority of the stock they distribute around the world.

You too can use the power of leverage once you've attended this life changing programme.

You'll learn:

- *How to generate 'Super Rent' so you can maximise profits from any property;*
- *How to find the right properties online - you'll actually find potential deals there and then;*
- *The magic words you'll need to say to seal the deal, so that you can start making money almost immediately; and,*
- *How to systemise your business to ensure a hands-off approach to property management and the creation of passive income.*

Now notice the use of a *'feature'* versus a *'benefit'*. There are a couple of examples.

'How to Generate Super Rent' - this is the feature and people might not know what it means, so I explain what is in it for them as a benefit by saying *'so that you can maximise the profits from any property'*.

And

'How to systemise' this is the feature, and the benefit is *'to ensure a hands off approach to property management and to create passive income'*.

Steve Jobs was the master of this. When he sold the *iPod* to the world back in 2001, he used the slogan *'1,000 songs in your pocket'*. The slogan was not *'the iPod has a 5GB hard drive and FireWire technology'*. He went straight to the benefit.

So, make a list of all the features of your product and why they are of real benefit to your potential customer.

The other thing to be sure to include is some *social proof*. This can be through the inclusion of testimonials or mention of awards or through endorsements by celebrities or well-known companies.

It is one thing if you say how great your company is, but you will take it to another level when you can share third party data; this is almost always a very powerful sales tool.

It is now time for you to package your 'no brainer', you are going to start with the pain or the gain your prospect told you about during the investigation stage. So, for example say:

'Now as you've just said you're desperate to leave your job and be your own boss but just don't know where to start. And you know that if you just carry on the way you are, it'll never get better...'

So, you are highlighting the problem they have just told you about. Once you have done this, you will then tell them about a few of the features and benefits from your list, but be sure to choose those that are most relevant to them.

Less is more in many cases; you do not want to just go on and on. People do not have the time or the patience to listen to you rambling on about irrelevancies. Just pick two or three of the most relevant features and tell them why they need your product in their life, and explain why it will help them solve their problems.

_E_liminate:

People from your contacts who do not purchase but only come up with phrases such as, '_I need to speak to my partner and will come back to you_', instead of owning up that they are not interested.

So, by this stage, you have got an amazing product that you love, you have investigated your prospect and you know they need your product. You then package together a '_no brainer_' offer that will make it virtually impossible for them to say no to, right? - wrong. They will almost always say '_no_' at this point. It may not be an outright no, but they will probably come up with an excuse as to why they can't commit at that precise moment.

Why do people do that? It is because most people hate making a decision - and they would like to think about things first. They put off making a decision because it is easier than actually making a decision.

Once you have closed there are two options:

1 - They buy.

2 - They say '_no_' or come up with objections.

Most of the time, when someone comes up with an objection, whatever they say may not always be true. It may often just an excuse not to buy. Your job as a salesperson is to try to get to the bottom of the real reason for objecting to the sale. Let me give you an example:

They might say to you:

'I need to speak to my wife'.

You need to find out whether this is a true objection or if they are just looking for an excuse not to buy and the real objection is something else.

So, I would reply with:

'I totally understand, no problem, can I ask you a question? What will you do if your wife says no?'

They have three possible responses:

1. *'My wife won't say no'.*

2. *'If she says no, I'll do it anyway'.*

3. *'If she says no, I won't buy'.*

If they go for option 1 or 2, it sounds to me like they are ready to buy.

If they reply with option 3, I would ask:

'And why do you think she would say no?'

When they tell you this reason, this is not really coming from the wife but it is coming from him.

If he says: *'she'll think it's too expensive'*, ask yourself who really thinks it's too expensive? Is it his wife (who doesn't even know the price) or is it really him?

So now you know the real reason why the person may not be ready to buy. They think it is too expensive. Well, that is not strictly true; most people will not think it is too expensive. What they really think is that it is too expensive for what you are selling.

They think that the price you are asking is higher than the value of the product. Something to bear in mind is that the decision whether to buy or not is always about value and never about price.

Here's an example:

If I said, *'Give me £10,000 for my iPhone that's worth £1,000'*, you would say *'No that's too expensive'* or *'I can't afford it'*, but if I said *'Give me £10,000 for a Ferrari that is worth £200,000'*, you would suddenly be able to find £10,000. You would beg, borrow and steal to get that £10,000 to get the bargain of the century. Why? Because the value of the product has changed, not the price.

It is never the price; it is always the value.

So, if someone thinks your product is too expensive it means you have not done a good enough job of selling.

I recommend making a note of every objection you encounter and writing it down. Then think about a good way of answering that objection - and ensure that you include this in the next update to your script. Believe it or not, there are normally only about ten different objections that people will come up with for any given product. So just make sure you know what objections to expect and be ready with an answer to each of these so you can get to the truth.

There are two things to remember when considering your responses:

1.   Always agree with your prospect - or at the very least understand and acknowledge what they are saying.

So, let's say I'm selling a *'Winner Sales Intensive'* two-day programme and after I close, someone says:

'This sounds good but I need to think about it'.

I would respond:

'Of course, I totally understand, how long would you like to think about it? A couple of days? A couple of weeks?'.

So now I have agreed with what they have said and I have demonstrated that I understand where they are coming from. This takes away any argument.

Most sales people would say something like *'What is there to think about?'*.

The problem with that approach is that it is aggressive. You should always start the closing process with agreement not aggression.

I know a sales person who when told by a prospect *'I need to check with my wife'*, asked him *'Do you run every little decision past your wife?'* What a way to turn off the customer and lose the sale! Always start by agreeing or at least understanding.

2.   Offer an alternative idea:

Once you have agreed with your prospect, you can offer an alternative point of view. This often works best in the form of questions.

So, if we go back to our *'sounds good but I need to think about it'* example, I would then say:

'Can I be totally honest with you? There are only three things to think about, do you mind if I share them with you?' They usually say yes and I ask them:

1.   *'Are you serious about becoming better at sales?'* (*Yes*)

2.   *'If you absolutely had to, could you afford it?'* (*Yes*)

3.   *'Do you think you would find the programme valuable?'* (*Yes*)

'Well, if you answer yes to all those three questions, there's nothing left for you to think about - you're going to get a load of value, you want to do it, so come on let's do this, how would you like to pay? In full or in instalments?'

So, I have agreed with them and now offered them an alternative point of view.

It makes your life so much easier if you properly prepare for when people throw excuses at you - and remember they are just excuses; excuses made to save them from making a decision. When you really believe in your product and you know that it offers real value, just remember that it only gives value to people when they buy. If they do not actually buy, all you have done is waste their time. If they need or want your product, make sure that you hang in there.

Take your time to craft your responses. Believe me, if you do this, it will put you in the top one percent of all sales people.

*R*epeat:

It is easier to win repeat business from someone who has already bought from you once - so long as their experience has been a good one. The lesson in this is to make sure that you look after your customers.

This is the final step in the WINNER sales system and probably the most important.

So, by now you have just eliminated the excuse to get to the bottom of and understand the real reason why they're not ready to buy - and now you need to repeat the system.

If you remember when we wrote down and list all of the selling points during the *'No Brainer'* section, I said to only use a couple of them and leave some out.

Think of those selling points as ammunition in your gun. You do not want to unload all your munition in one go or there will be nothing left to resort to. If they do not buy at the first attempt, you will have nothing left to say without just repeating yourself. However, if you keep some back, once you have eliminated their excuses, you can now repeat the process but this time with fresh features and benefits to use.

You should move back into the *'No Brainer Section'* then *'Negotiate'* then *'Eliminate Excuses'* and if necessary *'Repeat'* again.

This is why it is so important to have lots of selling points in your script, but not to use them all at once. You should use the most relevant ones first, but if you need to resell, leave some features available to turn to without just repeating yourself.

To summarise up, you sell and then you close. If they don't buy, you should then move onto the second sales script and then close. If they do not buy again, move onto the third sales script and then close. Obviously, only do this if they are genuinely interested. Do not just keep hammering away if they are clearly not interested and are giving you an outright *'no'*. This staged approach is designed for people who are on the fence and you are trying to gently nudge them over.

After Sales

The after sales process is almost just as important as the sales process itself. If you are going to take one piece of advice from this chapter, it would be this: TRACK EVERYTHING.

I use a sales spreadsheet to track all my enquiries. This has been set up on *Google Sheets* and is stored in the Cloud. The reason I use a *Google Sheets* Spreadsheet and not a *Microsoft Excel* Spreadsheet is because having it stored in the Cloud is really useful.

The main advantage is that all your staff or even just your business partner if you prefer, can access your sales spreadsheet at the same time. Therefore, you see when someone else makes a change in real time. You are also not risking losing loads of work as it automatically saves and backs up as you go.

Your sales spreadsheet is going to be the cornerstone of all your sales and marketing activity.

So, let us take a look at what your sales spreadsheet should look like. Along the top row, each in their own column, I have the following:

Staff Name, Date of Enquiry, Phone, Email, Name, Product Required, Additional Information, Where Are They Based, Date Required, Quote, Next Action, Have They Bought? If Not, Why Not? Time That They Booked, How Did They Find Us?

Now I am m going to explain why I have each one of these, although you will most likely have to edit this to fit your business.

Staff Name: – The name of the member of staff dealing with the enquiry. This is useful to know who the customer has spoken to.

Date of Enquiry: – This is especially useful for looking back to see how many enquiries you received on a given day and comparing year on year.

Phone: – I have found that potential customers who have provided us with a phone number are far more likely to buy. This is because selling over the phone is much more effective than selling by email.

Email: – Take down the prospect's email address and email them regularly to stay in touch. We'll explore this further when we look at the Next Action box.

Name: – Write down the person's name and make sure you regularly use it when having a conversation with them.

Dale Carnegie, author of the brilliant book, *'How to Win Friends and Influence People'*, says this:

'Remember that a person's name is to that person the sweetest and most important sound in any language. Using a person's name is crucial, especially when meeting those we don't see very often. Respect and acceptance stem from simple acts such as remembering a person's name and using it whenever appropriate'.

Product Required: – The product or service that they're interested in.

Additional Information: – Any additional information that would be useful to you. This may be regarding the product itself, such as for example, if they only want a yellow one. I primarily use this box to write down information about the client. I can give you an example:

I called a lady and she advised me she could not talk right now as she was taking her little girl, Amy, to hospital and could I call back in a few days. She sounded stressed, so I quickly ended the call and made a note in the Additional Information box.

A few days later, when I called back, I started off by asking how Amy was and what had happened. She, of course, appreciated that I had not only remembered the situation but also remembered Amy's name. She went on to buy and I got the sale.

At that time, I was calling about fifty people every day. Would I have remembered if I had not written it down? Highly unlikely. Instead of appearing to be thoughtful and caring, I would have come across as rude and uncaring. Would I have got the sale? Probably not.

Make sure you use this box to take an interest in your customers.

Where Are They Based: – This may or may not be relevant to your business.

Date Required?: – Again, this is only really relevant for a service-based business.

Quote: – If you quote different rates or amounts depending on where someone is based or the size of the job, do make sure you know how much you have quoted them to avoid sounding incompetent.

Next Action: – This box is certainly the most important one when it comes to sales. If anyone makes an enquiry and leaves a phone number, make sure you call them. If they don't answer the phone, I send them a text message explaining who I am and why I'm calling them.

I will then attempt to call them three times that day at different times – normally morning, afternoon and evening.

I will try this again for the next few days. However, if someone has not answered after twelve calls I give up, as either they are deliberately ignoring me, I have a wrong number - or for some reason they are clearly unable to take my call.

This is all marked in the next action box. Let's say I attempt to call someone on June 11th in the morning. I would write NA x 1 - 11/6 m.

NA – stands for Not Answered

x 1 – how many times I have attempted to call

11/6 – the date

M – indicates that it is in the morning

If they didn't answer again in the afternoon, I would change it to *NA x 2 - 11/6 ma*. And so on.

Once you have managed to get hold of your prospect and have delivered your well-crafted sales pitch, sometimes they may not be in a situation where they are ready to buy yet. The *'Rule of Seven'* is an old saying in marketing. It basically means that most people will need to hear from you seven times before they are in a situation where they are ready to buy. Obviously, it is not always seven times, but do not give up on someone just because they do not buy the first time you speak to them.

Normally they will say something like: *'I just need to compare a few more quotes'*, *'I need to talk to my partner'* or *'let me have a couple of days to think about it'*.

Most people say: *'Yes sure, no problem'* and guess what? Most of the time you will never hear from them again.

Make sure that when you put the phone down, you are in control of the conversation. For example:

If they say: *'I need to talk to my partner'* and after investigation, as above, this is genuine, I would say: *'No problem, when do you think you'd be able to talk to them?'*.

'Well, he is working late tonight, so tomorrow (Tuesday)', they reply.

'No problem, well if I don't hear from you before, shall I give you a call back on Wednesday at say 11am?', I ask.

Now 95% of the time they will agree to this. So, I would write on my sales spreadsheet – interested call back Wednesday 12/6 11:00am to close the deal.

Do always call people back when you say you are going to. It certainly builds up the trust element, proving that you deliver on what you say you are going to do.

If they are still not ready to buy, repeat this and stay in control of the conversation.

If at any point through this process someone asks not to be called back and says something like: 'If I decide I want to buy, I will call you', it is their way of politely telling you they are not interested.

So just write a big 'NO' in the Next Action Box and do not call them again.

Even though I do not waste time calling again, I will continue to stay in touch with them through email. When someone makes an initial enquiry, I will email them every day for the first week and then continue to email after that, albeit more infrequently.

It does not have to just be sales letters; you should be sending useful information regarding the product or service that they are considering purchasing. This is a great way of staying in the forefront of your prospect's mind while they are in the process of making a buying decision.

This is, of course can be fully automated, set up in the background to be working automatically without you having to actually do anything. The beauty of automated email is that it will not take rejection personally. It carries on regardless and it does not quit because someone shows a lack of interest.

Quite regularly someone will call to say they wish to make a booking and, when I find their name on the sales spreadsheet, they have a big 'NO' in the *Next Action* box. I smile to myself that our software system has gained us another client quietly in the background.

If you have not already got an automated email system set up, you are missing a trick. Do it now! We currently use *Infusionsoft*, but there are lots of other cheaper software options and even some that are free. *Mailchimp*, for example, is free, depending on the amount of email addresses in your list.

Have They Bought? If a person has not bought, I write '*No*' in this box. If they have bought, I write the information contained in the 'How did they find us' box, this could for example be *Facebook* or through e-mail.

I do this so that I can use the *COUNTIF* formula to search that column and find out how many bookings have come from *Facebook*, an internet search, a recommendation or another way, without having to manually add them all up myself. This probably saves me 30-45 minutes a month - and is another good example of systemising processes.

If Not, Why Not? You will not get an answer from everybody, but it is really useful asking people why they have decided to go with someone else and not buy from you. Once you know the reason, write it down in this box.

Keep an eye on this and if you notice the same reasons coming up again and again, maybe it is time to adapt so that it stops happening.

When my brother first started using the sales board approach, he noticed that quite a lot of people were saying what we provided was too expensive.

His main product was a two-hour complete party package priced at £199 [c. US$280].

So, he added an extra package which we did not advertise on the website, but could offer if someone said the party was too expensive.

He introduced a 90-minute package for £169. He booked in at least five of these packages per month. These were all extra bookings that he would not have obtained had he not used the sales spreadsheet.

Time They Bought? Every time you make a sale note the time in this box. If the time was 10:32, I just input 10 to show the hour that it was made. This is a new column that I have added recently to my sales sheets. The idea of this column is that we can track the busiest times in the office. What times are we most likely to be making sales? Again, you can use the *COUNTIF* formula to calculate this for you.

If we have to arrange staff meetings, training or even when staff have breaks, it is useful to know when the quietest times are and when sales will be affected the least.

How Did They Find Us? From what marketing activity, did the person find your company and make that enquiry? This could be *Facebook*, a recommendation, or a previous client.

It is really important that every time somebody makes an enquiry, they get put on this spreadsheet. We have an enquiry form on our website. When a prospect fills in the form, *Infusionsoft* automatically adds all their details to the spreadsheet for us. However, if somebody calls us, we have to manually add the information.

Once it gets to the end of the month, you have a wealth of really useful data to have a look at. You will have information such as:

- How many enquiries you have had,

- A breakdown of where all those enquiries have come from,

- How many sales you have had,

- A breakdown of where all those sales have come from,

- What your conversion rate is i.e., how many enquiries you need to make a sale,

- You can also compare conversion rates depending where the enquiry has come from,

- The peak times for sales in the office,

- What the average sale price is – and,

- Compare average sales price depending on where the enquiry has come from.

This means you can look at your marketing spend. For example:

Say I spent £500 [c. US$700] on *Facebook* ads and it generated 50 enquiries at a cost of £10 [c. US$14] per enquiry.

We then made twenty sales from those fifty enquiries at a conversion rate of 40%, costing us £25 [c. US$35] per sale.

The average sale price was £200 [US$280] which means you have an eight-times return on investment.

Now do this for all of your marketing activities, so you can see which strategies are working the best. Once you know this, it becomes increasingly clear where you should invest your marketing budget.

You can in this way see what is working and what is not working. This information is vital in growing your business.

Chapter Fifty Nine: Summary Key Behavioural Check List For Success In Business

I have compiled a list of key behaviours you should always try to aspire to and emulate to help you succeed in business:

1)   Your energy introduces yourself. The person with the greatest energy almost always wins,

2)   Know your own value in the market place; this is justified by the service you can bring, your authenticity and your integrity,

3)   Get to know your client and who you are serving; think and enquire about where are they on their journey? Are they new to a sector? Do they have thirty years' experience? Having an understanding of these points is important, so that you can serve them in the best way possible. Treat all of your clients as VIPs,

4)   Market based on the value you can offer,

5)   Give gifts and provide solutions to your clients,

6)   You *earn* the right to be paid when you are authentic - and when you have learned how to help your client,

7)   What is the client experience are you providing? This must be exceptional, if you are to succeed,

8)   Develop and practice your pitch... (say, for example, that you would *'love to work with your client via a joint venture and you will be there for your client for the long term'*),

9) You should and need to be in love with the service you provide. Passion feeds energy,

10) Facts Tell the Story: (Facts and figures speak for themselves but these offer up a story which you can use to sell) – it is important to understand the wisdom of the old adage to: *'Sell the sizzle not the Sausage'* – Develop narratives that sell the transforming effect your services can offer,

11) Be of service and bring value now to your clients,

12) Create desire – and,

13) Finally, be sure of and understand your mission. Apart from money what are your key drivers? These should include helping others, a sense of purpose and being the best version of yourself as you can. These need to be key driving forces that become core values.

Chapter Sixty: Building A Reputation

In the words of Cal Newport; *'Be so good that they can't ignore you…'*. Focus relentlessly on excellence; if you do, people will not be able to ignore you!

Always… be looking for ways to continue to develop and improve – through learning from your mistakes; from what other people do well and how they do this; and investing in yourself through education.

It is really important that if you wish to grow and scale your business, that you have a good reputation in your field.

Things can go wrong – but you should do everything in your power to make any project you are involved in be a success.

There are five things you can do to help ensure projects go smoothly.

These are:

1) **Doing Your Due Diligence and Risk Assessing Everything:** While it is important to be positive, optimistic and take real action, you also need to risk assess everything, be detailed and reflective at the same time. Life is a risk, and there will always be some risk.

   You need to assess how high the risk is in comparison to the reward, using critical thinking. You should ask yourself, what is the best-case scenario, worst-case scenario and most probable scenario. Then look at what is the likelihood of the worst-case scenario coming true. You can also look at how you could reduce the likelihood of the worst case happening. For example, you could put in a break clause into your contract if things for whatever reason do not work out as planned.

You always have to risk something, but you have to make sure how much risk you can afford to take.

2) **Make Sure You Document Your Journey:** If the project goes well, you will have built great project portfolio. Having photos, and well documented costs will help you show your worth - and demonstrate both your experience and capabilities to other potential future joint venture partners.

3) **Deliver on Your Promises:** If you say you are going to do something – make sure that you do indeed do it. If you say you are going to meet someone for coffee at 1pm, then be there at 12.55pm. If you say you are going to book arrange for a builder – then make sure you do it.

4) **Be Direct:** If a problem arises then say things the way they are. If your joint venture partner gives you a ticking off and they have a point, do not just get defensive – take the point on board and address it.

5) **Ask for Testimonials When Things Go Well:** Ask you joint venture partner, or accountant, or broker – or whoever you have worked with to provide you with written testimonials when things go well; this will all help you build your brand and reputation.

Chapter Sixty One: Launching Your New Business

Once you have set up the business, you need to tell the world!

Many people are worried about what people will think when starting a business - or fear that people will laugh at their company name. Most people approach things by thinking that they will secure a few deals, make some money and then tell people.

My suggestion is that the moment you have completed all of the preliminaries such as establishing the company and your website - then hold a party to celebrate launching your business. Invite all the property investors and landlords you know along with friends and supporters. Have champagne and give a speech saying you have launched a business and what you want to do.

If you do this, your friends and other investors you have invited will get come alongside you in business will help you and give you deals.

Anyone who laughs at you, does not support you or does not come to the party really is not your friend. Friends are people who want you to succeed.

Post on social media and tell the world what your business is about. When you tell people about your business, you are speaking it out into existence. Do not forget to update all of your social media accounts – and ensure that you have a *LinkedIn* profile that tells the world that you are now a company director.

Part Three:

Strategies For Property Investing:

Chapter Sixty Two: Remember The Ultimate Goal: Your Mission

Just before we look at specific strategies, please remember that financial freedom should *not* be your ultimate goal. There are four stages or levels to success:

- The first of these is '*F*ull *T*ime in *P*roperty' – or FTP; this reflects a time and personal commitment to determining your financial future.

- The second level is then becoming financially free; there are multiple ways to become financially free through property. Selling one deal a month as a property sourcer, for example, for many people could make them financially free. Many people think becoming financially free is hard – but all jobs have some degree of difficulty, so if you are going to work hard you might as well work smart and become rich! Anybody can make something appear difficult. Do remember that once you know how to do something in almost all cases it no longer seems so difficult.

- The third stage is then to become ultimately financially free; ultimate financial freedom is when your passive income is equal to or exceeds what is needed to fund your desired lifestyle. Write down on a piece of paper – where you would like to live, where and how often you would like to go on holiday, what car you would like to drive etc. You may be surprised at how little you need for this; (refer back to chapter fifty one).

- The fourth stage is being able to pursue and drive your mission in life: this means being able to change the world for the better in the way that you would like to see most. This could be helping those who you love most in the world, funding humanitarian work in developing countries, education – or saving the planet; or indeed whatever is most important to *you*; this is your mission.

Chapter Sixty Three: So - What Is The Best Strategy For You? How To Get Going Step By Step

So many people ask me, what I think would be the best strategy for them?

When people ask me about this, I often say something along the lines of, *'What strategy do you think that I use?'*. They often look a bit confused and reply with something such as: *'Well I've heard you talk about using lots of different strategies'*, to which I say, *'Exactly – that's because I <u>use</u> lots of different strategies; I use the most appropriate strategy for the situation.*

Think about this: Golfers do not go out to play with one club in their bag; they select a different club - the most appropriate club for each shot.

In the same way, when you go to view properties, one property might present an opportunity for a simple 'buy to let', while another might be perfect for a lease option agreement, and then another for a buy-refurbishment-refinance-rent project - and so on.

There are two sets of circumstances to consider: Firstly, your own - and secondly those of the opportunity you are considering.

First let us consider your circumstances; if you have little or no cash, then you can still start out in property investing through, for example, finding deals and selling them on to other property investors as a deal sourcer. Other options include raising finance – joint venturing with a partner, securing lease option agreements – or adopting a rent-to-rent approach.

If you do have sufficient funds for a mortgage deposit, then this opens up further possibilities such as purchasing properties for single lets, purchasing Houses In Multiple Occupancy (HMOs) – and Buy-Refurbish-Refinance-Rent (BRRR) projects.

As you become more experienced and build your portfolio, you will find that you sometimes go to view a property with one approach in mind, but as you find out more about the circumstances of the house or the sellers, it turns out that actually another approach might be more appropriate.

I will in the following chapters, first consider the approaches that require little or no cash and then move to more advanced strategies where you actively have to make money work for you.

All deals start with finding and securing an opportunity. To find deals you must look for them and this means viewing as many possible houses as you can. You need to continually keep viewing houses. If you do, you will find deals; for this reason, I believe all property investors should become deal sourcers and this is the strategy that I will cover in the next chapter.

Chapter Sixty Four: Finding Deals And Deal Sourcing

Stage One: Finding the Deals:

As mentioned in the previous chapter any property deal starts with first finding a property that offers an opportunity.

It follows that the first thing you need to be doing is finding these opportunities - and this is best achieved by viewing as many properties as you can. In this way you will inevitably gain experience, in everything from spotting opportunities, to valuing properties in a given area.

Viewing many houses is a great opportunity to network with and build relationships and network with estate agents in an area. This is the way for you to find opportunities which is of course the first step to finding and securing deals. The most important thing you need to do is to venture out and view properties – in fact to view as many properties as you can.

Having made this commitment to view as many properties as you can, you next need to decide upon a patch...

When looking for your area, the first place to start is looking close to where you live.

You are going to have to visit the area regularly to find deals – and if this means making multiple journeys to the other end of the country, this will be time consuming and become impractical.

Another advantage associated with a property being closer to where you live, is that you may well have some local knowledge of which areas might be good and which to avoid.

If you have a regular job, then you will need to plan first one - and then several 'big days out'. Big days should involve booking in as many viewings in a day as possible with local estate agents in your chosen patch (ideally at least seven or more).

A good place to start is to look for houses that would be suitable as HMOs since these, offer some of the highest returns on investment (ROIs). Look for houses that could offer at least 20% rental return on investment (ROI) using the formula I gave you in chapter twenty-three - and then phone each estate agent and introduce yourself as a property investor. Before your big day you need to undertake as much research as possible on the area - and indeed of course each property that you are going to view.

You should firstly determine the rental demand through visiting on-line resources such as *Rightmove* and *SpareRoom* if in the UK (or similar house sales and rental sites if in another country). You should determine the average value of a particular type of property in a given area, the demand for rental – and the market rental rate. Look also for houses on alternative sites such as *Gumtree* since sellers who advertise property in this way are often highly motivated.

One approach for determining demand is to pre-phone estate agents as a mystery shopper. Firstly, you can phone round and introduce yourself as a property investor – and ask the agent where they would recommend to invest – along with advice for areas to avoid and why. Ask questions such as what the rental demand is like in different areas – and whether the area is popular with working professionals, blue collar workers or students etc. Agents will often be very open with the advice they can give, which will help you to understand an area.

Next, get someone else such as your partner or family member to phone around some of the letting agents, (it is often better to get someone else to do this as many estate agents also act as letting agents) and have them enquire about rental prices in an area with questions such as, *'If you were to find a good property, how quickly might they have to move to secure it?'* – or conversely *'Would a renter have a pick of good properties to choose from?'*

Questions such as these will help determine how active the rental market in an area is; you clearly want to find an area that has a high level of demand.

If an area has an excess of properties for rent, then move on and find another area.

To help you find deals – in any market conditions, I have put together a programme called the *'Deal Finding Extravaganza'*.

This on-line or in person course is continually updated and will tell you all you need to know about how to find below market deals, stack the figures and find which properties are perfect for Houses In Multiple Occupancy, etc. (for more information visit: https://www.property-investors.co.uk/)

When you have found some good deals, you can make money from these even if you are not in a position to buy them; this involves packaging the deals and selling them on to other investors as a deal sourcer, which is what we will look at next:

Stage Two: Selling Deals As A Deal Sourcer:

Having become an expert at finding deals, as a deal sourcer you can sell the deals on; this is a fantastic way of making £2-3K [c. US$2.5-4K] with each deal you source, package and sell on.

The two most popular packages for deal sourcers and investors are for Houses In Multiple Occupancy HMOs, which we will look at in chapter sixty-nine – and Buy-Refurbish-Refinance-Rent (BRRR) projects which we will look at in chapter seventy.

Depending on where you live in the world, you may need to become legally complaint to sell deals; this essentially means complying with the rules that real estate agents must follow. In the UK, this means having the correct indemnity insurance, registering with one of the professional bodies and the registering with the information commissioner's office. One of the easiest and fastest ways to start and gain experience is to sell your first few deals in partnership with another deal sourcer who is compliant. This is known as co-deal sourcing.

A package for selling should contain the following information:

- Purchase price for the property

- Location

- HMO / is it tenanted or not?

- Size / bedrooms and a floor plan

- Refurbishment costs (if needed)

- Achievable rent (along with conformation of a letting agent if one is in place and the percentage of the rental fee that will be charged for management)

- Condition of the property

- Finder's Fee

One of the most important steps is to have a client base of investors who are ready to purchase and this is another reason why partnering with an established deal sourcer is often a great way to start while you establish your own client list.

If you contact me (details at the end of this book), I will help connect you with established deal sourcers to help get you started.

If you are going to find deals, you need to know what to look for when viewing properties - and this is what we will look at in the next chapter.

Chapter Sixty Five: A Guide To Viewing Properties

It is very easy to book a viewing and go to the property, but it is not easy to estimate the cost of the work that will need to be undertaken... until now - as I am going to show you how. This guide will take you through everything you need to know and key things to look for when viewing a property.

1. Make sure your phone is fully charged and there is ample storage for you to record your viewing. During each of your viewings take lots of pictures.

2. Arrive at least five minutes early at the property. Estate agents do not like tardiness, and neither should you. To be successful in property you must ensure you make and maintain quality relationships with estate agents, so, do be there on time! Being early is preferable, and this will give you time to make a start on the checklist below. It is also helpful to have a look at the other properties in the street: For example, are other properties for sale? Can you see any travel links near the property? Is it a busy road? etc.

3. Before viewing any property, study and think about each item in the context of the structure of a house. The diagram overleaf may help contextualise each item.

4. Now start your viewing checklist:

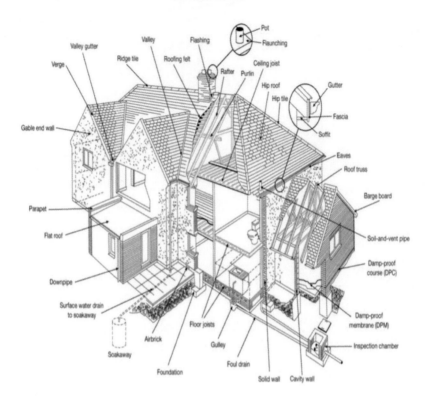

Schematic of a house with many of the key features to check when undertaking a house viewing

Viewing Checklist:

If you tick "yes" to anything on your checklist, make a note of where you see the defect and remember to take a picture.

Outside The Property:

Questions	Options		Notes
What are the parking facilities like?	Drive	Off Road	
Are there any external cracks, bulges or signs of vegetation on the building?	Yes	No	
Are there are visible cracks on the driveway? (if applicable)	Yes	No	
Are there large trees with roots close to the foundations?	Yes	No	
Are there any cracks around the windows			
If there is a basement, are the airbricks visible?	Yes	No	
If yes, are they are in good condition?	Yes	No	
Are they covered by vegetation?	Yes	No	
Garden			
Is there any damage?	Yes	No	
Are there any uneven surfaces?	Yes	No	
Paths			
Is there any damage?	Yes	No	
Are there any uneven surfaces?	Yes	No	

Ponds (if applicable)			
Is there any damage?	Yes	No	
Are there any uneven surfaces?	Yes	No	
Is it sealed properly?	Yes	No	
Is there a pump?	Yes	No	
Gates			
Is there any damage?	Yes	No	
Is there any rust?	Yes	No	
Are they working?	Yes	No	
Where are they located?	Yes	No	
Guttering			
Are there any blockages?	Yes	No	
Are there any nests?	Yes	No	
Is there a missing section?	Yes	No	
Are there any leaks?	Yes	No	
Are there any broken pipes?	Yes	No	

Roof:

Questions	Options		Comments
Has the roof bowed?	Yes	No	
Have the shingles cupped, curled or warped?	Yes	No	
Are there any cracked or broken tiles?	Yes	No	
Are there any missing sections?	Yes	No	
Are there mismatched sections of the roof?	Yes	No	

Bathroom:

Questions	Options		Comments
How new is the bathroom suite – will you need to replace it?	Yes	No	
Is the condition of the sealant around the baths, showers and sinks good?	Yes	No	
Are there signs of mould on the tiles?	Yes	No	
Is there a window or extractor fan?	Yes	No	
Are there signs of damp?	Yes	No	
Smell?	Yes	No	
Visible?	Yes	No	
Are there water stains under basin?	Yes	No	
Are there stains around the toilet?	Yes	No	
Is there a foul odour coming from the basin?	Yes	No	
Are there any leaks or blockages?	Yes	No	
Do the toilets flush?	Yes	No	
Are the taps leaking?	Yes	No	

Kitchen:

Questions	Options		Comments
How new is the kitchen – will you need to replace it? (warping to cupboard doors etc)	Yes	No	
Are the hob and oven gas or electric? Will you need to replace it?	Yes	No	
Are any white goods for sale with the property?	Yes	No	
Are there signs of damp? Smell? Visible?	Yes Yes Yes	No No No	
Are there water stains under sinks?	Yes	No	
Is there a foul odour coming from the sink?	Yes	No	
Are the taps leaking?	Yes	No	

Fire: (Property Type Will Depend On Fire Safety Regulations)

Questions	Options		Comments
Does the property have smoke alarms? (Where? / How many?)	Yes	No	
Is / are there a fire extinguisher(s)?	Yes	No	
Is there a fire blanket?	Yes	No	

General (Damage / Water / Mould / Electrical):

Questions	Options		Comments
Are there exposed wires?	Yes	No	
Are there wires with electrical tape?	Yes	No	
How old is the electrical consumer unit?	Yes	No	
Are there any signs of damaged wiring or lack of sockets?	Yes	No	
Are there water stains on the walls?	Yes	No	
Is there visible mould?	Yes	No	
Is there wood rot (if applicable) around exterior doors and trim?	Yes	No	
Is there peeling paint?	Yes	No	
Are there any signs of damp or discolouration to walls and ceilings?	Yes	No	
Are there any internal cracks that run through the house?	Yes	No	
Do all the doors move easily?	Yes	No	
Are there any draft points, cracks or worn seals around the windows and doors?			
Has the boiler had a recent survey? When was it installed?	Yes	No	

Examples of Subsidence

Simply put, a house that is subsiding is sinking into the ground. Homes built on clay are more likely to suffer from subsidence than those built on other types of soil.

Subsidence can occur when the ground below the house shrinks or swells due to the weather; during wet weather the ground expands due to the moisture, but then contracts during the dry summer months.

Though many homes may have a crack or two - which probably first appeared as the house was settling - the cracks which indicate that a house is subsiding are quite distinctive.

Cracks From Subsidence Can:

- Appear and spread rapidly compared to regular cracks

- Occur both inside and outside the property

- Look narrower at one end than the other and run diagonally across the wall

- Be found around doors and windows

Other Tell-Tale Signs Include:

- Doors and windows start to jam as you try to open/close them as they will become disturbed

- Wallpaper crinkling at the wall/ceiling joins

- Cracks where any later extension to the building joins the main body of the property

Classic External Signs Of External Subsidence

Examples of Mould / Damp

Efflorescence:

If there are white deposits like the ones in the picture below, then these could be caused by efflorescence. Efflorescence is one type of white deposit found on masonry. It is formed when water reacts with the natural salts contained within the construction material and mortar. The water dissolves the salts which are then carried out and deposited onto the surface by the natural evaporation that occurs when air comes into contact with the surface of the wall or floor.

Evidence of Efflorescence

Penetrating Damp:

Penetrating damp (also known as water ingress) is the result of water infiltration from the outside of a property to the inside. It can be caused from sources such as rain penetration due to for example faulty guttering or damp coming from high ground levels.

Visible Damp on Walls and Ceilings

Rising Damp:

You can often identify rising damp without using any professional equipment and just looking at and touching the wall. Typical signs that can identify rising damp include:

Tide Marks and Damp Staining:

One of the most common tell-tale signs are tide marks left on walls. Tide marks are caused by evaporation and salts from the ground. You will normally notice these anywhere up to a 1 metre above the skirting board.

If you do not notice tide marks, another very common tell-tale sign can be damp patches or staining. Typically, these damp patches are yellowish or brownish in colour and similar to tide marks; you will often find these up to 1 metre above the skirting board.

Peeling Wallpaper:

Look out for wallpaper coming away from or peeling from the wall. You will most likely notice it coming loose from the skirting board first with the corner of the wallpaper turned or curved up.

Decayed Skirting Boards:

As with many forms of dampness, rising damp has the potential to cause rot within timbers it comes into contact with. Look out for skirting boards that are cracked, easily crumbling or localised fungus growing on or creeping out of the side. In addition to this, look out for damaged or flaky paint.

Salts Within The Plaster:

Salts in the form of white fluffy deposits in the plaster similar to the images below are another clear tell-tale sign of damp. These salts are washed out of your bricks and into your plaster leaving what can look like blistering patches on your walls.

Chimney Repointing:

Chimney repointing is a process whereby the original failed mortar is raked out and replaced with new mortar. If this is not addressed, the chimney will ultimately be at risk of collapse; this will also give rise to a risk of water seeping into the gaps, which in turn will give rise to damp in the chimney breast.

Samuel Leeds

Chapter Sixty Six: Rent-To-Rent Strategies:

Rent-to-rent strategies are those in which you first rent for a property from a landlord or agent - and you pay them a fixed, guaranteed rent; the rent you pay is the 'normal rent'. Then you rent the property out for a super rent – often by changing the use of the property.

There are two main rent-to-rent approaches for turning general rent into super rent:

Two Main Strategies:

The first approach is to rent-to-rent for an HMO. In this strategy, you rent a house set up as a single dwelling and rent each room separately as an HMO (House in Multiple Occupancy) – see chapter sixty-nine. You have in this way changed the use of the property from being a single let to a multi let property. All of the additional rent you receive minus expenses, provides you with your profit.

The second strategy is to turn the property into a serviced accommodation letting unit. You can think of this as almost being a hotel without staff. You give the landlord a general rent, and maximise your rent by advertising and letting the property on a site such as *Airbnb* or *Booking.com*. Depending on the location, you can typically charge £100 [c. US$140] a night (£3,000 [c. US$4,200] a month) compared to £500 [c. US$700] a month on a single let rent.

Before you go any further, you need to decide if you are going to target Rent-to-HMO, Rent-to-Serviced Accommodation.

Locating Your Patch:

The very first thing you need to decide is where your patch is going to be for your rent-to-rent business; are you going to find somewhere that is working well for somebody else? Are you going to find somewhere new?

Where do rent-to-rent approaches work?

I would advise that you should in the first instance, shortlist three areas where you could set up a rent-to-rent business. You then need to rank these in order of preference and focus in on one area.

If your first area, after further due diligence does not look like it might not work so well, you will have two back up areas to look at next.

To select your three areas for shortlisting, consider if there are any large vibrant cities within half an hour's drive of where you live. You need to be looking for areas which are highly populated and have big centres for employment, tourism, entertainment and leisure.

Rent-to-rent approaches can work well in busy, thriving urban areas that could be described as 'buzzing'.

Exercise:

Write down the top three major towns or cities near your house where you could establish a Rent to Rent business.

Pick the busiest area out of those three - and make this your patch.

Selecting Your Strategy:

Now that you have selected your patch, you need to pick your strategy.

The main choices are between rent-to-HMO or rent-to-serviced accommodation.

Firstly, you want to *Google* search your area and see what sort of tourist attractions may be local. One approach is to find properties near tourist areas for rent-to-serviced accommodation.

The example below is in York in the UK, but you should do this for whatever area you have chosen.

The tourist attractions are usually near the city centre, and this can give an idea of where you may want to look for a property. Next you can look on *Airbnb* to see the type of accommodation that is renting for short-stays in your area.

You can see in the example from York in the UK below; that at the time of searching places were being offered for rent for over £100 [c. US$140] a night.

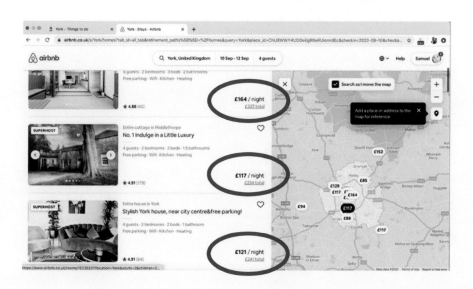

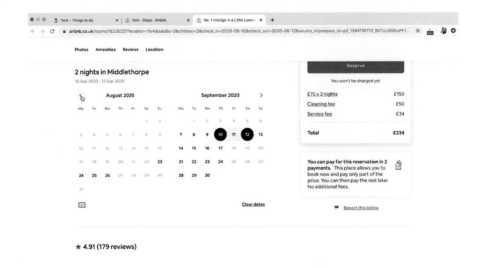

★ 4.91 (179 reviews)

You can next click on each of these properties and see how fully booked they are usually by scrolling to the bottom of the listing and looking at the calendar under availability.

You see in the property shown above, almost all of August is booked out while September is already starting to book out as well. This property is charging £100+ [c. US$140] a night.

In this instance, if you change the search term for the number of people staying, the price increases.

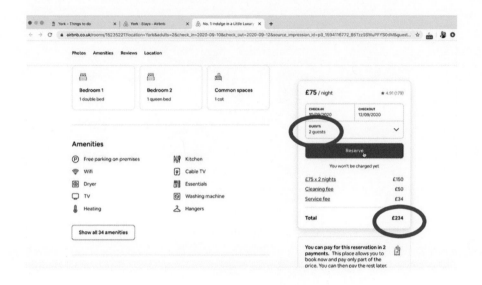

If you look at all the properties in your area on *Airbnb* and they are all charging good prices per night - and are being booked up in advance, then you may have found a good area for rent-to-serviced accommodation.

Now, if you are planning on targeting rent-to-HMO, the situation will be different because your tenants are going to be staying at least six months. If you go on *SpareRoom* you can find out how much people are willing to pay for a room; see below. People are in this area willing to pay £400/£500 [c. US$560-700] for a room. Also, as you can see, there are many adverts for rooms being added every day. In this instance the demand is clearly high!

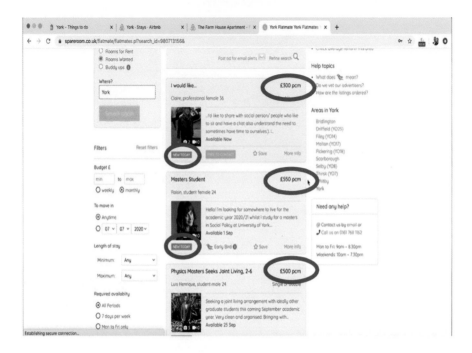

Next, compare this to the price of renting a whole property on *Rightmove* in your area. You can clearly make more money from renting a property out as an HMO than a single let. There are also properties being added every day!

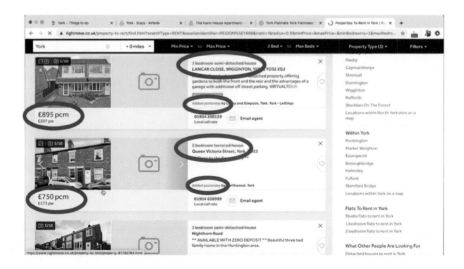

Now, you need to decide what your strategy is going to be. Are you going to find properties to rent out by the room as an HMO? Or are you going to rent out rooms by the night through serviced accommodation?

The biggest thing in favour of serviced accommodation over HMOs, at the time of writing is that there is less regulation, you do not need a licence and you can rent a property, advertise it immediately on *Airbnb* and start earning money very quickly. You only to have make sure any mortgage taken out on the property does not prohibit this and that you have the right type of insurance. A key advantage of this approach is that since different people are staying at your property every night each typically paying £100 [c. US$140] or more, you are likely to make more money than via the HMO approach.

HMOs have a few more rules and legislation to follow. However, HMOs will provide you with more of an idea what your cash flow be each month, since your tenants will be signed up to six-month or longer contracts.

Many more landlords are more familiar with HMOs, therefore, if you are trying to secure a rent-to-rent, the letting agent or landlord is going to understand this approach, whereas they might be a bit cautious about entering into a serviced accommodation.

There is no better or worse strategy, so you just need to decide which is best in your chosen area. If you go to *SpareRoom* and people are not looking for rooms in your area, but *Airbnb* is showing good nightly levels of booking - well, then go for serviced accommodation. If it appears to be the other way round in your area, then you should choose the HMO route.

Exercise:

Undertake the research and due diligence into three areas.

Select one area – and then,

Decide upon your chosen strategy; either HMO or serviced accommodation.

Selecting Your Management Plan:

Now you have your area and strategy in mind and chosen, you need to decide whether you want to manage your business yourself - or if you want to get managers to manage it for you so that the income becomes more passive.

If you are just starting out with rent-to-rent, you do not have managers and staff and your business is not systemised, it is likely to be HARD work. You are going to have to do things you might not necessarily always want to do. In the early days you have to just accept that this is going to be time consuming. It will be worth the time, give you the rewards you want and eventually you can turn this rent-to-rent approach into being far more passive through having people do everything for you.

You will still have to decide if you are going to need a manager for the property or if you are going to do it yourself.

One of the reasons I have seen people fail with rent-to-rent is because they approach this strategy with unrealistic expectations. They believe they can bring in a management company in to do everything from the start, generate a totally passive income and never have to even view the property. Even if you have a management company, you will still need to be involved to some extent. You will to a greater or lesser extent need to manage the managers.

In a year or two, once you have grown the business, you will be able to systemise the business and make it much more passive. You will however need to work hard in the beginning.

Reasons in favour of doing everything yourself of course include that you will make more money. Hiring people can be expensive and this will eat into your profit. You also are going to get to learn at a far faster rate - and in the future when you get a management company in, they are not going to be able to 'pull the wool over your eyes' as you will have done all of the tasks yourself job already.

The greatest benefit of bringing in a management company is that it will lighten the load and make the whole process feel less like a job. You can definitely run a rent-to-rent alongside a full-time job; however, you would almost certainly need a management company involved.

To make your decision, you have to ask yourself how much time you have. If you are trying to get as much cash flow as possible, you have time on your hands and are trying to replace your current job, then definitely manage the property yourself.

If you are time poor, do not have much spare time and you have a job which is paying you a reasonable income, then you may choose to pay for a manager. If your job is paying you much more than it would be to hire a cleaner, then pay someone to be a cleaner.

To help you make informed choices determine how much you are worth per hour. Divide your total pay last year by the number of hours you worked to find this out. If your earning potential per hour is £10 [c. US$14], then it will not make sense to pay a cleaner £12 [c. US$17] per hour when you could do the job yourself. Conversely if your time equates to £30 [US$42] earnings an hour, then it would not make sense to do the cleaning and management yourself when you can pay people to do this for you.

Chapter Sixty Seven: Lease Option Agreements

The Power of Lease Option Agreements

Lease options agreements offer a powerful approach of buying houses without the need for a deposit – and therefore represent a great strategy for helping you start out as a property investor.

Actually, lease option agreements should be an approach for all property investors since everybody, however wealthy they are, will have a finite amount of money – and this will limit the number of houses any one person can buy.

So, how exactly does a lease option agreement work? If you needed to explain this to a five-year old – a good way would be to describe this as being an approach where *you buy a house now but pay for it later*.

Now if you buy a car and pay for it later, this will of course devalue in time. This gives rise to bad debt.

If by contrast you buy a house and pay for it later, this will most likely increase in value over time. The house will also give you a rental income as we have already seen.

A lot of people ask if lease option agreements are legal. Other people sometimes say, *'if it sounds too good to be true it probably is'*. These are people speaking from ignorance.

Quite simply lease options are completely legal if drawn up properly. I have bought many properties through lease option agreements - and have seen the whole process (and timeline) through from beginning to end.

Lease options are common in business and commercial properties and are now becoming more common for residential properties.

Lease options _do_ however need to be drawn up and prepared through a solicitor.

The legalities from country to country do differ, so check with a solicitor that practices in your country. In Scotland if you wish to buy and pay for a house later, you _have to commit_ to buying the property and so these arrangements are called '_deferred purchase agreements_'. This does not, however, stop people in Scotland from agreeing lease option agreements in England or Wales.

To reiterate, lease options are legal but you need to approach these with knowledge - and to do this you need to arrange lease option agreements in conjunction with property solicitors who specialise in lease option agreements. Note: most solicitors who undertake regular conveyancing _are not_ specialists in lease option agreements and so you do need to select one who is a specialist in this area.

The Sellers Motivation and making it a Win-Win

You might ask who would agree for me to buy their house from them in five or seven years' time, knowing that I would at the end of this time gain from capital appreciation – while in the meantime I would be making a rental income from their property?

There are two types of people who would...

1) People who do not need the money now such as, for example, people who have inherited the property – or who wish to move abroad.

2) People who cannot sell the property now for the price that they need; these are people who are typically in negative equity; i.e., they cannot sell the property for a value that will cover their outstanding mortgage.

It is so important to make lease option deals to be a win-win for both parties. You should only offer these to people who are going to benefit from a lease option agreement. This person will need to be represented by a lawyer who will advise them - and the lawyer will need to be convinced that a lease option will benefit them.

Ensuring that you will have a win-win for both parties is the only way to properly structure lease option agreements – and so your task is to identify the people who will genuinely benefit from a lease option agreement.

In chapter seventeen I described how I secured one of my first lease option agreements.

Recessions Bring Deals:

In 2006, banks were across the world giving out 100% mortgages. In 2008 there was a global credit crunch followed by a property crash. This left people with large mortgages on houses that that had fallen in value - and that were in many cases in negative equity.

There are at the time of writing many areas of the UK where house prices are still worth less than they were fifteen years ago.

In downturns, people will be wanting to offload their houses – and this provides opportunities for buying these using lease option agreements - with the likelihood that over the longer term prices will again increase.

As a property investor, you need to think about and identify which areas have crashed and that may offer opportunities for purchasing through lease option agreements.

Finding Negative Equity Leads:

Finding negative equity leads is actually quite easy.

First go to *Zoopla*: Find areas where houses are in negative equity (such as Bradford or Burnley in the UK), where house prices have yet to recover fully from the 2008 crash.

Next go to *Rightmove* and look for properties that have been on the market for a long period of time (by choosing to sort the listing for houses first that have been on the market for the longest period of time). In some areas many of these may be in negative equity. This can be seen by looking at the house price sold history tab for each house.

Now build a list of one hundred houses that are in negative equity as leads for possible lease option agreements.

To help with this there is an app available called *DealSourcr* that will help scrape negative equity leads to simply this process.

Log all of these leads into your spreadsheet or document where you are collecting leads.

Now you need to contact your leads and you need to do this in the correct way:

Negative Equity Letters

Use brightly covered envelopes e.g., that are yellow, pink or blue... these can be ordered in bulk from *Amazon* or *eBay*. The brightly coloured envelopes stand out and encourage people to open them.

Address the letter by hand – do not use printed labels; this looks too business like and puts people off.

Address the letter to 'The Homeowner'.

Dear Homeowner,

I am not sure if you are still selling your house as it has been on the market for a very long time. But if you are, I am very interested.

I would like to pay you a monthly rent with an agreed purchase down the line giving you the price you want, but giving me time to save the deposit and wait for the market to recover.

If this is something that would be of interest then please get in contact using the contact details below.

Many thanks,

[YOUR CONCACT DETAILS IN HERE].

Securing The Deal:

As discussed in chapter seventeen, you need to explore options such as the home owner renting the property out themselves - before offering a lease option agreement. This is the correct and ethical approach to take.

If the home owner does not wish to become a landlord, then this is where you can make an offer of a lease option agreement.

If the person wishes to proceed, this is where you need to put the person in contact with your solicitor. Do resist the temptation to answer their questions, but instead refer the home owner to your solicitor; they are the legal expert and not yourself. You will need to ensure that the mortgage company agree to you taking on the mortgage payments – and that you will be renting out the house. I would not recommend that the home owner continues to pay the mortgage and then you refund them – as there is always the risk that they will default and not pay the mortgage. In a lease option agreement, you will be legally responsible for the house in all respects, so this is an important consideration.

Lease Option Agreements; Next Steps:

Lease option agreements are a very powerful strategy that should be for all property investors and are especially applicable in times of recession. Securing lease option agreements do however need to be secured in the correct way – with full details being beyond the scope of this book.

I have prepared a specialist raining programme, *'The Lease Option Bootcamp'* – details of which can be found at: https://www.property-investors.co.uk/

Chapter Sixty Eight: Raising Finance Through Joint Venturing:

The concept of investor financing is simple. By using a third-party investor's money, in what is effectively a loan, you provide them with a return on their investment.

There are many investors who would be happy to invest and receive a fixed percentage return or stockholding in equity of the house.

There are no fixed rules for negotiating a joint venture and each arrangement will be unique. It is important however to ensure that a contract is put into place for any joint venture to protect both parties and avoid any mis-understandings at a later date.

Buy-Refurbish-Refinance-Rent – (BRRR) projects, (see chapter seventy) can also sometimes be part financed by partnering with builders or architects in which you fund the purchase of the property, while the builder funds the refurbishment with an agreement for how you are to share the profits and/or equity in the venture on completion.

Before Setting Up A Joint Venture:

Before entering into a joint venture there are a number of factors to consider to protect both parties against any risks. It is also important to plan how the venture will be run and how you will both exit it at the end.

All joint ventures should be covered by a contract to prevent future mis-understandings. Simple contracts can be drawn up inexpensively through property lawyers using with template contracts based around, for example, either a loan agreement or a simple profit and/or equity sharing agreement

Longer term or multiple project joint venture arrangements might include the establishment of a private limited (Ltd) company or limited liability partnership (LLP).

Again, it could be wise to discuss your plans with both a specialist property lawyer and property accountant to ensure you put in place the best arrangement for all parties.

Ultimately no two joint ventures are the same. You need to decide on a mechanism that works for you and your joint venture partners. It should allow you to create the correct vehicle to complete your venture.

A solicitor specialising in property investment will be able to undertake the conveyancing for the house purchase and joint venture contract.

Where and How To Find Joint Venture Investors:

If you are looking to raise finance, the most common question people ask is: *'Where do I find investors?'* Finding investors can actually be the easy part. Proving that your project is worthy of their investment is the more difficult part.

Investors come in all shapes and sizes and quite often end up being the people you least expect. Investment can come from:

Family or friends: these are the most common source of funding for many investors. It is important that the family member or friend is clear about the potential risks involved. Otherwise, if the project fails and you are unable to repay the money, it may affect your relationship with them.

High net worth individuals: these can be a great source of finance. High net worth individuals have the money but not necessarily the time to manage investments. As these individuals are often knowledgeable about investing, they may want a higher return on the money they are investing. These types of investors are everywhere. The way to find them is to talk to everyone and tell them what you do. People will gravitate to you and then ultimately you can provide a solution to their problem.

Group investors: a group of angel investors who may, for example, have formed a syndicate. Investors such as these contribute funds to the syndicate account, creating a pot of money for multiple investment projects. A professional syndicate manager will control the account. You would need to apply to the syndicate manager to gain access to this type of funding.

The very first thing that you need to understand is that you are a GIFT to an armchair investor. In this model the armchair investor needs to know that they have hit the jackpot when they find you! This is something you need to believe in yourself.

The typical armchair investor is currently investing in the bank where they might be getting 0.5% annual interest if they are lucky. They would love to find a better rate of return, but in their mind, they are never going to invest in property as they see this as far too risky. However if they could find a way of giving you the money and you are going to give them a guaranteed return through, for example a secured loan – or through a guarantor, they would be very happy.

Armchair investors are typically going to be looking for rates of return of between 5-10% per annum depending on the nature and size of the project - though this may vary. You may be making 20% or more – but you are putting in all of the work and shouldering the risk – while you are giving them a risk-free opportunity to make far more money than they could by putting their money in the bank. Remember, in this scenario or model, they need you as much as you need them...! In this way you, really will be a GIFT to the armchair investor.

The G.I.F.T.S. Formula

So how do you find armchair investors? How do you approach them and how do you speak to them?

I have put together an acronym of G-I-F-T-S to help you through this:

We will first summarise this and then look at each of the five points in each of the five following sections.

__G__ – _G_et them asking you what you can do...

_I_ – You need to _I_nitiate or bring up the idea,

_F_ – You need to find their interest,

_T_ - You need to learn how to do some _T_hird party selling – and lastly,

_S_ – Send them the opportunity.

Now let's look at each of these in detail.

So how do you find armchair investors?

Get Them Asking

The first step is to get potential armchair investors asking you what you do. So how do you do this?

The answer is easy; ask them what they do...

Imagine you are at a party. When you get talking to someone – ask them what they do. They may say they are a doctor or a journalist or a golfer. Ask them about what they do and be interested in them – ask questions. If you know what they do already, then ask them how their line of work is going. They will almost certainly return the question and ask what you do...

Now let us consider the situation where you tell them that you are a property investor and they reply by saying, '*How interesting*' or something similar. Now say '*Yes*' and then tell them that you have some really interesting deals you are looking at. Now be quiet... what will happen next? They well might ask about these deals...

You need to be opportunistic and think of everybody as a potential armchair investor; you never know who may be interested: a colleague, a friend from your golf club, your GP or dentist – who knows?

Be interested in everybody and tell the world that you are a property investor – and see who comes back and who is interested in you and your business.

Initiate the Idea

Now that you have told them what you do and that you are a property investor, this gives you the opportunity to initiate a conversation around something topical to do with money, interest rates, house prices or the latest news item with predictions of where the property market is likely to go etc. Their reaction will be telling. Those who are interested in finance or investing may often pick up on this, while those who are completely uninterested or who have no money may be more interested in talking about their favourite TV soap opera.

It is always a good idea to always be up to date with the latest news concerning finance and the economy – so that you always have something to hand that you can bring up in impromptu conversations about property investing.

Find Their Interest

Having initiated the idea, you next need to find their interest. Your initial conversation about property or finance is most likely to have been very abstract or theoretical; now is the time to say something such as, '*I have been in property investment for the past two years and have a couple of houses I let to students – have you ever thought about getting into property?'.*

If their reply is something along the lines of, *'Me – Are you joking, I would never do that, it sounds far too risky and I haven't got any money anyway'*, they may not be your best prospect – which is of course fine; at least you have now established this. If they say reply with an answer such as, *'Well we have often thought about getting a student house but not sure about the timing – what are your thoughts?'* – this could be perfect to pick up on. You have just determined their interest!

Again, they might say something like, *'We have stocks – and we have always wondered about property, but not quite sure how or what might be the best way to get into property'*.

Third Party Selling

If it is clear that they are interested in property – then perfect! The next stage is to gently lead into a process of *'third party selling'*. So, what is third party selling? This is when you talk about deals but in an abstract way, so that the person who is interested can almost listen to the conversation.

The last thing you want to do at this stage is say something like, *'So how much would you like to invest?'* Do not do this!

The best way to describe third party investing is to explain by means of an example: The first time I 'third party sold' was by mistake to my grandma and grandpa. I had not had a good week, was in a bad mood, was about to lose a deal as I could not raise the deposit and emotionally offloaded to them when round at their home for Sunday lunch.

I explained the whole situation and that I was about to lose the deal and that I could not find an investor even though I was offering a 10% guaranteed per annum return. My frustration was showing through. To my amazement, I suddenly realised my Grandma and Grandpa were interested themselves – suddenly I had two investors – and by accident... Not only did I secure the money, I learned a tactic that I have used ever since.

If you have got this far in the process, you are nearly there; all you have to do next is to then offer them the opportunities and let them pick up on this; this is what we will look at next.

Send the Opportunity

If the person you have been third party selling to comes back with questions to replies such as, *'How do you find deals such as these?'* – or *'How long might someone's money be tied up for?'* – this is the time you could casually introduce something along the lines of: *'The next time I see a refurbishment property opportunity come along, would you like me to e-mail the details to you? Would this be of interest to you?'*.

This is a way of gently introducing them to an opportunity. You now have a potential armchair investor.

In the case of my Grandma and Grandpa, after they had asked a number of abstract third-party questions, they looked at each other nodded and said, *'We have some savings'*... They invested and the rest is history.

Samuel Leeds

Chapter Sixty Nine: *H*ouses In *M*ultiple *O*ccupancy - HMOs

We have seen earlier that HMOs are properties where each of the rooms is let out separately; this is a great strategy for obtaining *'super rent'* far and above the rent that could be obtained if the property was let a single unit. This indeed was the approach I first adopted. This approach can of course also be coupled with other strategies such as Rent-to-Rent (chapter sixty-six) or Buy-Refurbish-Refinance BRRR (chapter seventy).

The renting of HMOs is highly regulated in many parts of the world. The sections that follow are written from a UK perspective, but are not dissimilar to those found in many other areas across the globe.

So, now let us look at the main points you need to consider:

Average Room Rates

There is no direct correlation between house prices and rental prices for an area - and this is particularly true for HMO rental properties; this is why it better to normally buy in cheaper areas.

As an example, in the UK rooms within an HMO in Stoke-on-Trent will each rent out for c.£380 (US$530) in a house costing £130K [US$ 180K] – while similar rooms in a house in Brighton will rent out for c. £475 [c. US$665] per month although the house would cost you £500K [c. US$700] or more to buy. This demonstrates how cheaper areas often offer far greater returns on investment (ROI).

If you do need to break the one hour travelling radius rule from where you live, do make sure you choose an area that is really vibrant and 'buzzing', that will allow you to obtain good returns on investment by 'buying low and renting high'.

Checking the Demand

The next step is to check the rental demand for your shortlisted areas as we have discussed before using sites like *SpareRoom* – and talking to estate and letting agents in an area.

Now that you have seen what the demand is like – you next need to determine the supply for the area. Many – indeed the majority of people looking for rooms will not go to the trouble of creating profiles for themselves – and so the number of rooms advertised will almost certainly be greater than the number of people looking for rooms.

There is a formula that will give you an idea of whether an area is close to saturation or not.

Ideally – you should be looking for an area where the number of advertised rooms is less than three times the number of people looking for rooms. Any supply to demand ratio of less than 3:1 will be encouraging.

If there are more than three times the number of advertised rooms people looking for rooms – be cautious.

Checking the Supply

If the ratio of rooms to people looking for rooms looks encouraging, then your task as a landlord will be to supply some of the best rooms - and simply be one of the best landlords in that area. Aim to offer quality in the top 10% - but with a competitive rent in line with the average rent.

You will see when browsing through many of the adverts for rooms being offered for rent, many of these will be quite poor, with furniture looking like it has been bought from a charity shop – and it follows that beating the competition in terms of quality will not be too difficult.

Your task will be to supply a better quality of accommodation than the average by ensuring a good quality of décor, furniture and fittings - and if you do, you will become the landlord of choice for renters looking online for a room.

Licencing Checks

We next need to check the HMO licencing rules for an area. (Again, the rules do vary from country to country but in many cases will be broadly similar to those discussed here).

HMO licences are normally only required in England if the HMO has five or more unrelated tenants and has three or more floors. You however need to check to see if there are any specific licencing rules for your area.

This can be easily checked at: https://www.gov.uk/house-in-multiple-occupation-licence

This will bring up the government website as below where you can enter any postcode.

Let us look at an example: if we enter the postcode WS1 2EW, this will then bring up the licencing requirements from the local council, (in this case from Walsall council).

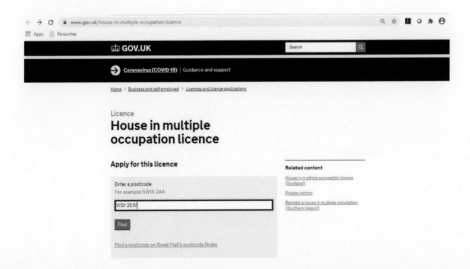

This shows that in Walsall a licence is only required for larger HMOs – with these being defined as ones where all of the following apply: (i) there are five or more tenants, (ii) if some or all of the tenants share a toilet, bathroom or kitchen facilities and (iii) if at least one tenant pays rent – or their employer pays rent for them.

This *.gov* site should indicate if there are specific licencing requirements for your post-code area – but to be absolutely sure that there are no special requirements, do as part of your due diligence phone the housing department of the local council and check – and make sure that they reply to you by email, so that you have this information in writing.

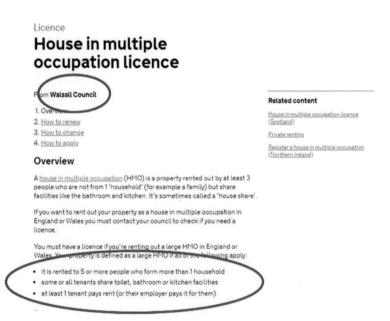

Article 4.

Now that you have determined the licensing rules for your town or city, the next step is to see if there is a so called *'article 4 directive'* in force in any part of the town or city.

Councils in the UK have the right to put in place an article 4 directive which prevents the conversion of use of a property as a single dwelling into an HMO without first obtaining planning permission. In practice it is extremely difficult if not nearly impossible get planning permission for the conversion of a single dwelling into an HMO – since the purpose of article 4 is to limit the number of HMOs in an area.

You can determine if a property has article 4 rights by Googling 'article 4' and the town or city name; this will bring up any article 4 information for the area – normally from the council website, see below: by following the information given on the *.gov* website, you will find areas in the town or city that are covered by an article 4 directive. Sometimes this may be just a few streets – sometimes a much larger area. A complete list of streets and postcodes will be listed by the council – along with normally a map on-line showing the areas covered.

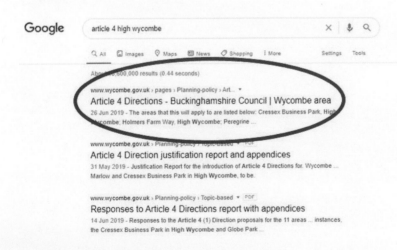

If the property has been used as an HMO before the introduction of article 4 for an area, then it may be continued to be used as an HMO – and if it the property is sold, then the new owner inherits so called 'grandfather rights' permitting its continued use as an HMO.

Buying On The Edges

If there is article 4 in operation in an area, then one approach is to look for streets just on the outskirts of the article 4 area; in this way you are likely to still be in an area that is vibrant and with very similar connectivity - but you will be free to turn a single residence property into an HMO without planning permission restrictions.

Nottingham is a good example; article 4 directives cover much of the city, but there are still areas just outside of these zones where there will still be good demand for single rooms within HMOs but where article 4 has yet to be introduced.

Buying Existing HMOs
As we have seen, if you buy an operating HMO in an article 4 area, you will inherit so called 'grandfather rights' that allows you to continue to rent the property room by room as an HMO. This does add a premium to a property price – but if the return on investment is still good, then this is a strategy you might wish to consider.

Finding HMO Managers

You are unlikely to want to manage the property yourself – and so you will need to find an HMO manager.

The first stage is to Google HMO managers for your area. Next look at the reviews online from tenants and landlords. If you know other landlords in the area – or attend property network meetings covering the region, see if there are HMO managers that others recommend.

Letting houses as HMOs is a highly regulated area and so I do advise you keep abreast of the field so as to stay legally compliant; I have prepared a specialist course which can be taken on-line or in person. Details can be found at: https://www.property-investors.co.uk/

Samuel Leeds

Chapter Seventy:
Buy-Refurbish-Refinance-Rent (Brrr)

The Buy-Refurbish-Refinance-Rent strategy (BRRR) is an advanced but hugely profitable approach for recycling your initial investment – leaving you a property that gives you an ongoing rental income and the cash to re-invest in your next venture. This approach truly can offer you *infinite* returns.

The four steps for investing to give infinite returns are to:

(i)   **B**uy (the right property – selected using strict formulae),

(ii)   **R**efurbish the property (again to strict criteria),

(iii)   **R**e-finance (re-mortgaging) to pull all of the money out of the property – and finally,

(iv)   **R**ent the property out to give you an on-going income.

Here is an overview of the BRRR Strategy:

Stage One: *Buy* - Buy a property, usually in poor condition or even un-mortgageable, that you can refurbish to add value to. The properties are typically initially purchased using cash, joint ventures, bridging finance or lease option (or deferred purchase) agreements.

Stage Two: Refurbish – The first step is to refurbish the property to a high standard, usually setting the bench mark for the area. The key is to add the most value to the property in the most cost-efficient way.

Stage Three: Refinance - Once value has been added to the property, the next step is to refinance the property to its new higher 'End Value'. The aim is to try and achieve the highest end value as possible.

<u>Stage Four: Rent</u> – Finally you can rent out your newly refurbished property and enjoy the cashflow. If you market your property well and have refurbished the property to a high standard, you will generally be able to achieve a higher rental value than average for the area or street.

This strategy has the potential for working in any region of the country so long as: (a) there is sufficient rental demand in the area and (b) that properties are available with sufficient potential for uplift in value.

Rich people rarely use their own money – and they recycle money again and again; BRRR strategies are particularly suitable for coupling with joint venturing and raising finance approaches to buy, refurbish, refinance and rent the properties out - and then doing this all over again. This is one of the most amazing strategies that exists as it allows you to recycle money to continually grow a property portfolio.

If you purchase a run-down property – refurbish this and increase its value sufficiently to a value where you can re-finance it and pull out the initial investment, you have effectively bought a property 'for free' which will now pay you an ongoing passive monthly rental income. If you do not have the money for a deposit then joint venturing will allow you use other peoples' money to buy and refurbish the property.

This really is one of the surest and sustainable ways to build long term wealth – but you do need to invest in the correct training to do this properly.

Buy – Refurbish – Refinance - Rent

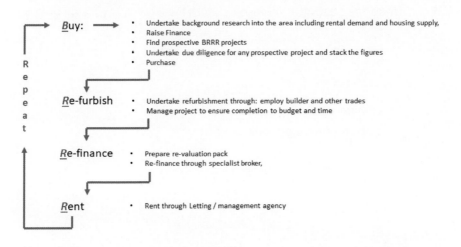

Let's look at each of the four stages:

Stage One: Buy...

The first stage is to find and buy the *right* property for this strategy.

The amount of money you make (the return) will be dictated by how wisely you buy. Many investors will tell you that the real money in property development is made when buying.

Since this step is so crucial, you need to approach this step by breaking this down into a number of sub-tasks.

This strategy has the *potential* to work in almost any area - but you need to research a potential patch and ensure that there is a sufficient supply of properties and demand for refurbished finished properties; if not move on.

The sub-tasks you need to undertake are to:

(a)   Undertake background research into local economy for an area,

(b)   Understand the mix of house types and house prices within an area,

(c)   Determine the rental demand in your area of choice for a refurbished rental property,

(d)   Stack the figures for a project,

(e)   Raise finance for the purchasing and refurbishment,

(f)   Find suitable properties with sufficient scope for increase in value.

Finding Suitable Properties with Sufficient Scope for Increase in Value:

There are a number of places where potential BRRR properties can be found. These include: *Rightmove, Zoopla, Gumtree* and other on-line resources, direct leads from agents and auctions.

The general rule of thumb is to look for properties with the maximum potential for uplift in value. This will often include properties that are un-mortgageable such as those that are un-inhabitable due to a lack of functioning bathrooms or kitchens. Note that in the UK uninhabitable houses are not liable to stamp duty, which makes these especially attractive to for this type of approach.

We will look at finding properties by each of these approaches in turn:

(i)   On-line property resources: *Rightmove, Zoopla, Gum-tree, Purple Bricks* etc.

(ii)   Direct leads from agents

(iii)   Auctions

(i)   *On-line Property Resources: Rightmove, Gumtree, Purple Bricks etc:*

The first and most obvious place to look for BRRR leads is on-line via all of the normal property websites such as *Rightmove* and *Zoopla* and some of the independent on-line estate agents such as *Purple Bricks*.

Remember you need to look for houses that the owners may be finding difficult to sell with motivated or sometimes desperate sellers resorting to advertising properties on sites such as *Gumtree*.

When searching for properties, start by select properties that have been on the market for the longest time in your selected area. A recently added feature of *Rightmove* is the ability to search for keywords. A keyword search should include the words in inverted commas in the list below and then looking for phrases in the results such as those in brackets:

- 'In need of' [modernisation]

- 'Refurbishment' [opportunity]

- 'Investment' [opportunity]

- 'Vacant possession'

(ii)   *Direct Leads From Agents:*

First, look up each of the estate agent's operating in your area: phone each in turn:

Introduce yourself by saying:

'I am a cash buyer looking to buy property which is in need of work and may not be mortgageable with a view to refurbishing and re-financing it – Do you have any properties that may work?'

Arrange a visit and a chance to have a coffee with the agent. When you meet, ask if the agent has any properties that they have been on their books for a long period of time and that might be difficult to sell to normal vendors.

Which houses to look for and which to avoid: You want a house where the problems can be fixed. There are few problems that cannot be easily remedied that you should stay clear of. These include: houses built of non-standard construction, houses with severe structural problems that cannot be remedied such as leaning walls due to subsidence. Properties with faults such as these will be difficult to mortgage and will be again be difficult to sell in the future if required.

The lesson from all of these examples is to ensure that you undertake your due diligence before purchasing. This should include having a full structural survey undertaken.

Building a rapport with an estate agent can be so valuable and one you have purchased your first otherwise unsellable property from an agent, the agent will bring to you other BRRR opportunities.

Having built a rapport with one agent, do the same in turn with all of the other agents in an area and gently let them know you are working with their competition so that they are competing for your custom.

(iii) *Auctions:*

Two words of caution: Firstly, I will say: 'Buyer Beware' – and Secondly: Buying from Actions is often not the best choice for the beginner...!

If you are considering buying from an auction, visit several auctions on a number of occasions before looking at any properties, just to familiarise yourself with the way auction houses and experienced purchasers operate.

Many properties are put into auctions because of un-solvable problems such as being of non-standard construction or having severe structural issues such as leaning walls due to severe subsidence.

Many properties however may be simply in need of a full refurbishment and currently un-inhabitable and un-mortgageable through not having functioning bathrooms or kitchens, severe damp or vermin infestation.

The lesson here is to ensure you fully undertake due diligence prior to even *considering* buying a property from auction.

One final word of caution: having bid on and won an auction, you are obliged to purchase the house. You will be required to pay a (typical) 10% deposit plus fees on the day and then be obliged to complete the purchase within a set period of time. Failure to do so will mean you will lose your deposit with no recourse.

Due diligence should include:

(a)   Firstly undertaking a careful inspection yourself, using a property inspection checklist.

(b)   If the property shows potential, has no obvious unsolvable problems – and if the figures stack up for a refurbishment, then before considering bidding for an auction make sure you arrange for a full structural survey on the property.

Whether you finally end up purchasing the property or not this will represent money well spent and should be thought of in terms of an insurance policy.

(c)   Determine the ceiling price to pay for the property – and do not exceed this when bidding under any circumstances. You need to be disciplined here. Sometimes the bidding may reach a value higher than your predetermined ceiling, but will fail to reach the reserve price and will remain unsold.

This can create a great opportunity for you. You can then approach the auctioneers and make an offer to the seller. Often this will open up a negotiation and a deal can be agreed; remember that the seller will almost certainly be highly motivated and you as a cash buyer, will be in a strong position.

One last point concerning auctions: many investors attend auctions - and this presents an ideal opportunity for networking and finding potential joint venture partners. You may wish to visit auctions with no intention in purchasing but simply finding joint venture partners who are happy to finance and share the profits for a joint venture BRRR project – or even receive a fixed percentage return for an investment. (Look at chapter sixty-eight on raising finance and finding high value individuals and other investors).

Stage Two: <u>Refurbishing the Property</u>:

Now you have purchased your property, the next step is to undertake the refurbishment – and to do this you need to find a builder and other skilled trades as needed.

Your due diligence will have determined the rental market you are aiming for, i.e., students, young professionals, families etc. The refurbishment and level of luxury clearly needs to be in line with your target market.

Note; it is now mandatory for all rental properties in the UK to meet at least a rating of *E* for the mandatory *Energy Performance Certificate* or EPC; from 2025 all properties will have to meet a grade *D* or above, so if you are undertaking a refurbishment, make sure you undertake this work to the required standard now.

The simplest approach for managing the refurbishment is to find a builder who will manage this for you and sub-contract trades such as gas fitters or electricians as needed. Builders such as these often advertise as refurbishment specialists – and/or as offering 'design and build' services. Finding a one stop shop builder who will manage the development will often be the most efficient way, especially if you live some distance away. Do not try to manage the development yourself if you live more than 30mins to an hour away, since this inevitably will lead to a lack of co-ordination between trades, frustrations, delays and in all probability unnecessary costs.

This means that you need to find a builder and/or project manager who you believe to be reliable, with a track record and what you can trust for completing the refurbishment on time and to budget.

In business it is normal to have to obtain three quotes for any significant purchase of equipment or service contracts.

For refurbishment projects expect to have to approach at least ten builders to find one who will undertake all of the work for you to a high quality, is reliable and who will complete the project on time and budget.

This may sound excessive but the time taken to finding a perfect ready-made power team for this part of the BRRR strategy will pay huge dividends – and remember once you have found them and they have delivered for you once, you will then already have all lined up and in place for your next project.

Here are the steps for finding a builder:

1) Go to check a trade for the area and search for builders, who advertise for full property refurbishments. Builders of this type will often advertise for undertaking extensions, loft conversions and garage conversions etc.

2) Look for those with a long list of excellent ratings for recommendations with mention of standard of finish, completing projects on time and to budget - as well as reliability etc. Immediately rule out those with those with repeated criticisms for any of the above.

3) Invite at least ten builders round to quote for the work. To help them, be specific and have a list of works, pre-determined for them to quote for.

4) Expect 20% + of these people not to show up to quote. Do not chase these people. This is a selection process to find people who will be reliable and you can trust. [This was one of my biggest early mistakes; people who did not show I chased. They have of course just proven themselves to be unreliable; remember the way people do one thing will be the way they do everything]. Even if all ten people do not show up, do not chase them – move on and search for another ten builders to come round and quote.

5) When the builders who do show turn up, ask them when they will come back to you with a quote. Again, if they fail to quote, move on and carry on looking for a builder. When they visit, ask them if they are doing any work or have completed any projects in the area recently – especially for BRRR type refurbishments. Ask if you could see any recently finished projects. Some builders will point you towards other property investors who they have undertaken a series of projects for; this is a good sign. You need to find a builder who you can work easily and get on with; if you have any doubts – move on and try to find another.

6) Next wait for quotes; expect only 50% of those who come to the property to come back with a quote; it is an astonishing statistic but one that often holds true. Again, do not chase those who fail to quote – this is a selection process and they have just proved themselves unreliable.

7) Now look at the quotes – not only for the figure but for how professionally the quotes have been prepared. Again remember – the way people do one thing will be the way they do everything.

It is often the case that the most professionally prepared quotes come in as the most competitive, reflecting on the builder's desire to win the contract.

8) Having shortlisted one or two builders and before commissioning the work, check the payment schedule to be agreed. Many builders ask for interim payments during the work to cover the cost of materials. This is completely reasonable but terms should be agreed in advance. One approach is to ask the builder to set up a *WhatsApp* group for the posting of weekly update photos. If a builder does not wish to do this – do be beware especially if you live some distance away. Reliable and reputable builders should have no problem with this.

Keeping a 'before during and after' photo record will moreover help build a portfolio for re-valuation of the property so store these photos carefully and prepare a pack to pass to the surveyor when the time comes for valuation and re-financing.

If your builder delivers to time and budget with a high level of finish, you have just established a key part of your power team – underlying how important an investment of time and effort in selecting a builder and/or other contractors is for success when undertaking BRRR projects.

Stage Three: Refinancing the Property.

Having undertaken the refurbishment, the re-valuation should be relatively straightforward if the work has been undertaken to a high standard and to budget.

The mortgage lender will need to value the property prior to agreeing a loan. This will almost certainly include a valuation survey to be performed by a surveyor of their choice.

There are a number of crucial steps to help this valuation and re-financing process.

(i)　Firstly prepare a valuation pack to pass to a valuer that should contain:

(a) the building survey prior to purchase to demonstrate that all highlighted defects have been addressed,

(b) a list of invoices and receipts for work undertakes,

(c) a 'before, during and after' picture portfolio showing visually the improvements to the property and,

(d) evidence for the rental valuation for the newly re-furbished property – with reference to comparables from *OpenRent* and your selected letting agent (see step four – Rent, below). Each of these will help justify the new uplift in valuation.

Use all of these to prepare a valuation pack which can then be passed to your broker and mortgage company ahead of the surveyor visiting the property.

(ii)　You need to select a mortgage broker specialising in refinancing of refurbishment projects.

Products are available for new property investors with no experience of buy to let landlord experience, although these are often only available through specialist brokers – and hence the need for specialists in this area.

Once you have re-financed the property and successfully withdrawn all of the money from the deal, the final step is to rent the property out – and of course then start looking for the next BRRR project.

Stage Four: <u>R</u>enting The Property

If you undertook your due diligence carefully for determining the type of rental demand (see stage one), this last step for renting your property, should be relatively straight forward.

The approaches for renting out your property and finding good tenants are just the same as in all other cases – but a summary will be given here.

First, you need to find a good letting agent as part of your power team. You will have found and spoken to a number of letting agents; the way in which your enquiries are handled can be quite revealing. Avoid letting agents who fail to pick up the phone, are un-professional in their manner – are slow to - or fail to return calls or e-mailed enquiries. Look to select a letting agent who come across in a professional and friendly manner and who inspires confidence. Look on-line for reviews from both landlords and tenants. Ensure the letting agent will undertake quarterly visits and will send photo evidence for the property and how is it being kept – as well as providing six monthly state of property reports to ensure the property is maintained in good order. Ensure the letting agent keeps good records and scheduled yearly mandatory maintenance including portable appliance testing electrical (PAT), smoke detector and gas / boiler servicing and safety checks.

Ensure that your letting agent obtains references for not only a prospective tenants last landlord, but the previous landlord before this as well. The previous landlord may give a good reference to help offload a bad tenant, whereas an earlier landlord is far more likely to provide an honest reference.

Advertising through *SpareRoom* is one of the best sites for advertising rooms within Houses In Multiple Occupancy (HMOs).

Dress the property well with bedlinen and other soft furnishings, pictures and similar – and then arrange for professional photos to be taken; this will help you both market your property or rooms. First impressions count.

Other approaches for marketing your property could include holding for example, an open evening with sparkling wine or champagne and canapés.

BRRR: - Next Steps:

BRRR is one of the most profitable – and possibly the most sustainable property investing strategy that exists. Put simply, once you have completed a successful BRRR and pulled out of the deal, you can do the same again and again and again.

I would suggest you undertake further training to help you make the most of this amazing strategy; I have put together a specialist training programme called *Infinite Returns* that can be taken on-line or in person. Details can be found at: https://www.property-investors.co.uk/

Samuel Leeds

Chapter Seventy One: The Very Best Investment

Property is one of the best forms of asset there is – but the greatest asset you will ever have is yourself, your brain and the skills and knowledge you have. Therefore, do invest in yourself – sign up for in training, listen to podcasts, look after your body in mind, body and spirit.

The aim of this book has been to set you up; to prime you for success in business – and property investing in particular.

I have in this book shared with you my life story so far - and how I became financially free in my early twenties.

Circumstances constantly change and so you need to continually update your knowledge and your strategies, approaches and tactics.

Always... always continue to invest in your education, listen to podcasts while driving in the car, listen to documentaries in the car, eat more healthily, get fitter – do everything you can to look after and thereby invest in yourself.

If you are not growing in yourself as a person then you are shrinking.

There are four key approaches you need to develop as life habits:

1) You need to gain knowledge through learning...

2) You need to follow up on this knowledge by implementing what you have learnt...

3) You need belief in yourself... some people say that up to 80% of success is down to belief. You need to be positive – winners believe they will win. Many of my students before you, have gone onto

become outrageously successful in property - so believe in yourself and follow these steps I have shown you.

4) Keep on going – persist... In my in-person teaching, I always tell my students to: '*Go for no*', Each little set-back is a stepping stone to success; this us how you learn... Learn how to be creative and above all persist and keep going. If at first you don't succeed – you just need to keep going. Success will follow.

Chapter Seventy Two: Useful Links And How To Stay In Touch:

I do hope you have enjoyed this book – and that this is just the start of your journey to becoming financially free, then ultimately financially free – and finally being in a position to pursue your mission – whatever that may be.

As I have explained, you will always be either growing and moving forward – or shrinking and slipping backwards. Do move forward and continue to invest in yourself; listen to podcasts, property training videos, attend in-person or participate in on-line networking events.

I would advise that you enrol on a *Property Crash Course* by visiting: https://www.property-investors.co.uk/ these are free and you can attend as many times as you like either in person, – or on-line. The *Property Crash Course* will keep you abreast of all of the latest developments in the field.

Many, many of my students have gone on to enjoy outrageous success – some of which are detailed within my latest book:, *'Samuel Leeds' Success Students (Volume 1)'*.

I would love to hear of your success, so please do get in contact through any of the ways below:

https://www.samuelleeds.com/contact

Email: team@samuelleeds.com

Index:

Printed in Poland
by Amazon Fulfillment
Poland Sp. z o.o., Wrocław
27 September 2022

6af90134-0382-4f3a-aa3e-0f01b05b8309R01